BORDERBLUR

Borderblur

Essays on Poetry and Poetics
in Contemporary Canadian Literature

Edited by
Shirley Chew and Lynette Hunter

Quadriga

© The Authors 1996

First Published by Quadriga
14 Woodhall Terrace
Edinburgh EH14 5BR

Typeset by Æsthetex, Edinburgh
Printed and bound in Great Britain by Antony Rowe Ltd, Chippenham, Wiltshire

Distributed by The Centre of Canadian Studies,
University of Edinburgh
21 George Square, Edinburgh EH8 9LD

Also available from The School of English,
University of Leeds, Leeds LS2 9JT

The Publication of this book has been made possible by a grant
from the British Association for Canadian Studies,
and its Literature Group

ISBN   1 85933 006 1

Contents

Foreword

Since its inauguration in April 1984 at a Seminar on Canadian Literature at the University of Leeds, the Literature Group of the British Association for Canadian Studies has played a significant part in promoting the study of Canadian literature in this country. An obvious example of its achievement is the strong and continuing presence of literature at the annual conference of the BACS. But, away from these big occasions, the Group has also been concerned to make space and time for a good deal of literary and critical activity. In this respect the tangible evidence of its success is the several volumes of criticism published over the last twelve years. *Borderblur: Essays in Contemporary Canadian Literature* is the most recent to date of these publications and the editors are pleased to have had the opportunity to bring it out. With one exception the essays submitted to us began as papers given at a Colloquium held at Leeds in October 1991. One of the highlights of that occasion was the presence of three Canadian writers – Joan Clark, Kim Morrisey, Nancy Mattson – who read from their own works and contributed to the various panel discussions, and the editors regret that circumstances have made it impossible to include their works in the volume.

To compare *Re-visions of Canadian Literature* which appeared in 1984 and *Borderblur* is to note several shifts of emphasis which have taken place in Canadian literary studies in this country. First, while the established writers continue to claim attention, it is no longer the case that they are all white Canadians. Included among the subjects of these essays are writers of Trinidadian, Australian and South Asian origin who by their presence call for a widening of critical approaches and a focusing upon cross-cultural exchanges. Second, while there is clearly a growth and consolidation of interest in Canadian women's writing, this interest ranges from criticism on the work of single authors to work produced by collectives of women. Last, while established academics are as usual represented in this volume, there is a strong presence of younger critics who gave their papers as postgraduate students and have since gone on to university posts in Britain and Canada. 'Borderblur' was a term adopted by bpNichol who involved himself in exploring work which ranged across different mediums and genres. Perhaps it is vainglorious even to borrow a term from a writer of his dazzling creativity. Nevertheless we hope that, through our own explorations here of different kinds of writing, critical approaches and cultures, we have been not altogether unworthy of the word.

Once again, thanks are due to the Canadian High Commission for financial support; thanks also to Michael Hellyer and Vivien Hughes of Academic Relations for their unflagging interest and help; to the Literature Group of the BACS and Peter Easingwood, its Chairman of longstanding dedication; and to Elizabeth Paget of the School of English for secretarial assistance.

Shirley Chew

1

Writing Wilderness: Margaret Atwood's 'Death by Landscape' and 'Wilderness Tips'

Coral Ann Howells

In *Survival: A Thematic Guide to Canadian Literature* (1972) Margaret Atwood offered her readers a map of the Canadian psyche through its literary traditions, at the same time putting Canadian literature on the map internationally by distinguishing it from British and American 'with which it is often compared or confused'.[1] What is interesting is that the concept of 'wilderness' is already there as the distinctively Canadian cultural space:

> When you are here and don't know where you are be-
> cause you've misplaced your landmarks or bearings . . . you
> are simply lost . . . Canada is an unknown territory for the
> people who live in it . . . For members of a country or a
> culture, shared knowledge of their place, their here, is not
> a luxury, but a necessity. Without that knowledge we will
> not survive. (p. 18)

That spatial metaphor of wilderness has remained a crucial feature in Atwood's narrative constructions of Canadian identity, modulating a continuity between a New World history of exploration and settlement and a contemporary postmodern awareness of the processes of fabrica-tion behind Canada's dominant cultural myth. In her latest short story collection, *Wilderness Tips*[2] (we shall explore the implications of that slippery word 'tips' later), Atwood again acknowledges her relation to the wilderness tradition, but the narrative dislocations in several of these stories suggest a new anxiety about the survival of Canadian culture and possibly the need for revision of the wilderness myth in contemporary urban multicultural Canada. I have chosen to examine 'Death by Landscape' and the title story because they form an interest-ing pair, presenting two classic (and opposing) versions of wilderness.

Indeed, together with 'True Trash' they are the most 'traditional' stories in the collection, being situated within the cultural mythology of wilderness while at the same time questioning that framework and so positioning themselves as postmodern fictions which challenge the very traditions to which they allude. They may be seen to offer another version of the 'shape shifting' which Linda Hutcheon discusses in her chapter on 'Canadian Women Writers and the Tradition' in *The Canadian Postmodern*.[3] 'Death by Landscape' alludes to the representation of wilderness by the most famous school of Canadian painters, the Group of Seven, while 'Wilderness Tips' analyses the construction of wilderness in nineteenth- and early twentieth-century literature and speculates on the viability of this tradition to represent a distinctive cultural inheritance in late modern post-traditional Canada.

We need not go further than *Survival* to find the evidence for what is now accepted as a truism, that Canadian geography was mapped, imaginatively reconstructed, and colonised as Canadian cultural space by European explorers, traders, missionaries, travellers and settlers – followed by writers of fiction and poetry – and then endlessly replayed and reinforced as popular cultural myth through summer camp and lakeside cottage scenarios right up to the present day. *Survival* names many of these wilderness texts in the course of presenting its Canadian literary history, laying out the main elements in the classic code of wilderness representation. 'Wilderness' meant forests and lakes (or less frequently the Arctic North) as synedoche for vast unexplored territory, though wilderness was not empty – only indecipherable. There were plenty of traces of indigenous inhabitants and the tracks of wild animals, so to describe the wilderness as 'desert' is merely to inscribe it as blankness within the conceptual framework of colonial discourse. Wilderness was presented as the space outside civilised European social structures and Christian moral laws, as the place of the mysterious Other and marked out by signs of human, animal and spiritual presences which were conceived as dangerous to whites, male and female alike. Inevitably such constructions of wilderness produced ambivalent, not to say contradictory representations (as Terry Goldie has amply argued in his study of the representation of indigenes)[4] summarised on the one hand by Northrop Frye's 'garrison mentality', and on the other by stories of wilderness as a condition of freedom from traditional social constraints. These wilderness constructions were of course produced by Europeans and not by Natives, and the discourse of wilderness is now under revision largely owing to the increasing intervention of voices from the First Nations over the issue of land rights and the renaissance of Native cultural traditions which intermesh with contemporary environmental awareness.

Atwood's feminist critique of the representation of wilderness does not refer to wilderness writing by nineteenth-century women (e.g. Susanna Moodie, Catharine Parr Traill, Anna Jameson), but operates within the male textual or visual spaces which she has inherited from Canadian tradition. However, these two stories expose the cultural construction of wilderness as white male fantasy by adopting two opposing versions of classic wilderness narrative: the heroic survival story and the story of disaster – what Atwood has called 'Death by Nature'.[5] By putting both versions into circulation Atwood destabilises any 'truth' about wilderness, for stories may offer different interpretations, which by implication are themselves open to revision at different times and from different perspectives. Not only do these stories when read together offer a double view of wilderness, but each of them is told as a double narrative where traditional wilderness stories intermesh with the private stories of two contemporary women on the verge of breakdown. This is to simplify very complex narrative processes, but I have done so in order to emphasise structural patterns of doubling which work to undermine the authority of the 'master narratives' projected through painting and literature.

'Death by Landscape', set in a Harbourfront condominium in contemporary Toronto, offers a feminised alternative interpretation of wilderness to that represented by the Group of Seven in their paintings. This early twentieth-century tradition in Canadian visual art is established and glossed at the beginning of the story, as within a safe urban domestic space ('the building has a security system', p. 109) the middle-aged woman called Lois looks round the room at her collection of pictures. The names of the painters (all male) are given, and the elements of the Group of Seven aesthetic are described in a catalogue of the paintings hanging crowded together on the walls:

They are pictures of convoluted tree trunks on an island of pink wave-smoothed stone, with more islands behind; of a lake with rough, bright, sparsely wooded cliffs; of a vivid river shore with a tangle of bush and two beached canoes, one red, one grey; of a yellow autumn woods with the ice-blue gleam of a pond half-seen through the interlaced branches. (p. 110)

This is the representation of wilderness as untouched nature, 'voided of human presence' as the art critic John Bordo has recently argued in a semiotic study of Group of Seven paintings.[6] He reads these pictures as expressions of a white male aesthetic of the dominating gaze, with landscape focussed by 'a single foregrounded tree' (e.g. Tom Thomson's 'Jack Pine') which represents the displaced 'significant subject' as an integral part of the natural landscape. Atwood's story however adopts a very different perspective on these paintings, reading them through the remembering eye of Lois, who gained her experience of wilderness as an adolescent at summer camp in the 1940s, and who was so traumatised by one event there that she has refused ever since to go anywhere near 'a place with wild lakes and wild trees and the calls of loons' (p. 128). To her the paintings give an entirely accurate representation of the geography of the Laurentian Shield as she remembers 'the rounded pinky-grey boulders', the 'spindly balsam and spruce trees', and the 'blue fragments' of the lake glimpsed through the trees. There are however no 'single foregrounded trees' here; indeed there is no centring principle at all for Lois in these paintings, which she reads as images of decentring, dispersal and absence.

Lois's memory of summer camp, that typical outdoor holiday experience of Canadian white middle-class children, lays out the features of the wilderness myth as recreation, for the summer camp represents wilderness domesticated, with its white appropriation of Native place and Native culture – the name of the camp itself ('Camp Manitou'), its stuffed moose head as camp mascot, its dressing up in blankets, its war paint and its Indian greetings. These are all white fantasies of playing at being Indian, and according to a masculine ethic where girls are addressed as 'my braves' (never as 'squaws'), though the war paint with which they are daubed is lipstick. An older and more politically correct Lois can re-evaluate these activities as 'a form of stealing' (p. 117), though at the time she responded imaginatively to the impossible heroic ideal they represented: 'She wanted to be an Indian. She wanted to be adventurous and pure, and aboriginal' (p. 118).

It is on the (supervised, white-sunhatted, 'Clementine'-singing) canoe trip that Lois has her traumatic experience of loss, for her best friend Lucy, an American from Chicago, mysteriously disappears. From narrative details, it would seem to have been an alienated teenage girl's suicide by drowning, for Lucy must have jumped off the cliff at Lookout Point into the lake far below. Lois was the last person to see Lucy alive and possibly the only person to hear her last cry, for at what must have been the crucial moment Lois, who was politely waiting for Lucy to 'go to the bathroom', heard a sudden shout:

Not a shout of fear. Not a scream. More like a cry of surprise, cut off too soon. Short, like a dog's bark.   (p. 123)

This is the point when realism, confronted with the blankness of ignorance, shifts into the realm of speculation and the reconstructions of fantasy, for traumatised by Lucy's disappearance and blamed by the camp leader for her death, Lois begins to re-imagine wilderness as exceeding the comforting fictions of the summer camp ethos. The version she adopts is that of 'Nature the Monster', the sublime and alien Other, actively hostile to human presence (particularly white female American teenagers from Chicago?). In *Survival* Atwood cites many literary models for 'Death by Nature', glossing this wilderness convention as follows: 'Death by Nature can also come in the form of suicide, and again drowning and freezing are favourite methods'.[7] Atwood follows the convention here, though she refigures it from the perspective of a female survivor who is also the victim of the interpretations of others. Lois becomes so fixated on the riddle of Lucy's vanishing that Lucy becomes her own dark double, the absent part of herself which shadows her conscious life:

> She was tired a lot, as if she was living not one life but two: her own, and another, shadowy life that hovered around her and would not let itself be realised – the life of what would have happened if Lucy had not stepped sideways, and disappeared from time. (p. 128)

Wilderness becomes symbolic landscape, figured for Lois in the Group of Seven paintings she collects. As she says, 'These paintings are not landscape paintings. Because there aren't any landscapes up there, not in the old, tidy European sense' (p. 128). To her questing eye they represent the Canadian landscape as maze, the site of riddles and secrets, a supernatural place of perpetual metamorphosis:

> And the trees themselves are hardly trees; they are currents of energy, charged with violent colour.
>
> Who knows how many trees there were on the cliff just before Lucy disappeared? Who counted? Maybe there was one more, afterwards. (p. 129)

The story of Lois's quest for her other self lost in the wilderness offers the possibility for a revisionary reading of the Group of Seven aesthetic of wilderness sublime. If we follow Bordo's reading, this aesthetic represents the 'experiential records of the subject's response to wilderness';[8] so does Atwood's version, though with its proliferating trees it offers the record of a dispersed subject seeking to locate the site of her loss, and lacking any of the unity signified in the 'single foregrounded tree'. At the end of the story, the catalogue of Lois's pictures is repeated in exactly the same order as at the beginning:

> She looks at the paintings, she looks into them. Every one of them is a picture of Lucy. You can't see her exactly, but she's there, in behind the pink stone island or the one behind that. In the picture of the cliff she is hidden by the clutch of fallen rocks towards the bottom, in the one of the river shore she is crouching beneath the overturned canoe. In the yellow autumn woods she's behind the tree that cannot be seen because of the other trees, over beside the blue silver of pond; but if you walked into the picture and found the tree, it would be the wrong one, because the right one would be further on. (p. 129)

There is however one significant addition here, and that is Lucy's ghost:
Everyone has to be somewhere, and this is where Lucy is.
She is in Lois's apartment, in the holes that open inwards on
the wall, not like the windows but like doors. She is here.
She is entirely alive. (p. 129)
Lois's feminised perspective takes the conventions of the Group of
Seven and turns them inside out, in order to code in a different subjective response to wilderness which contradicts their aesthetic of space
voided of human presence. After all, this is the story of a haunted
wilderness, where landscape painting becomes the means of figuring
loss as a decentred female subject searches endlessly for her absent
other.

'Wilderness Tips' offers a different version of writing wilderness,
from the slippery word 'tips' at the beginning ('He was not immediately
sure whether this word was a verb or a noun', p. 204) to a woman's
vision at the end of a forest landscape sliding down into a lake. Invoking
cultural tradition, Atwood tackles the question 'What is Canadian?',
prompted by the presence of an 'ethnic Canadian' the Hungarian immigrant George, the news of Québec Separatist agitation, and the Oka
crisis in the summer of 1990. George may not be worried by what he
reads in *The Financial Post*, for 'he's been in countries that were falling
apart before. There can be opportunities' (p. 199), but the white anglophone Canadian-born Canadians are worried, and the anxieties of
this formerly dominant cultural group are coded into this multivoiced
story with its ambivalent celebration of the wilderness myth. The story
opens at a lakeside cottage where a middle-aged family of three sisters,
their brother and George, the husband of Portia (one of the sisters)
are spending a summer weekend, having driven up from Toronto to
their pastoral retreat, roughing it (briefly) in the bush. Again using a
double narrative structure, Atwood replays wilderness, analysing its
construction through literary tradition, exposing both its appeal and
its anachronism as white male cultural fantasy, offering not radical
alternatives but implying that it is a fiction in need of revision along
the lines of race, ethnicity and gender. Wilderness is however only one
of the cultural fictions which she addresses here, the other main ones
being the rather more insidious female romantic fantasy of the perfect
marriage and of woman as victim. This slippery tale finds its double
focus in the husband and wife, George and Portia, having traversed a
number of subsidiary themes relating to tradition and inheritance.

It is the literary tradition of wilderness which is foregrounded here –
in the name of the cottage 'Wacousta Lodge', the books in the great
grandfather's library at the cottage, and in the responses of those in-
heritors of the tradition living in the present. Again Atwood names her
literary inheritance, when it is explained to George that *Wacousta* is

a nineteenth-century Canadian historical romance written by Major John Richardson and that 'It's about war'. The reference to *Wacousta*, a novel described by Michael Hurley recently as 'problematising the whole notion of a stable coherent national or personal identity',[9] is peculiarly apposite, for as well as being 'about war' between whites and Indians, it is also a tale of duplicity and revenge and its main protagonist is himself a double figure, an English aristocrat who has come to Canada and gone Indian. Wacousta is a trickster figure whose shadow falls across this contemporary story, and is the main agent in Atwood's demonstration that the wilderness tradition was always a hybridised form riddled with contradictory values. It is interesting to note that the only characters to have read Richardson's novel are the men: Roland, the brother, who is an ardent traditionalist and the in-heritor of Wacousta Lodge by birth and who fears being dispossessed, and George, the immigrant, who has learned his adopted Canadian heritage through reading its sacred texts. Thirty years after his first visit he has fulfilled his ambition: 'He didn't want to desecrate Wacousta Lodge: he wanted to marry it' (p. 205). It is through these two male characters that the literary tradition of wilderness is interrogated, first through references to Wacousta (the novel and Wacousta Lodge which they both want to inherit) and then more elaborately through the old Canadian survival manual *Wilderness Tips*, the book that was Roland's favourite reading as a child.

Wilderness Tips is one of the great grandfather's books, and we are given a catalogue of his collection – along with the furnishings of the cottage built at the turn of the century (like Camp Manitou inciden-tally, and containing the same 'wilderness' signs: stuffed wild animals, Indian artefacts, Hudson's Bay blankets, snowshoes). The book titles are observed by George: 'Then he scanned the shelves. *From Sea to Sea, Wild Animals I Have Known, The Collected Poems of Robert Service, Our Empire Story, Wilderness Tips*' (p. 207). Laid out in this manner the titles trace the genealogy of this indigenous Canadian literary tra-dition, which is revealed to be the invention of white male imperialists fascinated by the otherness of the wild with its forests and animals and Indians. The wilderness becomes the scenario on to which are projected the Victorian masculine ideals of heroism, honour and concepts of the sacred. The inauthenticity of this tradition is highlighted by the last book on the shelf: *Wilderness Tips*. The book is described in detail as George looks at it: its date (1905), the photograph of its author (white male) seen paddling a canoe, and a summary of its contents. (Another fuller version of its contents is later provided by Roland as he remembers his childhood fantasies of being an Indian.) Evidently it is about woodcraft, Indian lore and survival, on the model of a book by Ernest Thompson Seton which Atwood recalls as part of her own childhood reading when she was living (as the daughter of a biologist) in the wilderness, where 'Seton's stick-and-stone artefacts and live-off-the-land recipes in *Wilderness Wisdom* were readily available, and we could make them quite easily, which we did'.[10] Atwood's challenge to the white male tradition is here most overt and daring, for this book is her own invention, a clever pastiche which imitates the conventions of the heroic survival wilderness narrative and looks indistinguishable from the foregoing list of authentic titles. (The word 'authenticity' itself becomes a problematic concept here when discussing conventions for writing wilderness.)

However, Atwood's challenge goes further, for this imitation is embedded in her short story of the same name, which is itself a critique of the wilderness myth. She also describes its romantic appeal through Roland's childhood memories, an appeal which is similar to that of Camp Manitou, with its narrative of the heroism and purity of the Indians as icons of wilderness in a white Canadian myth of origins. However, the wilderness myth is no longer a viable narrative for survival in the present, but a shabby historical relic like Wacousta Lodge. Its middle-aged devotees like Roland are plunged into self-division and alienation as they hanker after a lost innocence and an Amerindian past which perhaps never existed anywhere except in the white coloniser's imagination:

> How can you lose something that was never yours in the first place? (But you can, because *Wilderness Tips* was his once, and he's lost it.) He opened the book today, before lunch, after forty years. There was the innocent, fusty vocabulary that had once inspired him: Manhood with a capital M, courage, honour. The Spirit of the Wild. It was naive, pompous, ridiculous. It was dust. (p. 214)

It is not Roland but George who can see the precise value of the wilderness tradition (and this is not its commercial value, though that is all Roland believes George cares about): 'George doesn't mind the shabbiness, however. Wacousta Lodge is a little slice of the past, an alien past. He feels privileged' (p. 203). Roland's opposition to George is however only a condition of silent resistance, and his veneration for tradition is powerless to affect action in the present. He too seems to have been relegated to the position of historical relic, as we hear him chopping wood behind the cottage:

> The sound goes out through the trees, across the small inlet to the left of him, bounces off a high ridge of rock, making a faint echo. It's an old sound, a sound left over. (p. 215).

George's wife is herself meshed into her own disabling fantasy, that of romantic love and perfect marriage ('Even after thirty-two years, she is still caught in the breathlessness, the airlessness of love', p. 217).

Though their domestic drama of George's repeated infidelities (beginning with her sister Prue) would seem to be tangential to the narrative, it gradually comes in from the periphery to assume central focus. This is not only because George chooses to seduce Pamela, the third sister, at Wacousta Lodge and so breaks a taboo of that 'sacred place', but because Portia (like Sally the wife in the story 'Bluebeard's Egg')[11] is forced to look outside her carefully preserved romantic fantasy, though 'She would rather be kissed; she would rather be cherished. She would rather believe' (p. 215). Portia's sense of betrayal exposes the fragility of her romantic fantasy which, like the wilderness myth, is also shown to be a fabrication riddled with contradictions (if not with 'maggots', like the stuffed birds at Wacousta Lodge).

It is Atwood's patterned language and narrative method which bring wilderness and romantic fantasy together, for Portia's subjective response to this unwelcome revelation is projected as another wilderness vision, though this time it is a vision of collapse. As she floats in the lake contemplating suicide as the way of least resistance, her perception shifts into a vision of geological fracture where wilderness 'tips':

It seems to be on a slant, as if there'd been a slippage in the bedrock; as if the trees, the granite outcrops, Wacousta Lodge, the peninsula, the whole mainland were sliding gradually down, submerging. (p. 221)

This vision in turn shifts into a scenario of human disaster – with a nod to E J Pratt's long narrative poem 'The Titanic' – when Portia alone, like a latterday Cassandra, proclaims imminent collapse in which she is powerless to intervene. This female victim position possibly signals her continuing passive acquiescence in her marriage relationship; things may go on just as before, repeating themselves in an iterative pattern without motivation or meaning:

She would be invisible, of course. No one would hear her. And nothing has happened, really, that hasn't happened before. (p. 221)

The last sentence is what alerts us to powerful hidden correspondences between this domestic drama and the wilderness myth. It has all happened before, whether the comment is restricted to focalisation on Portia's response or widened to include the narrator's more general perspective. Just as geographical landscape has been transformed into Portia's symbolic landscape, so the marriage betrayal might be seen as yet another European violation of Canadian sacred wilderness space. However, Atwood's story has already undermined this interpretation by showing in detail that wilderness is a white cultural myth produced by literary discourse and arguably in need of revision to accommodate Native people, ethnic immigrants (like George) and women. What the story offers in its multiple versions of wilderness is the diagnosis of a malaise which has both private and social dimensions. Of course, such a deconstruction of cultural myth is bound to end in dislocation. (This possibly generates another meaning of 'tips' as metafictional comment on the intention of this wilderness story.) Paradoxically, the last sentence holds out a whisper of hope for the survival of wilderness, at least in its artistic representation of distinctively Canadian space: as cultural myth, the wilderness is always available to be revised and rewritten in an endless process of narrative transformation.

Notes

1. Margaret Atwood, *Survival: A Thematic Guide to Canadian Literature* (Toronto: Anansi, 1972), p. 13.
2. Margaret Atwood, *Wilderness Tips* (London: Virago, 1992). Subsequent page references are to this edition and included in the essay.
3. Linda Hutcheon, *The Canadian Postmodern: A Study of Contemporary English-Canadian Fiction* (Toronto: Oxford University Press, 1988), pp. 107–37.
4. Terry Goldie, *Fear and Temptation: The Image of the Indigene in Canadian, Australian and New Zealand Literature* (Montreal: McGill-Queen's, 1989).
5. *Survival*, pp. 54–5.
6. Jonathan Bordo, 'Jack Pine – Wilderness Sublime or the Erasure of the Aboriginal Presence from the Landscape', in *Journal of Canadian Studies/Revue d'études canadiennes*, 27.4 (1992–93), pp. 98–128.
7. *Survival*, p. 55.
8. Bordo, p. 102.
9. Michael Hurley, *The Borders of Nightmare: The Fiction of John Richardson* (Toronto: University of Toronto Press, 1992), p. 4.
10. *Survival*, pp. 29–30.
11. Margaret Atwood, *Bluebeard's Egg* (Toronto: McClelland and Stewart, 1983).

2

Werewomen: The Horror of Historical Subjectivity for Canadian Women Writers

Jill LeBihan

This essay is an examination of how the ground lies for women writing in Canada in the late twentieth century, and the way that literary land has been furrowed for contemporaries by the women who have gone before. My suggestion is that metaphors of landscape and metaphors of horror are specifically connected in the writing of Margaret Atwood, Mary di Michele, Alice Munro and Bronwen Wallace, as a means of emphasising the terrifying nature of the position of women under patriarchy.

My title, 'Werewomen', is suggested by the poem 'The Wereman' in Atwood's *The Journals of Susanna Moodie*.[1] In this poem, Atwood's recreated Moodie imagines her absent husband's metamorphosis, as he blends with the wilderness, becomes part of it, in order to make himself secure. With all the concern expected of a nineteenth-century bourgeois wife, the poem's narrator worries that her 'shadowy husband' will regress to a state of nature without her civilising influence. But without anyone to see her either, Moodie's own subjectivity falls into doubt. Her vigilance turns her into a fox, an owl, a spider. When her husband returns, Moodie 'can't think/ what he will see / when he opens the door' (p. 19). Out of one another's sight, Moodie and her husband are transformed. She becomes a nocturnal creature. He becomes a monster, or rather, the monster that the man always was is revealed. He is not a werewolf, a man that changes into a wolf at the full moon. Moodie fears rather that he is a were*man*, a kind of embodiment of 'pure masculinity', which in this formulation manages to suggest some kind of threatening beast which becomes human only under the woman's gaze.[2]

In this essay, 'werewomen' suggests not only the capacity in Canadian women's writing for horrific metamorphosis of women in the presence of men, but also an idea of a women's literary community: an inclusive 'we're', we are. Finally, as a conjugation of the verb 'to be' in the past tense, *were* women, I want to use the term to indicate the role of history in the formulation and change of women's subjectivities.

> So because I was more with you than on Bloor sidewalks,
> I was surprised when I looked down
> and my feet were drawn into quicksand
> from the Badlands. Even a little
> reading can be a dangerous thing
>
> (di Michele, p. 101)[3]

> Though they buried me in monuments
> of concrete slabs, of cables
> though they mounded a pyramid
> of cold light over my head
> though they said, We will build
> silver paradise with a bulldozer
>
> it shows how little they know
> about vanishing: I have
> my ways of getting through.
>
> (Atwood, p. 60)

Both the poems quoted above convey memories of literary women and a need, by poets who survive them, to ensure that the writing and the subjectivities of their colleagues are not obscured by the chaos of a literary city, the paving stones of critical indifference or the concrete of sterile readings produced by textual canonisation. Mary di Michele's 'Angel of Slapstick' is a tribute to Bronwen Wallace, in which di Michele situates her narrative self on the subway, reading *Badlands*. As she surfaces, being lost in thoughts of her dead friend, she steps into a layer of wet cement. The landscape of southern Alberta, with all its fossils, skeletons and dinosaurs, commemorated by Kroetsch's novel, is transported east to Toronto, in order to prevent the ossification of di Michele's literary heroine. 'Angel of Slapstick' also draws parallels between Wallace's writing and Christopher Dewdney's collection of insects, which have lived once and remain, in death, glinting like emeralds, like gold. In writing a poetic narrative which is at least partially about Canadian literary interest in evolution, ecology and landscape, di Michele is carving for herself and Wallace a niche in the Canadian literary tradition, their 'place in the story' as she puts it (p. 99).

In 'Conversations with the Living and the Dead', di Michele develops a specifically urban architectural location for her poetry. Her essay uses a building as a method of explaining 'The Tradition' and her place in relation to it. Instead of an Ivory Tower for poetry, she proposes:

> a home with rooms which do not belong to a gallery; imagine rooms where the traces from frying eggs are more lasting than the tempera of painting. You enter, Tom Waits is singing and the room smells of diesel. Every room in the house is haunted; in the bedroom where you sleep you dream the dreams of all who have slept there.[4]

This is a claim for space for the voices of the women who fried the eggs, a recovery project in which the writer says both she and Wallace are involved, a space which is both domestic and filled with horror. Di Michele is haunted by literary ghosts but in her essay, and particularly in 'Angel of Slapstick', she abandons an attempt at concretising Wallace's literary stature, a project as doomed to failure as wanting back 'the woman'. The poem's narrator lightly detaches her brain from her feet, which apparently work independently of each other. The feet transport her unconsciously into Toronto sidewalk cement, whilst her reading takes her to the Badlands. Her body may be on the street but beneath is the history of literature, 'layered like the earth and riddled with the speaking of bones, traces of former being, speaking through us'.[5]

In constructing a sense of tradition, or more accurately, a *community* in contemporary Canadian women's writing, I recognise that the spectre of Atwood influences considerably the poetry of both di Michele and Wallace. Di Michele's writing in particular shows that she is heir to Atwood's urban 'langscape', heir, that is, to her creation of a sense of location in language;[6] but the living poets' relationships with the ghosts who speak from within their work are clearly quite distinct from one another. Atwood's treatment of Moodie in *The Journals* is not the same as di Michele's treatment of Wallace, just as the influence of Moodie on Atwood is not the same as the influence of Atwood on the two younger women writers. Cross-textual references are a feature of twentieth-century women's writing in Canada, as I see it: however, they operate on an interactive model rather than a hierarchical, unidirectional tradition.

Atwood's poem 'A Bus Along St Clair: December', published twenty years before 'Angel of Slapstick' and with its speaking voice of Susanna Moodie narrating from beyond the grave, has a less benevolent ghost than Bronwen Wallace bequeaths to di Michele. Moodie is speaking, ventriloquised by Atwood, from beneath the sidewalks of the city, and she dares anyone to neglect her or her message. Wallace's ghost is a less assertive one who inhabits the world through di Michele's mind and poetry. In this last poem of *The Journals*, Atwood's Moodie denies that the Ontario wilderness has ever been replaced by St Clair and its buses. 'There is no city', she says, and unlike Wallace and di Michele, Atwood constructs no 'improvised sling / over the abyss' (di Michele, p. 99) of time and mortality. Atwood's poem suggests that Susanna Moodie is not only ever-present as a layer in the geological analogy of literature, but also that she is dominant and that she has relinquished none of her coloniser's ways over the years. She is still the usurper who claims, even in death, 'your place is empty' (Atwood, p. 61) as she suggests when she first sets eyes on Canada.

Atwood introduces her *Journals of Susanna Moodie* with a poem on the potential violence involved in the role of mediator, and the problems relating to narratorial neutrality and self-effacement. She writes:

> I take this picture of myself
> and with my sewing scissors
> cut out the face.
>
> Now it is more accurate:
>
> where my eyes were,
> every-
> thing appears
>
> (Atwood, p. 7)

By making herself see-through, by cutting out a window in her head, rather than offering her own visionary perspective, the narrator is inventing a myth of objectivity. In the act of self-effacement, we are given a window onto the world, a chance to see 'every / thing'. We are given the opportunity to see things with greater clarity, we are assured by the narrator with her transparent window face. Yet it is still through the picture of the woman that we read this pioneer's journal. The observatory may be larger, the whole face and not just eyeslits, but nonetheless we are looking *through* someone else. Atwood asserts her grip on our eyes from the outset, and like the ghost of Moodie, she doesn't let go easily. This sequence of poems, from the first to the last, simultaneously offers the 'neutral', transparent viewpoint of the narrator and deprives us of a stable reading and viewing position of our own.

In a culture that usually employs the camera lens as the 'objective' view, a way of observing the world, nature, 'everything', Atwood's poem places significant insistence on the necessarily gendered and mediated condition of representation. The camera is often accepted as providing an objective picture. As a piece of complex technology though, the (unseen) operator behind the lens is, more often than not, a white man. His invisibility is important here. If it is a woman behind the camera, then her view is considered more susceptible to bias, especially if she is also a feminist, or of 'marked' ethnicity. We are made aware that we are seeing through the gaze of a woman, or of someone of colour. The Western masculine view is still considered to be the 'human' view: neutral and universal. Atwood's insistence on the body through which we look at her poetry is a challenge to the notion of unmediated access to history or narrative.

Susanna Moodie entered the wilderness in 1832 and proceeded to mark herself off from it as well as to mark it up in terms of its usefulness for her. Margaret Atwood, 140 years on, returned to Moodie's wilderness journals and reclaimed them for feminist readers and for Canadian literary history. But the appropriations are not quite as clear as we might like them to be. The problem of who is watching whom, and through whose lens or page, is an interminable one in Atwood's poetry and prose, and it is this relationship between object and subject that is crucial to a contemporary feminist interpretation of her work.

Russell McDougall, in an essay comparing Canadian literature with that of Australia, asserts that Canadian writing is 'compulsively photographic'.[7] Basing much of his argument on Susan Sontag's well-known *On Photography*,[8] McDougall states that 'photography can be recognised as an act of possession', literally *taking* photographs; he goes on to say that it is 'an "active" way of seeing Canada, of enacting Canada'. McDougall takes on board Robert Kroetsch's and Shirley Neuman's concerns[9] about photographs being included in texts in order to fix and guarantee a verifiable reality, and he accuses Canadian literature of creating no more than a 'crypt(o)graphy: a fascinating and funereal enigma' (p. 118). He concludes: 'Canada . . . has been subject to the invasion of the body-snatchers, the image makers'. McDougall posits here what he considers to be the ultimate horror of the Canadian literary psyche. Rather than a dread of a lack of resonance, he fears the deathly sterility of fixation, a kind of photographically produced rigor mortis.

From my experience of Canadian literature I would argue that McDougall's reading of the Canadian writer's use of the photographic image as a 'short-cut', a 'razor to the eye' in the place of which is 'installed a camera lens', is a rather unimaginative one, which valorises the letter over the visual image rather than attempting to read a dialogue between the two. He also relies on a notion of photographs and other documentary inclusions as unaltering, static portraits of the past.

In her Afterword to *The Journals*, Atwood explains that the third section of the poetry sequence was inspired by the discovery of 'a little-known photograph of Susanna Moodie as a mad-looking and very elderly lady' (p. 63). Presumably it is this grainy portrait which is reproduced, sideways, within an oval of two red lines on the front cover of the Oxford University Press edition. The photograph resembles a Victorian locket enclosure, with Moodie dressed formally in a lacy bonnet and high-necked collar with a brooch at the throat. It is flanked by some hand drawn, rather charred-looking bushes sprouting out of a solid, flat horizon. The rear cover of *The Journals* shows an upright photograph of Atwood herself in high-relief black and white, clad in an anorak with the hood shadowing her face and surrounded by slender, ghost-like trees. The contrast between the portraits of the authors is striking: Moodie is enclosed safely within her geometrically perfect red egg and Atwood is clad for the great outdoors, her silhouette blending with the forest backdrop. The play that can go on between these two images, between the front and back covers of the book, refutes McDougall's claims about the stasis inflicted on language by photography.

The other collage illustrations in *The Journals* use a mixture of nineteenth-century prints and Atwood's own monographs of Moodie and her other characters. The first of these has a hand-painted forest backdrop with the dominating image of a woman in a long Victorian gown, her arms raised perhaps in the characteristic gesture of a ghost; this ghost is trying to haunt the present from the depths of a nineteenth-century Ontario backwood. Like many subsequent ones, this image has a thick, white margin where the monograph has been cut out, and this serves to insulate it from the surroundings against which it is placed. The only single-medium, integrated image in this collection is the rear-cover photograph of Atwood that I have already described. The cut-and-paste, divided images reflect Atwood's infamous comment that the national mental illness of Canada is paranoid schizophrenia (p. 62). The drawn figures surrounded by their thin white haloes reflect the sense of profound alienation, an experience which is crucial to the poetry as a whole.

The appropriation of the land is, as McDougall says, an important part of taking photographs, but because he ignores the element of gender difference in the way that the camera signifies in a text, he is too quick to dismiss the photographic image as stultifying. Alice Munro, who is often viewed alongside Atwood as an 'establishment' woman writer, is no exception to the tradition I see of writers using the photograph as a dynamic, rather than sterile or frozen image. Munro's *The Progress of Love*[10] includes the story 'Lichen' which uses the central figure of a photograph without literally reproducing it on the page. Fiction such as Michael Ondaatje's *Coming Through Slaughter* and *Billy The Kid*, Kim Morrissey's *Batoche* and Daphne Marlatt's *Steveston* include photographs which function in various ways as supplements to the text. Munro's story, which makes use of a Polaroid snap, is chosen here because the image in the text explicitly deals with the relationship between women and the landscape, and because Munro uses it to dramatise the power relations between men and women, providing a useful analogy for much of the documentary inclusion that features in Atwood's *Journals*.

'Lichen' involves Stella and her ex-husband, David, who comes to Sunday dinner bringing Catharine, his current woman-friend, only to disclose privately to Stella that he is having an affair with a much younger woman, Dina, who is of the same generation as his and Stella's children. David's disclosure ends with his showing a Polaroid snapshot to Stella whilst she is preparing lunch:

> 'It looks like lichen,' says Stella, her paring knife halting.
> 'Except it's rather dark. It looks to me like moss on a rock.'
> 'Don't be dumb, Stella. Don't be cute. You can see her. See her legs?'
> Stella puts the paring knife down and squints obediently. There is a flattened-out breast far away on the horizon. And the legs spreading into the foreground. The legs are spread wide – smooth, golden, monumental: fallen columns. Between them is the dark blot she called moss, or lichen. But it's really more like the pelt of an animal, with the head and tail and feet chopped off. Dark silky pelt of some unlucky rodent. (Munro, p. 32)

The photograph that David shows off proudly to Stella turns the body of Dina into a mutant animal or into part of the natural landscape. Dina is flattened by the two-dimensional representation of her, smoothed out into the background, just as David's careless descriptions of his lovers are designed precisely to frame them, contain them, stop them from overflowing. They are smoothed out into character shapes that can be appropriated, carried around in his pocket, to be pulled out smugly in front of his ex-wife.

When David first sees Stella again, he is horrified by her appearance. She has been berry picking and David sees her, significantly, as she steps out of the bushes:

> She is a short, fat, white-haired woman, wearing jeans and a dirty t-shirt. There is nothing underneath these clothes, as far as he can see, to support or restrain any part of her.
> 'Look what's happened to Stella,' says David, fuming.
> 'She's turned into a troll.' (Munro, p. 33)

Stella trampling around the bushes collecting berries suggests to David an ugly, supernatural creature, 'the sort of woman who has to come bursting out of the female envelope at this age' (p. 33). In growing older, and particularly in living independently, Stella has ruptured David's neat image of her as his ex-wife and the mother of their children. What he sees bursting out of her, manifest in her flesh, are her political beliefs. What he perceives as her feminism appears to have inscribed itself on her body and she becomes physically repulsive to him as a result.

But Stella's sense of herself is shaken by David's visit and by the photograph, which he leaves with her, propped on the windowsill where it fades in the sun. The picture has been transformed:

She sees that the black pelt in the picture has changed to gray. It's bluish or greenish gray now. She remembers what she said when she first saw it. She said it was lichen. No, she said it looked like lichen . . . And now, look, her words have come true. The outline of the breast has disappeared. You would never know that the legs were legs. The black has turned to gray, to the soft, dry color of a plant mysteriously nourished on the rocks.

This is David's doing. He left it there, in the sun.

Stella's words have come true. This thought will keep coming back to her – a pause, a lost heartbeat, a harsh little break in the flow of the days and nights as she keeps them going. (Munro, p. 55)

The photograph in this Munro story becomes a figure of transformation. The Polaroid snapshot, together with Dina and indeed Stella, refuse to fit in the nice neat frames that David creates for them. They exceed his control. But it is also this power which causes Stella's lost heartbeat. Her life is no longer 'David's doing'. She can no longer ask that he take responsibility for creating her image. They are her own words, not David's, that have come true. And here is the final irony. Stella recognises that by an act of will and a flash of invention she is as capable of turning people into landscape, fixing and appropriating them as David's representations of his lovers do.

Munro's story explores a woman's received image of herself and of other women, an image constructed by a dominant man and Stella is shocked when she finds herself questioning these portraits. Similarly, Atwood's Moodie finds herself questioning her self-image and her identity when the familiar mirrors of Reydon Hall and the Suffolk countryside are removed from her. 'Looking in a Mirror' finds a similar merging of the ageing woman into the natural landscape that is expressed in 'Lichen'. Moodie sees herself suddenly as having 'skin thickened / with bark and the white hairs of roots' (Atwood, p. 24). Her 'heirloom face', that oval-enclosed portrait of the front cover, is no longer a smooth ovum but rather 'crushed eggshell', and her fingers are 'brittle as twigs'. In her new environment, up until this point,

Moodie has been unable to see, her eyes 'blind/ buds, which can see/ only the wind'. Her language has to be newly formed to fit the New World, speech coming only with effort, 'the mouth cracking / open like a rock in fire' (p. 24). But the vision of herself in the mirror seven years on from her arrival is a shock most of all because, the poem suggests, Moodie really may not have changed at all, or may not know whether she has been transformed by her new environment or not:

> (you find only
> the shape you already are
> but what
> if you have forgotten that
> or discover you
> have never known)
>
> (Atwood, p. 25)

Until Stella recognises her own graying form in the lichen/pelt/pubic hair of the photograph, she has not realised how far David has created an image for her, as he has done for his other lovers. Stella seems never to have known the shape she is, just as Moodie does not remember how to recognise herself in the mirror. Both Atwood and Munro use the metamorphosis of women into the landscape as a metaphor for examining moments of crisis of identity through ageing and, more generally, the horror of historical subjectivity.

Roslyn Jolly, in her comparative essay on transformation in works by Atwood, Malouf and Heaney, is enlightening on matters of alienation, identity-splitting and loss.[11] She writes of *The Journals of Susanna Moodie*:

> Without the anchors of civilization, especially the power of naming (and thereby defining) objects and identities may be changed by the environment.

Jolly identifies acts of 'creative vandalism' inflicted on language by *The Journals of Susanna Moodie*. She asserts that it is 'necessary to dismember language as the received view of the world before it is possible to see or express clearly', continuing that Atwood's violent acts upon syntactical and grammatical conventions create 'poetic forms of typographical spaciousness which suggest topographical spaciousness'. This analysis of the assault on language performed by Atwood's poetry eerily echoes the fate of her character Moodie.

Jolly argues a convincing case for Atwood and Moodie making spaces for themselves in the land and the language through their writing, but ultimately she concludes that Atwood's disruptive use of the langscape (language as it relates to the land and the layout of the page) is a process of 'exploiting the colonial lack of history and self-definition as a means of achieving a Romantic ideal of mythic unity of self with universe: the colonial exile of "fall" from the metropolis will be Romantically fortunate'. Jolly seems to be suggesting here that Atwood, despite the radical approach towards writing in her *Journals*, is really a believer in the notion of the return to pure language and unviolated landscape outside the corrupt city.

Jolly seems to read Atwood's writing as being technically innovative but politically conservative, in favour of the attempt to achieve a kind of pre-Edenic state of metaphysical self-identity through colonisation. Jolly calls Moodie a colonial exile but Moodie is not the only person who has been displaced by the projects of settlement under the British Empire, and it seems to me that Jolly misses Atwood's strong criticisms of Moodie for being part of a process of colonisation that makes exiles of native peoples *on their own land*. Jolly ultimately reads Atwood's Moodie as one of the rehabilitative women on whose shoulders rests the reparation of the damaged ecosystem.[12]

However, Jolly's conclusion to her reading of *The Journals* seems to me to collude in a framing of women within the categories of the natural, the caring, the essentially ecological. As Bronwen Wallace writes, within inverted commas:

> 'women are more interested in peace
> and things of that nature . . .
> the human interest stuff'
>
> (Wallace, p. 86)[13]

In this poem, 'Koko', Wallace discusses the gorilla that was taught American Sign Language by Francine Patterson in the 1970s, and explores the challenge that this animal's acquisition of language causes in terms of patriarchal power. 'Who says / and what / is what it comes to, though,' she writes, citing the dismissal of Koko because of her low IQ, but adding that we accept all kinds of other techno-junk without question because of the power at their source. The problem that Koko poses is what divides humans from animals. Her mastering of sign language, as well as her adoption of a pet kitten, and her use of a camera, give her all the attributes expected of a woman within Western culture – communication skills, technological capability (in a restricted way) and nurturing abilities.

The problem with Koko, Donna Haraway argues, begins with her name, 'a key rhetorical device' which bestows upon her 'a particular kind of individuality in the form of an apparently timeless, universal selfhood'.[14] The merging of the boundaries between human and primate through the creation of a particular identity for a zoo gorilla is paralleled by the shift of women into mutant animals, lumps of lichen, trolls or trees. The identity of a woman is bestowed upon her by the men in her life or in her world ('Who says / and what / is what it comes to though') and as *The Journals of Susanna Moodie* and 'Lichen' clearly show, this identity sways when the men and their powers are challenged. This would seem to go a long way to explaining women's collusion in their own oppression – their very selves are at risk.

Notes

1. Margaret Atwoord, *The Journals of Susanna Moodie* (Ontario: Oxford University Press, 1970). Subsequent page references are to this edition and included in the essay.
2. Fiona Sparrow explains that the prefix 'were' originates in the Anglo-Saxon word for 'man'. She argues that the word 'wereman' is 'on the surface meaningless', but that it is 'presumably something distinct but related to a werewolf'. She then implies that it might have something to do with nature in '"This place is some kind of a garden"': Clearings in the bush in the works of Susanna Moodie, Catharine Parr Traill, Margaret Atwood and Margaret Laurence' in *The Journal of Commonwealth Literature*, XXV, 1 (1990), p. 32. I would argue that the term is rather to do with cultural codes of the supernatural and of masculinity.
3. Mary di Michele, *Luminous Emergencies* (Toronto: McClelland and Stewart, 1990). Subsequent page references in the text are to this edition.
4. Mary di Michele, 'Conversations with the Living and the Dead' in Libby Scheier, Sarah Sheard and Eleanor Watchel, eds, *Language in her Eye: Views on Writing and Gender by Canadian Women Writing in English* (Toronto: Coach House Press, 1990), p. 106.
5. Ibid., p. 106.
6. For a development and fuller analysis of the term 'langscape', see Gaile McGregor, *The Wacoust Syndrome: Explorations in the Canadian Langscape* (Toronto: University of Toronto Press, 1985).
7. Russell McDougall, '"A Portable Kit of Images": Photography in Australian and Canadian Literature in English', *Kunapipi*, IX, 1 (1987), pp. 110–121.
8. Susan Sontag, *On Photography* (Harmondsworth: Penguin, 1979).
9. Shirley Neumann and Robert Wilson, eds, *Labyrinths of Voice: Conversations with Robert Kroetsch* (Edmonton: NeWest Press, 1982).
10. Alice Munro, 'Lichen', *The Progress of Love* (London: Fontana, 1988). Subsequent page references are to this edition and included in the essay.
11. Roslyn Jolly, 'Transformations of Caliban and Ariel: Imagination and Language in David Malouf, Margaret Atwood and Seamus Heaney', *World Literature Written in English*, 26, 2 (1986), pp. 295–330.
12. Donna Haraway, *Primate Visions* (London: Routledge, 1989).
13. Bronwen Wallace, *The Stubborn Particulars of Grace* (Toronto: McClelland and Stewart, 1987).
14. Haraway, op. cit., p 146.

3

Writing About Writing: Malcolm Lowry's Novelistic Fiction

Peter Easingwood

Malcolm Lowry, in the most productive period of his literary career, in the 1940s and early 1950s, occupied a waterside shack on the beach at Dollarton, near Vancouver. Being the kind of artist inclined to place a symbolic construction on his own experience, Lowry was to exploit this marginal situation in the course of his work. He described himself as being in 'the crucificial position of a writer in Canada'.[1] Yet he also represented this place on the Pacific Rim as the site of a new experiment in writing in English. Lowry's inclusion in both Canadian and Modernist canons has for long remained problematic, but his fiction stands to gain as much now as it appeared to lose at the actual time of writing from an account of its transgression of the current limits of genre. Lowry's fiction characterised the vocation of writing itself as part of the general cultural crisis of the time. On this basis he is the most experimental anglophone writer of his generation. He produced writing that extends from the short story to the novel and from the novel to the 'novelistic'. The latter term, adapted from Roland Barthes, provides a way of reconsidering the significance of a writing career that had seemed to end in failure if judged by conventional standards. The implications of this argument will be developed first by reference to *Under the Volcano* and then through discussion of stories in *Hear Us O Lord From Heaven Thy Dwelling Place*.

Under the Volcano (1947) has acquired a special status for a certain community of readers as a 'linguistic carnival'[2] even if it has not secured recognition as a classic novel. In this connection, Barthes' observations in *Writing Degree Zero* (1953), on the limitations of the classic novel and on the 'problematic of writing'[3] which confronts the contemporary writer of fiction, have immediate relevance to Lowry's situation. By 1953 Lowry had reached a point of crisis at which he continued to write in the knowledge that his editor and American publisher now found him virtually unreadable.[4] In Lowry's case, the degree-zero style which Barthes considers as a model for new writing is clearly inapplicable: in his own search for a style, Lowry is given rather to excess. As early as 1940, Lowry envisages writing 'the last book of its kind': this would be a novel which aspired to 'inexhaustibility' though it would nevertheless be fully representational as a work of fiction and would proclaim its cultural and linguistic relationship to a European tradition. Lowry describes this project with the fear that it might sound 'too pretentious'. The statement resonates with ambition and anxiety, dressed up in apocalyptic terms:

> I have been writing this book, as it were, out of Europe's 'unconscious' . . . As the last scream of anguish of the consciousness of a dying continent, an owl of Minerva flying at evening, the last book of its kind, written by someone whose type and species is dead, even as a final contribution to English literature itself . . . [5]

The eventually completed project of *Under the Volcano* wears its apocalyptic mask with a grin of pleasure. The pleasure of the text is constituted by the writing's self-conscious enjoyment of its own textuality: the fantastic elaboration of the language seems to recondition the conventional elements of narrative fiction, encouraging the reader to look beyond the requirements of realism and to enter into a more 'writerly' and playful relationship with the text.[6] At the opening of the novel, M. Laruelle speculates on the arrival under his pillow of 'that long-belated postcard of Yvonne's'[7] which had been addressed not to himself but to the Consul. The significance of the postcard floats for over 300 pages before the reader reaches a position to interpret it. The novel is characterised by the apparently erratic play of signification within a structure that turns out to have the elements of a conventional plot. The uncertain circulation of written materials is a theme that marks the pathos of the Consul's existence, as signified by 'the thumbed maroon volume of Elizabethan plays' (p. 34) that the Consul had lent Laruelle; and the 'two sheets of uncommonly thin hotel notepaper' (p. 42) that drop out of it. Laruelle reflects that by this latter stage of events, the Consul had 'lost almost all capacity for telling the truth and his life had become a quixotic fiction' though he still continued to search for meaning in texts: 'How the Consul had delighted in the absurd game too: sortes Shakespeareanae . . . ' (pp. 40–1). The same opening chapter relates the Consul's condition to the myth of the Tower of Babel: 'How admirably he had concealed what must have been the babel of his thoughts!' (p. 17). Enraptured with the play of signification, deeply familiar with the seductiveness and treachery of language, the writing invites the reader to enjoy the artifice of fiction.

The reader is granted freedom to respond to the artifice of the writer's performance but it must be added that Lowry's writing displays
a certain kind of semiological intensity. In representing the Consul's
crisis, the text aspires to be the writing on the wall for the whole
period, as it spells out its ominous message for the times. Laruelle is
confronted by a cinema poster which looms over him with the force
of an expressionist image, overriding the boundary between objective
and subjective reality:

> so far as he remembered the film not even Peter Lorre
> had been able to salvage it and he didn't want to see it
> again . . . Yet what a complicated endless tale it seemed to
> tell, of tyranny and sanctuary, that poster looming above
> him now, showing the murderer Orlac! An artist with mur-
> derer's hands; that was the ticket, the hieroglyphic of the
> times. For really it was Germany itself that, in the gruesome
> degradation of a bad cartoon, stood over him. – Or was it, by
> some uncomfortable stretch of the imagination, M. Laruelle
> himself?   (pp. 31–2)

From the remote and obscure situation described in this opening chapter there extends a long chain of signification by which the text seeks
to link itself to the context of world war, to establish itself as the
complicated endless tale of its own culture.

For its author and perhaps for most of Lowry's readers, *Under the
Volcano* has a unique status within his work. Lowry was deeply ambivalent about the success of its initial reception. His poem, 'After the
publication of *Under the Volcano*', opens: 'Success is like some horri-
ble disaster . . . ' The immediate embarrassment of the occasion, and
the struggle against writer's block that followed publication, provide
extensive illustration of the problem. To begin with, this author of extreme self-consciousness, who was working at the limits of the novel
as a genre, found himself weirdly compromised by considerations of a
conventional and extremely damaging kind. Lowry was seriously worried over possible charges of plagiarism.[8] In retrospect, the cause for
concern may seem superficial but the same charge had already arisen
in connection with his first novel, *Ultramarine* (1933), with the result
that by this time any mention of that book had become unbearable to
Lowry. Paradoxically, *Under the Volcano* might be perceived both as
highly eccentric and yet as derivative or even plagiarised. The project
of writing a sequel with the title *Under Under the Volcano* became for
Lowry a desperate joke. All subsequent attempts on his part to produce
a novel capable of satisfying the North American and British markets
were marked by an anxiety, concerning his vocation as a writer, that
reveals itself both within the literary texts he produced and in letters
he wrote during this period.

Lowry's strategy at this point involved making a number of fresh starts. His idea was that everything should eventually contribute to an overall design in which *Under the Volcano* would be one among a series of interconnected narratives. The series would be called, appropriately enough as it turned out, *The Voyage that Never Ends*. Parts of it remain still unpublished. Each new beginning took the form of a short story, but *October Ferry to Gabriola* developed from story to novel length, just as *Under the Volcano* had done before it. Lowry had reached a point where conventional conceptions of novel and short story were no longer relevant to what he was attempting. A related issue is that the distinction between autobiography and fiction also becomes increasingly problematic in his writing. Even where narratives are still constructed in the familiar third-person style of fictional presentation, the investment of the author in the narration is brought into question as part of the design. Lowry had begun to mix genres in a style that is neither short story nor novel nor autobiography, but as indicated above 'novelistic.'

It seems appropriate to consider Lowry in this connection because the pieces collected in *Hear Us O Lord From Heaven Thy Dwelling Place* (unpublished when the author died in 1957) characterise the problem with 'the instrument of writing' that Barthes identifies as the principal stylistic and cultural challenge to the writer in this period. 'Novelistic' writing is discussed as a key term in an interview Barthes gave in 1975. Barthes is quoted as saying: 'I love the novelistic, but I know that the novel is dead'. Barthes' response to being questioned more closely on this term is as follows:

> The novelistic is a mode of discourse unstructured by a story; a mode of notation, investment, interest in daily reality, in people, in everything that happens in life. The transformation of this novelistic material into a novel seems very difficult to me because I can't imagine myself elaborating a narrative object where there would be a story, which to me means essentially verbs in the imperfect and past historic, characters who are psychologically believable – that's the sort of thing I could never do, that's why a novel seems impossible to me. But at the same time I would like very much to work more on the novelistic experience, the novelistic utterance.[9]

Undeniably there are problems in relating this statement to Lowry's actual practice; perhaps even unresolved tensions within the statement itself. How far such a narrative could be 'unstructured by story' remains doubtful. This kind of development may perhaps better be imagined as taking place along a continuum rather than as being initiated only after a complete break with the history of the 'story'. But Barthes' comments here have a direct bearing on the problem of modern writing as he had expounded it earlier in *Writing Degree Zero*. The following statement represents a compelling insight into Lowry's predicament, though no one writing in English could have articulated it in this way at the time:

> Nature speaks, elaborating living languages from which the writer is excluded . . . History puts into his hands a deco-rative and compromising instrument, a writing inherited from a previous and different History, for which he is not responsible and yet which is the only one he can use . . . [10]

The Lowry of 1940, who constructs his creative gesture so portentously as writing 'out of Europe's unconscious', exemplifies the terms of this difficult 'inheritance'. Barthes considers the stylistic implications of this pressure on the writer. Again, his remarks could be illustrated from the case of Lowry. Barthes writes of:

> this fatal character of the literary sign, which makes a writer unable to pen a word without taking a pose characteristic of an out-of-date, anarchic or imitative language . . . one in any case conventionalised and dehumanised.[11]

Lowry's texts usually convey a general sense of fatality which he at-tributes to the cultural-historical environment at the time of writing. However Barthes' discussion offers a more intimate insight into the ac-tual writing process and concludes that there is also a kind of 'fatality' inherent in the situation of the contemporary writer.

For Lowry, the escape from his writer's block came through a re-lease into novelistic utterance which he achieved by writing about writing. His new writing persistently took this direction even though his editor, Albert Erskine, tried to obstruct this development. Erskine's advice was that stories about writers were anathema to publishers. To Lowry, this line of development seemed attractive, even irresistible. He made out his case at length.[12] But Erskine had a point: writing about writing could appear an evasive strategy, a withdrawal from the re-sponsibility of constructing a conventionally acceptable story, and a retreat into introspection. Critics are still debating the charge of solip-sism sometimes made against Lowry; the whole issue of his reference to historical and social reality is keenly disputed.[13] In fact it can be argued that, by deciding to foreground the act of writing itself and by making representation such an issue in these texts, Lowry moves to-wards the kind of 'notation, investment, interest in daily reality . . . ' that informs Barthes' sense of the novelistic.

Writing about writing is for Lowry a way of acknowledging litera-ture's participation in the general crisis of the times. The most familiar theme in his work is the progress of an individual, who is carrying some obscure psychic wound, towards finding a place and a commu-nity in the postwar world that can satisfy the life of the imagination.

The fiction is always constructed on the thematic opposition between utopian desire and dystopian trauma. However, the later fiction begins to acknowledge such ambivalence and conflict within the actual process of writing: repeatedly, the underlying issue at stake in these texts is the capacity of literary language for self-renewal. To quote the closing sentence of *Writing Degree Zero*, it is as if 'Literature becomes the Utopia of language.' Lowry's story 'The Forest Path to the Spring', for example, strains towards a kind of utopian climax in its account of language as well as in its thematic development. The first-person narrator invokes the idea of:

> a region where such words as spring, water, houses, trees, vines, laurels, mountains, wolves, bay, roses, beach, islands, forest, tides and deer and snow and fire, had realized their true being . . . [14]

The flatness of the formulation shows that the writing is under acute strain at this point in 'Forest Path': the words here can hardly be said to release themselves from their common associations. But Lowry's writing cultivates a mood of expectancy, a suggestion that language may liberate itself from conventional usage to create a new view of hell or paradise.

'Strange Comfort Afforded by the Profession' is the central piece in the collection of *Hear Us O Lord* but is arguably the best place to begin. As Lowry practices it, novelistic writing must inscribe within itself the signature of its own textuality: 'Strange Comfort' is an outstanding performance in this respect. It addresses a theme in which Lowry had a peculiar interest: that of a dead poets' society.[15] The opening setting is contemporary: Rome, at the house of John Keats; the story also makes extensive reference to the death of Edgar Allan Poe. The entire motivation of the story is deeply involved with what *Writing Degree Zero* terms 'the literary myth', and with issues of creativity and freedom that affect the position of the writer in society. The point of view is that of Sigbjorn Wilderness, one of the series of writers and artists in this collection. The situation has strong autobiographical significance for Lowry and quotes from one of his own letters. The novelistic signature is inscribed in various ways. The text represents a drawing, which Wilderness makes in his notebook, of the lyre which appears on the front of Keats' house, 'similar to the one on the poet's tomb'. The narrative then focuses on the notebook, where Wilderness has developed his own special form of notation:

> he realized that the peculiar stychometry of his observations, jotted down as if he imagined he were writing a species of poem, had caused him prematurely to finish his notebook . . . That didn't mean there was no more space, for his notebooks, he reflected avuncularly, just like his

candles, tended to consume themselves at both ends; yes,
as he thought, there was some writing at the beginning.
(p. 104)

This leads to a series of reflections on writing as a vocation: on the materials and 'protocols'[16] of the writer's work; on the always troubled
relations between contemporary writing and the literary myth. As a
form of compensation for his own troubles, but without total convic-
tion, Wilderness tries to imagine himself as belonging to the historic
community of writers who were able to sustain their vision against
severe contemporary discouragement.

The other Roman story in the collection, 'Elephant and Colos-
seum', is again constructed as if from a writer's point of view. Kennish
Drumgold Cosnahan looks without success for the publisher's office
of his Italian translator. He meets an old friend, an elephant at the
zoo. The narrative is about nothing if not about writing. The story
suggests a cinematic potential in its representation of a scene filled
with human movement, together with its extravagant investment in
the play of coincidence. But these effects ultimately depend on the vitality of the writer's fantasies: the craving for recognition, the dread
of the publisher's cold shoulder, the anxious estimation of divergences
between the American and European markets. The apparently casual
form of notation is developed to a point where a fascination with the
process of fiction becomes apparent: 'No preposterous recognition in
literature . . . could have been more complete . . . ' (p. 168).

'Present State of Pompeii' opens with another writer, Roderick
McGregor Fairhaven, nursing a bottle of vino rosso in the Restaurant
Vesuvius and resisting for as long as possible his duty as a tourist to
inspect the ruins of Pompeii. His comment that, 'It was a silly place
to put a volcano' (p. 191) encodes the humorous self-advertisement of
an author who is a connoisseur of volcanoes; who followed Lawrence
to Mexico and is competing with him again in Italy. The setting
stimulates allusion to Eliot's *The Waste Land* (p. 188) as well as to
Volney's *Ruin of Empires* (p. 194). Some of the local ruins in the story
are man-made: the result of wartime American bombing. Fairhaven,
'half watching himself watch his wife in the mirror' (p. 178), struggles
against the 'migraine of alienation' (p. 177) that the scene produces in
him. The story attempts to construct the writer's attitude to his own
experience and succeeds at least partly in achieving this, by locating
Fairhaven in a setting where the recorded contest between Nature
and History is so ancient and by framing him, between two sets
of ruins, in an 'imperfect or dislocated relation to his environment'
(p. 200).

'Through the Panama' offers itself to the reader as the story of a
postwar voyage in an old Liberty ship from the Pacific coast of Canada

to Europe; as an allegory of rebirth; and as an experiment in writing
to bear out the claim that:

> Nothing indeed can be more unlike the actual experience
> of life than the average novelist's realistic portrait of a
> character. (p. 85)

The story introduces as its narrator Sigbjorn Wilderness, who in turn
introduces a second point of view, that of Martin Trumbaugh, a fictional character 'who becomes enmeshed in the plot of the novel he
has written, as I did in Mexico' (p. 27). The text expands at several
points into the margin, where historical references and quotations from
Coleridge's 'The Rime of the Ancient Mariner' serve as a gloss on the
main narrative. Trumbaugh's characterisation emerges in the context
of 'the continual painful conflict that went on between him and reality'
(p. 86). It has been argued that:

> Of all Lowry's late stories, 'Through the Panama' is the one
> which most radically ruptures the conventions of realism. By
> actually fragmenting the story on the printed page, making
> the reader face two parallel narratives, Lowry demolished
> the principle of linear progression (the very essence of the
> *book*) in a striking and original fashion.[17]

'Through the Panama' illustrates in the most spectacular way the kind
of provisionality that entered Lowry's view of the text in the later fiction. At first sight, the story which was intended to be the final part
of the unfinished sequence, 'The Forest Path to the Spring,' may seem
a less writerly text.

'The Forest Path' constructs the cool Canadian paradise imagined
by the Consul in the closing pages of *Under the Volcano*. Considered
as a story about an attempt to lead the simple life on the margins of
postwar society, under the constant threat of eviction, it is easily sen-
timentalised. What saves it is the novelistic discourse that enables the
writing to reflect critically on its own utopianism. Though the narrator Sigbjorn Wilderness asserts his idealising view of the scene, the
rhetoric of the story also displays a stylistic overcoding, a discursive
elaboration, which compels recognition of the provisional state of affairs; of the difference between Nature and History; of the gap between
things and words. The idyllic strand carries a reminder of history in
the form of the wrecked steamer which has become a landmark for
the community living on the beach:

> And on the stern, seeming to comment on my own source,
> for I too had been born in that terrible city whose main street
> is the ocean, could still be almost made out the ghost of the
> words: *Eridanus*, Liverpool —
>
> We poor folks were also Eridanus, a condemned com-
> munity, perpetually under the shadow of eviction. And like

Eridanus itself, in its eternal flux and flow, was the inlet.
(pp. 226–7)

This 'comment on my own source' undercuts the arcadian sentiment
of the narrative by using the coincidence of the name 'Eridanus' to
connect an uncertain future with a 'terrible' past. This is a precarious, rented paradise where some of the shacks have ironic names like
'Wywurk' (p. 220) which, among other associations, recalls the name
of the house in Australia in which Lawrence wrote *Kangaroo*. The pattern of notation constantly problematises the narrator's enthusiastic
account of this place.

Lowry tried to describe his own idea of 'novelistic' writing to Albert
Erskine. To support his argument, he cites Ortega's view on the creative
awareness of the individual; an awareness which supposedly informs
every thoughtful person's attitude to their own experience. The Lowry
narrator is an artist figure in this sense: 'he is Ortega's fellow, making
up his life as he goes along, and trying to find his vocation'.[18] As the
narrator expresses it in 'The Forest Path':

> there is a sense in which everybody on this earth is a writer,
> the sense in which Ortega . . . means it. Ortega has it that
> a man's life is like a fiction that he makes up as he goes
> along. He becomes an engineer and converts it into reality –
> becomes an engineer for the sake of doing that. (p. 271)

Lowry found this a valuable way of thinking about the relationship
between life and fiction. His later texts are designed as illustrations
of this sort of engineering. To make the design work, Lowry decided
that he needed to foreground writing as a vocation and to show 'the
bloody agony of the writer writing.'[19] But he insisted that he could
construct this situation in a style that would still be accessible to the
general reader: 'there is an artist, a poet in every man, hence he is a
creature easy for anyone to identify themselves with':

> Even kids, and our forgetful grocer and postmaster – perhaps
> especially our forgetful grocer and postmaster – can identify
> themselves with such: as can Jimmy Craige, the boat-builder,
> and Gulbrandsan the fisherman, etc.[20]

In statements like this, Lowry may seem trapped not only by the
gendered language of the period but by wishful thinking. Erskine was
certainly not convinced by this at the time. Recent Lowry criticism
concedes that he still 'remains a marginal figure'.[21] Yet such an assessment of Lowry could have positive as well as negative implications.
From the beginning, Lowry looked for his material at the margins of
contemporary English culture and beyond. During the wartime and
postwar years, he became one of the millions of displaced people in
transit between Europe and the New World. The stories construct the
figure of the artist as a Displaced Person: exile, lover, drunk, traveller,

squatter or beachcomber. Even on the most grudging estimate, this is potentially interesting material. But of course, in the case of Lowry, it is not possible to speak of the writer's attitude to his material simply in conventional terms, because his view of the fictional process undergoes such change. His writing increasingly opposes the concept of the finality of the literary work and instead chooses to represent itself as being in process. It is a form of writing that constantly returns to the notation of a given reality: a kind of realism, but not the bankrupt realism to which Lowry thought too many of his contemporaries were still committed. A significant part of the notation consists in the effort to display the process itself, involving the frequent play of allusion to the materiality of the text. In this way, writing begins to incorporate a range of observation and reflection that would certainly appear marginal according to received opinions about the realistic novel and the short story in English. For some readers, though, this marginal extension allows an increase in the pleasure of the text.

Notes

1. Cited by Gordon Bowker, *Pursued By Furies: A Life of Malcolm Lowry* (London: HarperCollins, 1993), p. 477.
2. This phrase is used by Sue Vice in *Malcolm Lowry Eighty Years On*, ed. Sue Vice (Basingstoke and London: Macmillan, 1989), p. 4.
3. Roland Barthes, *Writing Degree Zero and Elements of Semiology*, trans. Annette Lavers and Colin Smith (London: Jonathan Cape, 1984), p. 72.
4. See Bowker, pp. 536–43.
5. Cited by Bowker, p. 296. (Letter to Whit Burnett 22 June 1940).
6. The writerly text is designed 'to make the reader no longer a consumer, but a producer of the text'. Roland Barthes, *S/Z*, trans. Richard Miller (London: Jonathan Cape, 1974), p. 4.
7. Malcolm Lowry, *Under the Volcano* (London: Jonathan Cape, 1947), p. 19. All further references are included in the text of the essay.
8. For a discussion of Lowry's style which includes comparison between *Under the Volcano* and Charles Jackson's novella, *The Lost Weekend* see Victor Sage, 'The Art of Sinking in Prose: Charles Jackson, Joyce, and *Under the Volcano*,' in *Malcolm Lowry Eighty Years On*, pp. 35–50.
9. Roland Barthes, *The Grain of the Voice: Interviews 1962–1980*, trans. Linda Coverdale (New York: Hill and Wang, 1986), pp. 222–23.
10. *Writing Degree Zero*, pp. 71–2.
11. *Writing Degree Zero*, p. 70.
12. *Selected Letters of Malcolm Lowry*, ed. Harvey Breit and Margerie Bonner Lowry (Harmondsworth: Penguin, 1965), pp. 329–32. (Letter to Albert Erskine, Dollarton, Spring, 1953).
13. For example, see Dominic Head, 'Expanding Circles: Inductive Composition in "Hear Us O Lord From Heaven Thy Dwelling Place"', in *Malcolm Lowry Eighty Years On*, pp. 70–91.

14. Malcolm Lowry, *Hear Us O Lord From Heaven Thy Dwelling Place* (Harmondsworth: Penguin, 1979), p. 284. All further references to the stories in this volume are incorporated in the text of the essay.
15. See the account of the discussion between Lowry and Nordahl Grieg on the subject of Grieg's book, *The Young Dead* in Bowker, pp. 126–29.
16. 'Personally, I call the set of those "rules" (in the monastic sense of the word) which predetermine the work – and it is important to distinguish the different coordinates: working time, working space, and the action of writing itself – the 'protocols' of work.' Barthes, *The Grain of the Voice*, p. 178.
17. Ronald Binns, *Malcolm Lowry* (London and New York: Methuen, 1984), p. 83.
18. *Selected Letters*, p. 331.
19. *Selected Letters*, p. 339.
20. *Selected Letters*, p. 330.
21. *Malcolm Lowry Eighty Years On*, p. 6.

4

'The Crops Are Stressed': Charles Noble's
Let's Hear It For Them

John O. Thompson

0. When I visited Canada last, summer of 1991, there was a national atmosphere so strained, so cross . . . Edmonton, but Vancouver and Victoria too. Meech Lake, the new tax, free trade. Now, in 1992, Europe similarly: Maastricht, German unification souring, recession, devaluation, agricultural subsidy by some so loathed and by others the threat of its disappearance so feared . . . Further east, what horrors . . . Wilfred Watson's Sorrowful Canadians of the 1970s having been succeeded by something so much more angrily gloomy, I did find myself almost delighting in it as in a new energy, a new page turned. Now, Europe similarly, the USA similarly (Ross Perot, deficit, 'life'/'choice', medical costs, Japan, entitlements). Still 1789 perhaps, but our century's '17 dead in its '89. The great Thatcherite acronym, TINA, There Is No Alternative, recto, and its verso, ANIT, All Nations In Turmoil. (In a British Film Institute office called 'TV and Projects', my friend Tana, who claims her own name is alternatively acronymic – There Are Numerous Alternatives – has a secretary called Anita, a Trot true-believer still, chuffed to be lent Lukacs. These women aside . . .)

Philosophy and farming. And if the astonishing thing, the really astonishing thing, should turn out to be that the most tedious and dated of all global political-economic 'debates' (and therefore naturally the one that was most centrally Canadian), Free Trade versus Protectionism, turns out to be what we are left with under TINA as motor of (end-of-)history. That to which there is no alternative being not The Market but Markets-Plus-Regulation. Regimes of trade are the prime site for regulatory debate: regulation to protect, regulation to dismantle protection. Strange geographies where Maastricht and Meech Lake meet Uruguay, oh GATT, as in a poem by Apollinaire. The 'repressed' returning is as nothing to the savage force of the return of the tedious and dated.

Philosophy the most universal of pursuits, if only as, much of the time at least, the pursuit of the universal, pondering the forms of ultimate General Agreement. Farming however, is always of particular land – in order to Trade certainly, but behind Tariff (or Subsidy) perhaps, if that keeps the land farmed? Or do the state and its banks themselves constitute in their stupidity, in their confidence in being able to 'fine-tune', the danger to farming? (Oscillations in policy: encouragement to borrow which then gets redefined as over-borrowing and administered as bankruptcy.) And need the anti-particularity of capitalism stop short of the land? Expand: not just the market, the market plus techno-science. Agri-business . . . Not a new thing neither. Grandparents . . .

My claim would be that the Pound antenna, or the Cocteau/Spicer radio, was tuned into our '90s, so far as these matters are concerned, by CN (Charles Noble) about a decade earlier.

Slowing down, and moving into more expository mode . . .

1. Charles Noble's *Let's Hear It For Them* (*LHIFT*)[1] is a long poem in five sections, plus a Janus-faced 'Postscriptum'. It appeared in book form in 1990, though earlier – in some cases radically different – versions of some of it were published as early as 1985. I don't think the Canadian Long Poem comes any better than this. The principal purpose of what follows is simply to advance that judgement.

The crudest plot summary that might be given of the poem would run along the following lines.

Section I, 'Coffee': an image of a naked woman standing in a prairie irrigation canal melts into a description of the immediate surroundings of the writer ('On the corner of an irregular, almost triangular, / homemade, stained, plywood table / is a can of gourmet coffee / long since empty but refilled over and over / with an ordinary brand' [p. 8]).

Section II, 'Opera': from an account of taking his mother to a local showing of the film *La Traviata*, CN moves to a broader account of family matters, notably involving his grandfather (' . . . was a gambler with weather, markets, / new ideas and the Winnipeg Grain Exchange' [p. 14])[2] and his father ('He drafted new frames, standards and blades, / let the blue prints soak in our bathtub, / sculpted an all-metal, dainty hammer for our house / and carved a pirate sword for my school pageant' [p. 13]).

Section III, 'Interview': a question-and-answer format is deployed very baroquely, with literary and philosophical topics ('Would you then say that this metaphor taken head on and no doubt in the service of something else, is a metonymic act?' [p. 19], melting into something (even) more dreamlike, 'I wrote a cheque for goodness and then I was dreaming; the dream was the headless under water where the viewer was excused and the view was a friend with all his untouchableness and useless past perfect' [p. 18]).

Section IV, 'Props': the shortest section; a meditation from the tractor ('I'm swathing west of the house / taking my pleasure in larger cycles / patiently doing the rounds on this 135 acre field / of spring wheat in the early fall . . . ' [p. 22]).

Section V, 'Grounds': the longest section, indeed longer than the other four together; a 'letter' format (e.g. 'Dear Slice of Cake', 'Dear Doctor', 'Dear Image', 'Dear Globe and Mail', 'Dear It', 'Dear COFFEE's imaginary canal')[3] is deployed, with as a central focus the financial crisis facing western Canadian agriculture and the inadequacy of media commentary on this ('Dear Globe and Mail //re your SHOULD CANADA QUIT FARMING? / (except for a few rutabagas and cabbages / around the cities) or WE CAN'T AFFORD OUR FARMERS' [p. 50]).

While I think that anyone reading this who hasn't yet had a chance to read *LHIFT* ought to be intrigued by this skeletal account (clearly the poem's macro-organisation is forceful and original), plot summary is radically insufficient to convey what makes the poem so extraordinary.

0.1. (Cutting across *LHIFT* exposition with the other big element of the collage as soon as possible): Jean-François Lyotard's collection of late-'80s essays and addresses *The Inhuman* (*TI*)[4] concludes with a dark and dazzling chapter entitled '*Domus* and the Megalopolis'.

The overall 'story' of *TI*, as of all post-'post-Modern' Lyotard, involves sweeping dichotomies, unabashed left-functionalist gloom, and a serenely unlimited capacity for reiteration, notably via a sense of the Burkean-Kantian Sublime (CN writes 'spare-me the Kantian-sublime' [p. 55], but I am not sure why) as a boundless resource with which to think both the enterprise of the avant-garde and the impossible possibility of justice.

If these elements are not automatically attractive, *TI* disarms certain criticisms by its self-definition as a discourse of failure. There are two Inhumans: the self-presentedly benign 'humanism' of Development (capitalism plus technoscience) which has the most violent effects on actual human beings living on the planet; and the inhuman as the pre-'human', the pre-socialised – the inhuman of the 'infans', the child before s/he speaks, that which from the beginning is and keeps itself unreconciled in us. Lyotard asks, regarding the first Inhuman: 'what else remains as 'politics' [after Marx; and now after the definitive dissolution of '17 in '89] except resistance to this inhuman?' And, continuing: 'And what else is left to resist with but the debt which each soul has contracted with the miserable and admirable indetermination from which it was born and does not cease to be born? – which is to say, with

other inhumans?' (*TI*, p. 7). The other inhuman, however, is clearly established as *not enough* with which to resist: Development does rule.
2.0. If 'Props' begins straightforwardly enough, as already quoted ('I'm swathing west of the house'), a page later this 'account of experience' has passed through some sort of forcefield, or meteor attack, which leaves its final five lines reading thus:

> this bit sudden, status quota/ unquota bread basket
> with assorted bottle necks reading/ anything
> with skirts, little parachute caps grass-read riding
> who'd think X-tended wooloves blanch, cut out to be
> cutting in? I'm the punched-up mouse and *the Hegel*'s over.
> (p. 23)

The play of language and of concept here is not something which would yield to explication or interpretation, though a 'puzzle' element does operate and yields the satisfaction of micro-level quasi-solutions. By this I mean: the reader picks up how Little Red Riding Hood is getting into the picture (into the words, the morphemes) by registering 'basket', 'bottle', 'skirts', ' . . . -read riding', 'wooloves', 'blanch' (white *against* red, Snow White?). There is a semantic linkage via 'basket' which opens on to the cliché 'bread basket of the world' and the agricultural economy theme ('quote/ unquota': protection/ free trade). There is a semantic linkage via 'riding' which connects CN 'in [his] glass booth' (p. 23) to riding (and reading? has he had a book to hand as he drives? 'You can see while the working works I've been able/ to think away' [p. 23] – perhaps even something by Hegel??).[5] But what does not seem to be required, or possible, is *interpretation* of such linkages.

Whatever can be 'got out of' the Red Riding Hood wolf as 'wooloves' (and this idiom itself recalls the bloody version of the tale, in which by means of the wood-cutter's axe the grandmother is 'got out of' the body of the wolf) is there to be semantically experienced, and savoured. But semantic experience is not, where poetry (this poetry, and arguably the most interesting poetry of our moment) is concerned, to interpret, to construe, to gain a mastering *understanding* of the text. Wooing and loving *might* connect powerfully with elements in the rest of the poem; but 'wolf – woolove', provides no less valid a micro-level semantic experience if it is momentary, unconnected (which is my impression). Either way, trying to pin down a 'meaning' for 'wolf – woolove', as though the effects of a small explosion within a word were to be construed as simply as a new word, a new sign, seems unprofitable.
0.2. The banality of certain assurances within the Cultural Studies tradition that resistance is either with us or straightforwardly attainable is not what Lyotard has in mind. The 'what else' is not guaranteed

or even likely – even if, at the dark heart of Development it remains as an ineluctable limit to what can be managed, digitalised, disembodied, sent on a spaceship to a new world after the death of the sun. ('You will smile at how much the picture I have drawn owes to fiction' [*TI*, p. 65].)

Still later as a Lyotard text: *Lectures d'enfance* (1991). 'Let's call it [*Baptisons-la*] *infantia*, that which does not speak' (p. 9). The 'it' is what these diverse texts suffer [*dont ces ecrits divers sont en souffrance'*] – the texts are by Joyce, Kafka, Arendt, Sartre, Valery, Freud – and what gives them, or some of them (Lyotard really hasn't forgiven Sartre) status as *écriture*, writing in the fullest and most mysterious sense.

2.1 But what is most striking about *LHIFT*, what would least emerge in any plot summary, is the audacity, indeed the violence, of its breaking up of the word.

The pun is basic to this operation, and *LHIFT* is as resourceful in its punning ('the drop of a pun' [p. 37]) as *Finnegans Wake*. (And yet a CN pun and a Joyce pun have very different shapes, different 'feels': specifying the difference would be a challenge.) More unusual is the breaking up of words via the slash mark, or the hyphen, or just a space. An example, plucked rudely from context:

> my/ th/ ought-ical doub t expel a whole school
> of thought/hot issues   note ice by conspeakyou/ us
> morsel Duchamption   O'Neill cometh to mind
>
> (p. 38)

Here the break-up after a respelling of 'methodical' yields 'my' (which will be picked up shortly in a division of 'images' into 'I'm ages'), 'myth', 'thought' and 'ought'. 'Notice' breaks into 'note ice' (with 'ice' bouncing off the 'hot' immediately preceding it, which was a quasi-pun on 'thought'). 'Conspicuous consumption', the Thorsten Veblen concept from *The Theory of the Leisure Class*, comes apart so that (i) 'speak' emerges and the personal pronoun 'you/us' are put into relation with the aforementioned 'my/I'; (ii) via a punning incorporation, 'consumption' is twisted to 'Duchamption' after Marcel Duchamp, the exemplary figure within our century's art whose work ought most to have escaped a Veblenesque cynical critique of art-market prestige valuation, and yet, arguably, didn't. 'Conspeak': a virtually Orwellian coinage. 'Morsel': Duchamp-in-pieces (not an inappropriate manner in which to invoke him). 'O'Neill cometh': a joke about ice (*The Iceman Cometh*), perhaps unconnected to the poem's larger concerns – though 'mind', given the heightened level of verbal sensitisation which such passages induce in the reader, may refer us back to 'thought' (or 'th/ ought') . . .

So, micro-level semantic delights: 'violent', one might say, against the word (but what word ever bled?); endlessly inventive and ingenious regarding the semantic riches that pour out of the word qua piggy-bank once it has been shattered. However, the violence or turbulence of the text at this level would not *itself* be extraordinary, or as extra-ordinary as it is, if there were not something larger, more referential, to which its energies and indeed its anxieties answered.

3.0. For instance, as a larger theme of the poem: the problem of over-borrowing encouraged within the agricultural sector by banks and government in the late '70s and then brutally reversed in the mid-'80s. An especially rich (!) stretch of text organised around the topic is to be found on pp. 54–5.

'PPS Protrait of a Bank Robber' (this is the penultimate postscript to the 'Dear It' letter): 'the bank rolls into town', *as* robber of course; less obviously, 'wearing waves for water skis'. Banking as tidal wave, 'wherein laws of the land take their take / to the seas'; oceanic, drown-ing, as reflected in a Shakespeare rewrite: 'those are fuzzy grey eyes they have for eyes': 'the bank rolls itself: a ship of waves / peeling waves in the troughs making the proph-its'. ('Peeling' here is something done idiomatically with/to eyes, and the bank's eyes have been glued to the screen, on the electronically embodied global rationality of capi-tal: 'the teller can't tell the chips are down / when the screen thumb is up'.) And after the bank has rolled in and rolled out, a gloomier sense of transformation under water than the pearly Shakespearean can be expressed: 'the farm operation is squeezed into a crystal   juiced'.

All this is written 'in this large house / designed for my grandfather by an architect from California / who died in the 1918 flu' (p. 15):

> what's the use   value   always already useree
> oscillates to useree   old spectres waived
>   . . .
> interest takes on the eyed unlidded   oceanic
> baffling capital simply shaded   inbricated into
> baffled nature   blind   duck blind
> and getting behind   us all ways
>
> (pp. 54–5)

I take it that the unhappiness over farm finance explored within the poem is generalisable, that it speaks more broadly to These Great Times, in Europe and the USA as well, to the Generally Agreed disaffection. '[D]ear Nietzsche / my *ressentiments* exactly' (p. 55) . . .

0.3. Returning to Lyotard, to his '*Domus* and the Megalopolis': the essay sets up in its very title a sweeping dichotomy. *Domus* is the Mediterranean ideal-type pre-modern estate: 'Bucolic tableau' (*TI*,

p. 193). Against which the city, 'spend[ing] centuries, millenia slowly gnawing away at the domus and its community . . . stifl[ing] and re-duc[ing] *res domesticae*, turn[ing] them over to tourism and vacation', wins. The reader gets this far into the essay with a certain sense of having been here before in anti-contemporary-life writing of both the right and the left. But in detail the Bucolic Tableau gets presented in Lyotard's text in a curiously split manner, nostalgically and ironically at the same time. The irony can be felt in the insistence on the in-equalities built into this bucolic: 'The commoners move around at a distance from the masters' residences' (*TI*, p. 191); '*Ancilla* the female servant . . . When she gets up to serve at table, it is the nature-god who cultivates the house, is content there, is at home' (p. 192). Yet the evocation of a non-city ethos does not at times seem to be at all undercut:

> A savouring of the sounds. Some from the near distance, the depths of the stables, cacklings, a silence hollowed out round the call of the owls when Venus shines out at dusk, crackling of the alder branches thrown onto the hearth, clogs on the thresholds, conversation on the hill opposite, wasps round the melon, shouts of encouragement to the autumn oxen, swifts madly chasing each other around the darkening roofs. The sounds are toned to the measure of the bitter-sweet, the smoky, the tastelessness of the boiled beans, the pungent dung, the ferment of the hot straw. (*TI*, p. 194)

This makes the expression of a further split, whereby the bucolic is subverted in its own terms and through its own destiny (rather than by cancellation from the city, from Development), all the more mysteriously violent:

> [A]nother scene in the tableau . . . In this scene, the fe-male servant with the heart of gold is impure. The service is suspect, ironic. The common work is haunted by dis-aster. The respect is feigned, the hospitality despotic, commonsense obsessed by the banishing of the mad, its bur-ial within . . . The domestic monad is torn, full of stories and scenes, haunted by secrets . . . Father, mother, child, fe-male servant with the heart of gold, niece, old man-servant, shepherd and ploughman, gardener, cook, all the figures of wisdom, the corner of the park under the fig tree, the little passage for whispering, the attic and its chests – everything is matter for obscene crimes. Something in the *domus* did not want the bucolic. (*TI* pp. 195–6)

The bucolic, torqued . . . This is an evocation of Greek tragedy, or of a view from 'our distance, our anti-domestic violence' of a tragic kernel at the heart of the Mediterranean ideal: 'Freud makes us reread, via

Sophocles and Shakespeare, the tragedy of the Greek families in this penumbra of madness' (*TI*, p. 195).

0.4. The 'haunted by disaster' other scene is, however, *still domestic*, not megalopolitic, Developed. *Domus* is what 'gives the untameable a chance to appear' (*TI*, p. 196), more than does 'the city, the republic or even the flabby and permissive association of interests and opinions called contemporary society'. What is terrifying (fascism, 'ethnic cleansing') is how this untameable resurfaces with infinitely greater brutality as some sort of sick memory of *domus* after *domus*'s ruin. '*Homo re-domesticus* in power kills in the street shouting "You are not one of ours". He takes the visitor hostage. He persecutes anything that migrates' (*TI*, p. 197).

While at the same time there is a more overarching rationalising push. Lyotard calls Development in this essay 'the big monad', and writes:

> With Nazism the big monad in the process of forming mimicked the *domus* . . . Does that remain a constant temptation, after Nazism? At any rate the untameable has to be controlled, if the big monad is to be competent and competitive. Everything must be possible, without remainder, with a bit of ingenuity. But that's just it, the *domus* isn't ingenious enough, the extermination betrays too much hybris, there has to be a more rational and open way of operating. More operational, less reactively earthly. [Earthy?] Secrecy must not surround the destruction of the secret. Communication and culture accomplish this destruction, and much better. Timbre will get analyzed, its elements will be put into a memory, it will be reproduced at will, it may come in useful . . . (*TI*, p. 203)

The untameable loses its chance to appear as its appearance is promoted, cultivated, coded, recorded, *broadcast* (another agricultural term originally, or course) . . .

3.1/0.5.

> Will I catch stress?
> Where does stress pass against us?
> Doc: on the tossed post salad day seas
>   : but that's where our wheat is lost at
>   what do we have granaries for?
> Duck on hold: I heard that some American farmers
>   don't have granaries   ship it right
>   off the field
>   : Doc   I wanna control my shelves
> Doc: Esteem build up a head of esteem

: the crops are stressed and sow
are the sillybulls
The doc's covered with barn-aches
eat wheat hulls   chafe the chaff
no hull   no see the dock

(*LHIFT*, p. 29)

The crops, the syllables, 'I'. What *is* 'stress', across these? A silly question?

The garden is also a sea; or rather the field is. Counterfactually; actually, drought was the problem.

The 'I' is stressed by drought and by banking, nature and the economic regime; the latter being Developmental to the full. If Development decrees that (urban) CANADA CAN'T AFFORD ITS FARMERS, then so be it, so must it be. And yet the syllables (stressed, as verse, so un-wordly, in some sense pre-verbal whilst constituting the verbal) are what 'I' can cultivate as 'the other inhuman', the one thing left to resist with. (Or: one of many shapes which that final, ineliminable resistance can take.)

0.6./3.2. Which would be to say that *LHIFT* speaks against the big monad through (i) a certain evocation, non-Mediterranean, non-nostalgic, surprising ('I ascend the stairs in flashbacks / . . . And leave the unread issue / of *Amnesty International* on the newel post' [p. 15]), and direct, of *domus*; and at the same time through (ii) an evocation of that which in this *domus* does not want or cannot sustain the bucolic, a pained or stressed family-farm history romance, at moments directly but more often through the twisting, forcing or smashing of language.

An unhappy polity finds itself spoken to by the poem at various levels; smashed language 'reflects', one could well feel, smashed political hopes, to put it very crudely, but there is also a very direct address, 'Dear Globe and Mail', to the particular political/financial stupidity which CN and many other farmers have had to live with.

At the same time, torqued language opens onto such fun, such wit and oddity. Against the stress of the crops (ungrowable in drought, unsaleable if grown), the sillybulls (and what could be sillier than to think 'bull', with its weight and danger and animality and sexuality, alongside 'syllable', Yeats's 'mouthful of air', the sort of thing that is either immateriality to the nth degree or that sits placidly on the page, Ferdinand-the-Bull-like, awaiting someone to come to play with it by reading, listening, *hearing*?). Against the weight of family and economy and history, the lightness of the verbal acrobat, the juggler keeping the words in the air *and* in pieces . . .

'That does not happen without a certain lack of respect, assuredly, but not without respect either' (*TI*, p. 198).

Notes

1. *Charles Noble* (Saskatoon: Thistledown Press, 1990).
2. As I understand it, CN's grandfather not only gave his name to the town, Nobleford, but via plough design invention (the 'Noble blade') set up an agricultural machinery manufacturing operation of serious proportions.
3. This withdraws, or re-presents as imaginary, the poem's initial image.
4. Trans., Geoffrey Bennington and Rachel Bowlby (Cambridge: Polity Press, 1991; French edition, 1988).
5. CN once spoke to me in passing of a particular summer as being the one in which he was reading Kant's First Critique in the cab of his tractor.

5

The Weavers of SP/ELLES:
Feminism and Canadian Poetry

Marion Wynne-Davies

The Universal Spell

How do you spell 'spelles'? Take the verb and draw up a neat column of singularized/pluralized/genderized possibilities:

I spell	We spell
You spell	You spell
He spells	They spell
She spells	They spell

Of course, English has lost and/or gained in its lack of gendered endings, unlike other languages . . . French being the most important in relation to Canadian poetry . . . but if you add that final 's', then the prefix, the determining subject, is most likely to be either male or female. ['It spells' is not so impossible, since my computer does indeed spell, but it does so through my own, necessarily gendered, operational intervention.] Even in English then, the conjugation of the verb predicates a gendered 'spells'.

By extending our field we may go still further and bridge the linguistic divide so that an increasingly *female* signification emerges: this, through an awareness of *'elles'* as a separate entity. A segment of a word that becomes a whole, even as it mutates back into a part.

'SP': an abbreviation or symbol for 'spelling'.
'elles': third person feminine.
  << Translate >>

Elles orthographient : they spell [women spell][1]. Women laying claim to the authoritative determination of meaning/women asserting their linguistic control in the tomes/tombs of academia/but . . . ironically, women accepting the structures built up letter upon letter by male authority, by a male-dominated academe. Spelling and orthographier alike, there is only one C. O. R. R. E. C. T. way to participate in the written codes of any particular language. Or is there? How do you spell 'spelles'?

Take the noun, 'from Old English *spel(l)* to *Gothic spill*: tale, story, statement',[2] as Judith Fitzgerald does in her introduction to *SP/ELLES. Poetry by Canadian Women. Poésie de femmes canadiennes* (1986). That first term slides in its signification, avoids the starched correctness of dictionaries, the stiff white page inside the dark cloth cover, held tightly in with the slick neck-tie of grammar. Instead, the contributors to this collection have garbed themselves in weird/romantic/Remedios-Varo-like metaphors:

> '. . . i imagined my place out in a ditch lurking there on the far edge of town with the other witches . . . ' (Daphne Marlatt, *SP*, p. 66)
> '. . . the magic of discovery . . . ' (Lola Lemire Tostevin, *SP*, p. 96)
> '. . . listen to the storyteller weave her magic . . . ' (Ann Wallace, *SP*, p. 104)
> '. . . to weave, text . . . ' (Betsy Warland, *SP*, p. 116)
> 'poetry as the practice of magic . . . ' (Maxine Gadd, *SP*, p. 50)

Gadd's theoretical introduction to her poems (each writer provides a similar preface) explains this weaving/witchcraft/spelling imagery:

> There are weaver birds; they make baskets to keep their eggs and their chicks, we speak of weaving spells, of spelling each other off, fraternal, kindly, networking, making lace, nets to catch hair, butterflies, Cruise missiles . . .   (*SP*, p. 51)

To catch the readers, the writers in this collection weave their metaphors/their freeplay of images through the dense-textured weft of ideology – their loyalty to social and political activism: 'Cruise missiles'. The coloured wools are words, the taut frame is language; these poets 'spell . . . each other off' through the very substance of their writing. 'Spelles' is not a word, not a word in a dictionary, in a lexicon, in a thesaurus – it is not WOVEN into the fixed linguistic tapestry. Instead it is active, these women are in the process of WEAVING it, of WEAVING spelles.

As a present/presence 'spelles' may remain unfixed. Imagine the drawing of coloured skeins, the movement of content and form, the brief relation of tone . . . it may not be spelt, it is not merely a spell, it is neither English nor French, subject, object, noun, verb. It is all of these and none. It is impossible to finally, completely, utterly, spell 'spelles'.

What this essay intends is to catch, even if only for a brief moment, that process. *SP/ELLES* is a collection of poems which attempts to unite a group of Canadian women writing in the mid–1980s. While recognisably disparate, there are certain strands which unite the poets. While the task of creating a 'group' is impossible, the editor has exercised an eerie awareness of the almost imperceptible bonds of political awareness that they have in common. Inevitably, Judith Fitzgerald's work fails: large rents appear over the broad cloth she has woven. But she has captured a particular moment in Canadian Women's poetry, an interstice which emerged, perhaps from *Tessera*, and which lies between the united feminist causes of the 1970s and the too-ready acceptance we now give to the playful multiplicity of postmodernism.[3] As such I intend to use *SP/ELLES* as a context for the excavation of feminism in Canadian poetry of the 1980s; it acts as the centre of my own web of language, the poets in the collection act as the radials, and their subverting of patriarchal language has affected the consistency of my own thread of signification. Rather than formulating static questions which will produce mummified answers, suspended in their cocoon-like sacks, this essay attempts to $O = P = E = N$ up the spaces in which other questions may be voiced – and heard.

Some Theories of Spelling

Deconstruction is [k]not intended. Perhaps, turning back upon my own prose, a dialecticism, the spelling out of initial theoretical practices, has already begun – a subconscious / subtextual writing / reading by a late twentieth-century critic. Setting ▮limitations ▮, ▮borders ▮, ▮ rules ▮, about th e words in the text, which have then been = broken = , = challenged = , = deconstructed = . A policing of interpretation, which has then blurred and shifted into a free-flowing, uncontainable, semiotic reading of the text.[4] But don't imagine that this is freedom, a liberating expression of revolutionary ideology. Rather, it is the form and language of critical entrapment. It is a net which does not carry the reassurance of 'Women Friendly'. That which appears to proffer a radicalisation of cultural modes, itself depends upon an OUTmoded, structure . . . grounded in the framework of patriarchy. As Nicole Brossard has pointed out:

> Binarity might be something the human mind cannot escape. But within the patriarchal system, binarity provides for a hierarchical logic that privileges men's values and behaviour . . . [and that] patriarchal binarity has provided for systematic violence against women.[5]

Brossard is certainly not averse to a little theoretical thuggery herself. She is quite prepared to bludgeon her male audiences and readers into acute discomfort . . . this quotation was given in response to a male questioner who enquired parodically if computers, which use binary systems, could be accused of being patriarchal. The answer provided for more and less than the questioner wanted: it was a serious response to a debate over the deeper structures governing gendered value-systems, as well as a brisk rebuke of a particularly jokey kind of insecurity. Moreover, her last words – 'violence against women' – bring the audience/reader into a sharp awareness of social issues >> REAL violence against REAL women. Linguistic games may be played out through the formulating and destabilising of significations, but for feminists the gritty materiality of experience anchors meaning to political action.

Internal contradictions are not intended. Instead the poems in *SP/ELLES* focus our attention upon a spatial plurality suffused with associative significations and symptomatic states. They call on us to abjure the endless chain of *différance* in favour of a multiple vista of difference, which will always be, is now, changing and engendering. They affirm women's ability to shape language in relation to their experience, to create possibilities, to open up, not to withdraw into an inner investigative nihilism. Rather, they enter into a dialogue with a Utopian postmodernism. Perhaps, they were all anticipating, already answering the unspoken CRITICISM, Linda Hutcheon's Introduction to *The Canadian Postmodern*:

> Postmodernist 'recording' and 'inventing' are clearly processes, not products. They are not fixed, closed, eternal and universal. Instead of feeling threatened by this unfixing of certainties, postmodern culture tends to find it liberating and stimulating. Perhaps the loss of the modernist faith in fixed system, order, and wholeness can make room for new models based on things once rejected: contingency, multiplicity, fragmentation, discontinuity.[6]

Similarities emerge: the process of weaving, not the product/the finished tapestry . . . the *picture theory*, not the picture itself. The O = P = E = N, unfixed possibilities of naming, the unconnectedness of difference, the co-existent fragmentation of meaning. The fiction . . . the theory, entwined without recourse to chronological demands. The answer before the question. An excavation of the hidden polemic of *SP/ELLES*. Betsy Warland introduces her poetry by entering into this same dialogic communication:

> as a lesbian i do not speak Universese. few people do. we (collective not universal) come from different cultures, classes, ages, lifestyles, bodies, beliefs, and educational systems.

conflict in the world has been largely due to the desire to stamp out difference or at least have authority over it. (*SP*, p. 112)

The unfixing of certainties, the a-l-l-o-w-i-n-g (albeit with a certain degree of resistance) of homosexuality, and the a-c-c-e-p-t-a-n—- (maybe not quite yet) of the sexual force of homoerotic texts *IS* welcomed by the poets in *SP/ELLES*. But can Warland really be serious in offering us the elimination of world conflict by allowing this Utopian, postmodern plurality? If we were all to accept one another, one another's value systems, one another's cultural codes, without criticism, contempt, covetousness, would we see ourselves as 'an open circle / word without end' (Warland, *SP*, p. 118)? No, not really.

An apology is not intended. Necessary? After all, isn't that the 'function of criticism' – to take the ideal and undercut it, revealing to the innocent reader that this tale, these poems, have been nothing more than an illusion, the fabric of a dream, a conjurer's trick, a gossamer spell. And isn't that image, in its turn, no more yielding but a dream? The uninitiated reader reading a book, coming with their unchanging dictionary to the words of the text, seeing without ambiguity the colours on display.

Instead, try rereading the title (with the lights on, before turning into the white-pillow-world of the unaware receptacle – the blank page of sleep), reread *SP/ELLES*. This reader startled into reassessment. To understand it is necessary . . .

> to think back
> to recall previous associations
> to review the individual and collective memory
> to recognise other readers with other
>   genders/sexualities/races/class allegiances
> to face our own privilege
> to acknowledge foreknowledge

. . . for only then does the outlawed word yield its possible significations. Then, as if to reassert the metaphoric free play of the first 'word', the metonymic subtitle solidifies on computerised subject catalogues: *Poetry by Canadian Women*. Not much doubt about the contents and the authors there; we can all spell that one. Indeed, we can even translate it: *Poésie de femmes canadiennes*.

A History of Spelles

The skeins of colour might ply in and out, but the associative tension of the political weft (and, often, *left*) drag the anger of his/herstory through the poetic cloth. Warland's concept of a universal language of ideas not only conjures the improbable vision of a unitary ideology, but also demands that we recognise 'language' as a weapon of imperial domination. Those 'different cultures' have finally been heard through the voicing of a postcolonial discourse; they isolate, challenge and heap guilt upon the languages of authority, they catch these old European languages in the act, in the net, in the context of, the subjection of native peoples and of minority groups. When the poets in *SP/ELLES* write of linguistic oppression and of a challenge from within the text by << 'shaking the syntax' / refusing to gloss / vernacular transcription / verbal hybrids >> they excavate the roots of the colonial apparatus and, by exposing them to the glare of an unfettered awareness, dry their tenacious hold into insignificant dust. The brightness of the brave new world.

■■■ ■■ ■■■ ■■■■■ ■■■■■■■

Answer B: Black Women

Ayanna Black, who was born in Jamaica and moved to Canada in 1964, picks up the rhythms and sounds of the dub poets; in 'she writes' she writes:

> mi child
> dem
> always want fi mi advice
> surprize
> da first time
> mi cry buckets of wata
> 'nd me think:
>
> advice from dis a black woman?
> dis a black nigger?
> black mama?
>
> mi child
> mi da say to all a dem
> from mz anne to mz jane
>
> mi nuh you psychiatrist.   (*SP*, p. 27)

[My child, they always want my advice. I was surprised the first time and cried quite a lot; I couldn't understand why they wanted advice from a racially and sexually disadvant-

aged person. So, my child, I said to them, from Ms. Anne
to Ms. Jane, that they should pay a professional to sort out
their problems.]

This is not a poem that gains in translation. My standard English,
my politically correct formulations, not only impede the flow, the
rhythms of the poetry, but also reintroduce acceptable [literary]
language.
      This is a poem to be read aloud, not reread on the page. By spelling
it out, I've flattened it out . . . only by retaining the 'mz' spellings can
we make strange our perceptions, unravel the tightly wound spools
of our pre - conceptions. The tongue must remain unaccustomed: the
spelling, stress patterns and line arrangement deny normative pronunciation and demand a twisting into/out of a different cultural mode.
This is alienation in double exposure. First, the scholarly templates of
experience exclude White/Western/European (and Canadians of European extraction)/Middle Class/'Educated' readers from the language
of Black/Southern Hemisphere/African (and Canadians of African
extraction)/Working Class/'Uneducated' authors. The stereotypes of
the former are parodied by the stereotypes of the latter . . . and the
underlying anger at the necessity, still, to take the former's value judgements as a basis for this REbounding. Secondly, the white person's
REspeaking the black person's speech . . . the exclusion of the vocal
self through the adoption of another's tongue . . . tongue as patois,
tongue as bodily turning into new shapes, quicker, slower, to imitate,
to split the self into self and other. And – on the << OTHER >> side –
the strangeness of hearing, simultaneous to writing and reading, of the
Standard English/Standard French tongue/s struggling to become acquainted with that which they have previously: condemned, outlawed,
diminished.
Perhaps, simply,
not heard.
The muted tongue now heard.
But nothing comes free, especially in these commodified, postmodern
societies, and the price for that audibility is a TRANSference of ex-
clusivity, of being, of self, of identity, into the multiple tongues of
multiculturalism.[7]

■ ■ ■ ■ ■ ■ ■ ■ ■ ■ ■ ■ ■ ■ ■ ■ ■ ■ ■ ■

The Question

Who listens and where do they listen? Who has the investment in a
single voice? Who welcomes the many voices?

■■■ ■■ ■■■ ■■■■■ ■■■■■■■
Answer A: A Feminist

If you're *out*side listen to 'all the ways the walls say no' – Marlatt's 'seeing your world from the outside' (*SP*, p. 68) catches the pain of the outcasts, those excluded from the sheltered world of social conformity:

the night is full of losers & empty buses, palisades of light adrift . . . nothing left to lose.

Then, taking the thread of liberal guilt wound tight with the images of the homeless/the down-and-outs/the have-nots, she transforms it with the tints of gender oppression, with, maybe, a *hint* of racial prejudice:

black & white. & you. standing inside your world are photographing doors or holes in the wall night pours thru. 'a scream is an appraisal.' you. a scream is a refusal. we. refuse to keep in all that silence pressing thru the walls o women, women who write 'because the night belongs to us'

'We' – the blacks/the poor/the women – are out [side]. 'You' – the white/middleclass/man – is [inside]. It's safe inside, light in t[here] . . . yet the darkness 'pours thru', refusing to remain caught in the net of these disturbing, but unthreatening, images from a newspaper article. Instead, it takes on a voice, an inarticulate sound, a scream from the queen of the night. The blackness sound . . . how do you spell 'spelles' = ■ ■ ■ ■ ■ ■ ■. 'Women who write' UNwrite because they are OUT[side] patriarchal language. To be heard as women writers 'women who write' must eschew the daytime language, the LC (Literary Correctness) language, and 'Reclaim the Night'.

And that language – if it does press 'thru the walls', if it is heard by the 'you' [inside] – can mutate the threat, making the OUT[side] safe and the [inside] dangerous . . . those walls can look like caving in.

Note to Answer A:
1. But, if the 'night belongs to us', then perhaps we have a political investment in staying OUT[side], in the act of PRESSING in, of WEAVING an unwritten text out of the dark.

Outside or inside? 'Dehors, dedans' (Louise Cotnoir, *SP*, p. 37). The fear of collapse, of the breakdown of accepted practices all depends on whether we are within the dominant system or if we have been excluded by it. As a University Lecturer in English Literature I

am familiar with the language/the tongue of Chaucer, of the GREAT
ENGLISH AUTHORS . . . I know what to say in order to be heard. I
have the right to use the higher-case – I am not i. I am [insIde]. But,
a spin of the shuttle, the slither in between the threads, passing them
of Ypres and of Gaunt, and, i exist out[side]. The i's in feminism are
often lower-case (Black, Brossard, Gadd, Marlatt and Warland, *SP*,
passim).

Reread Marlatt and wait for the 'black tint under your eyes' to show
(*SP*, p. 68). '<u>Your</u> eyes'? – Who are 'you'?

'You' are the 'ladies of the night', the women outside, the
dispossessed sisterhood under whose banner writers and prostitutes
march shoulder to shoulder. Yet, on the same page, only eleven lines
down, 'you' are the privileged reader, the self whose gender, class,
race and career are immaterial in the face of your acquiescence to the
READER, to your constructed self, to the subject position you learned
to adopt, so adroitly, when you first began to read, and carried on reading, and still do even now, unless you remember your other self, your
(if you're really 'at the bottom' [Marlatt, *SP*, p. 68]) female, working
class, black, whore self.

Who are you and where are you?

■■■ ■■ ■■■ ■■■■■ ■■■■■■■

Answer C: The Canon Strikes Back
Geoffrey Chaucer (1340 – 1400)

The House of Fame

The supreme canonical author: Chaucer, 'fadir Chaucer'.[8]
The origin. Returning to the source of the patriarchal river,
swimming upstream against an age-old tidal power to the
first welling up of English poetry.

The text. The multiple voices whispering about
The Hall of Fame.

. . . Thus north and south you and w
Wente every tydyng fro mouth to mouth,
And that encresing ever moo,
As fyr ys wont to quyke and goo

From a sparke spronge amys,
Til al a citee brent up ys.[9]

Imagine the image: a solid block, neatly drawn hall.

Imagine the voices as flames . . . the walls crumble.

How can the CONstruction hold if the CONflagration is so great . . . ?

What does the CONstructed reader feel?

Fear.

Caught in a web of identity, in the weavings of language, 'you' are both ostracized from, and welcomed into, the dominant culture – simultaneously. You are, if you like, ouitnsidsiede.

It's clear by now, as Marlatt points out, that 'this game is rigged'. It is always you who listen, but you never know where you'll be when the voices begin. Sometimes you'll be the single call from the wilderness, sometimes you'll be the only 'true' voice, sometimes you'll be one of many who uphold the status quo, and sometimes you'll be out there marching with the other dissidents. But, more often than not, you will be all these things.

Marlatt's poetry reveals these snags of dislocated identity at the same time as she draws tight the collective responsibility of early feminism.

Even though *SP/ELLES* was published in 1986 and perhaps conceived in early 1984 (the editor, Fitzgerald points out in her introduction that the title emerged from the first editorial discussion on *Tessera* in January of that year) it still pledges its faith to the earlier decades.[10] While the proclaimed political message of the collection is to move beyond 'male-dominated myths' about literary creativity and language, as well as to recreate 'the feminine case', there is an old fashioned thread trailing at the edges of these taut primaries. For example, the choice of poets is not what Fitzgerald terms 'designer poets (poets with attendant labels)', but 'quite simply, a sampling of the best'. There is nothing 'simple' about literary judgement, deciding what is the 'best'. The very conditions which she feels women have moved beyond – '*immigrant, kitchen sinking, Marxist* and *heliocentric*', even 'the same old ego-orientated Romantic traditions and Renaissance ideals' – still determine what is considered art, Fitzgerald's <<'exquisite alphabet'>>.

The ABC of the text: how do you spell 'spelles'?

Despite Fitzgerald's claim that the poets in this collection 'write our alphabet correctly', that is exactly what they do NOT do.[11] Race, gender and past influences intertwine . . . the Black woman writing, A feminist herstory, the pervasive power of the Canon . . . all are present in the BAC . . . in the MZspelling, the INcorrect spelling, of the alphabet. The REwriting of history into herstory . . . the MZplacing of chronology when answers come before questions, come before answers . . . *The Herstory of Spelles.*

Spelling Hurts

I have never been very good at spelling. As a child I learned to read in two languages: English at school and Welsh at home. *Janet and John* and *Y Llyfr Gwyrdd.* Different alphabets, different pronunciation, with me somewhere in between. To be born into one language, to live in one language is, still, the privilege of the nationals of wealthy and powerful countries. Few people can, or bother to, read in Welsh. In order to communicate, to be understood, to be heard, I must write in English, circumvent my muted tongue and release the strangled, mz/pronounced words for the mockery of those who know only that they are right. To be a self, which in order to construct an identity must 'simply' bury a part of that self, thereby allowing the other self to emerge triumphant, is to live in TRANSit. To speak and not speak. To write and not write.

Anger and guilt: to hear myself acknowledge – with just a hint of the old twang – that a Labour Party leader with a Welsh accent is an encumbrance at election time. The anger at the truth of it. The guilt that I accept it, that I don't fight back. Looking through the (not all-inclusive) biographies in *SP/ELLES*, Canadian linguistic affiliations emerge:

English Canadians	French Canadians	Caribbean Canadians
Gay Allison	Nicole Brossard	Ayanna Black
Maxine Gadd	Louise Cotnoir	Ann Wallace
Dorothy Livesay	Louise Dupré	
Daphne Marlatt	Lola L. Tostevin	
P. K. Page		

Scottish Canadians	Norwegian Canadian
Lesley Mcallister	Betsy Warland

The impossibility of an easy camaraderie between black and white women has already been traced upon the tongue's memory in the reading/speaking process of Black's 'she writes', but the most sharply felt split, the cleft-tongue of Canadian literature and culture exists between the English and the French. Hardly new, this revelation . . . it emerges, this twisted aporia of tongues, in the writings of the second group . . . the 'not first' group. The poetry of the English Canadians ignores, almost, this divide; they have no need to interrogate their own power.

Nicole Brossard's angry voice calls out into this particular political/poetical void:

> I resent profoundly how as French Canadian we were
> despised and discriminated against by Anglo Canadian
> politics. I have always made the language issue a
> personal thing. Today I am still vividly hurt when
> someone who is living or who has been living in Montreal
> for many years addresses me in English.[12]

The razor-edge of the political agenda slicing through the autobiographical flesh of the fingers that weave the spells . . . blood on the texts . . . 'bleeding into print' . . . the stain on the blank sheet (paper/linen).[13] 'Despised.' 'Discriminated Against.' 'Personal Thing.' 'Vividly Hurt.' How do you spell 'spelles'?

With difficulty.

Lola Lemire Tostevin TRANSlates the anger into an almost languid, nostalgic, bitterness directed at language itself:

> it isn't that
> the faded voice betrayed
> its speaker
>
> it's just that it failed
> to get an answer
>
> (*SP*, p. 97)

Faded and failed, the voice dies, recedes into the darkness that for Marlatt is a strength, but for Tostevin carries a gothicised fear, a:

> small hook
> in the flesh
>
> (*SP*, p. 97)

DIScrimination for Brossard: DISmemberment for Tostevin. Dis: noun. The name given to the underworld, the darkness. Dis: prefix. Meaning to split asunder. Meaning deprivation.

DISSPELLING. To melt away the alphabet. And Tostevin does unravel the text, she 'unspeaks' speech in order to tangle the all-too-familiar linguistic codes. Three of her poems in *SP/ELLES* are drawn from *Color of Her Speech* (1982) which as an entity subverts expected textual practices: there is only one title in the collection and there are no page numbers.[14] The text exists without apparatus, a text split asunder from texts:

> the Unspeaking
> the Unbinding of Umbilicals
> ba be bi bo
> '*déparler*'
> *décomposer*
> *sa langue*
> da de di do
>
> '*l'enfant do*
> *l'enfant dormira bien vite*'
>
> 'and if that lullaby don't sing
> papa's gonna buy you a diamond
> ring . . . '
>
> *la source renversée*
> the course unlaid
>
> baby lulled
> by a lie
>
> byaliebyaliebyaliebyaliebyalie

By DISregarding the rules of syntax and translation Tostevin unspeaks the symbolic language. This unspeaking, unravelling of sig-nification perfectly caught/TRANSfixed in the exquisite image of water flowing back/turning back upon itself – '*la source renversée*'. Marlatt seems to echo Tostevin providing a fleeting glimpse of pattern:

> if the language is one of multiple meanings rather than
> the one (right) meaning, then the form it takes will tend
> to be open, to come into being swimming upstream against
> the fixed, the prescribed & towards the unspoken, that
> which lies always on the far side of the settled, the
> defined. (*SP*, p. 67)

There is something free and adventurous about Marlatt's:

'swim
ming up
stream', a wild
salmonette push
-ing its way
again-
st
the flow,   that which attempts to restrain it.
pouring..
thru..

Marlatt's image is redolent of the connectedness=with=nature experienced by the subjects of Canadian novels such as Atwood's *Surfacing*.[15]
The similarity between the two writers is pointed out by Hutcheon:

> Atwood's [and] . . . Marlatt's . . . language is both the vehi-
> cle of exploration and the site of combat; its limitations and
> powers become metafictional obsessions, and never more so
> than in the poems about the paradoxical interplay of life/art,
> process/product.[16]

Poetry as the site of combat . . . '"the night belongs to us"' . . . turning
the tides of patriarchy . . . 'la source renversée'.

'*La source renversée*': TRANSlated by Tostevin this becomes 'the
course unlaid'. RErun the image and REpeat the soundtrack.
▌▌▌ ▌▌ ▌▌▌ ▌▌▌▌▌ ▌▌▌▌▌▌ The language rents the celluloid,
the spool spins with the flick-flick UNsound of UNspeaking and
UNseeing. 'Source' (a spring) must become 'course' (a river bed).
'Renversée' (reversed) must become 'unlaid' (not set down). But in the
split-second before the texture tears apart, it is possible to glimpse
the point of mutation, the TRANSference of one signification into the
other. Begin with the aural hint of internal assonance and link 'source'
to 'course': through the water's bubbling transparency to the channel
of rocks beneath. Then move to the prefix, a REpetition of segments
which are UNlike: are they part of the same inverted narrative? The
reversing of a chronological process which leads, eventually, to a time
when there were no springs or rivers or river beds, when there was
nothing but an inarticulate void? Tostevin's poetry exists at the very
point of integration and DISintegration, at the moment when you know
it should break apart, but you experience it as together. Hers is the
moment of suspense, that exquisite moment of the 'small hook / in the
flesh'.

Unlay the human course, unbind the umbilical, and the processes
upon which the voice relies . . . the rewards it hopes for by acqui-
escing to the symbolic language ('papa's gonna buy you a diamond/
ring') . . . melt away into the rhythmic sound patterns of an early

linguistic form – the lullaby. The scene begins warmly, cocooning signification within the 'b', 'b', 'b' of 'b'aby talk . . . 'ba be bi bo'. Cut affectionately to the language of the father, of the 'd'a'd'a ('da de di do') and the familiar song which lulls the child safely to sleep. Now the camera draws back, the music gathers intensity and momentum and you realise that there is something in the room with the baby, something dark, something threatening . . . for the rosy/cosy image was only a decoy, the initial workings of a horror yet to be recognised . . . the recognition of 'byaliebyaliebyaliebyaliebyalie'. The tactile fluidity and over-long insistency of the line disguises and reveals a process, in language, where innocence has been DISpossessed, where the hook digs into the white skin of the page/the cream tones of the flesh and warns:

> do not be deceived by appearances
> I am not a woman I am a woman
> a space in space . . .
>
> (Tostevin, *SP*, p. 102)

Language is deceptive, it can dispossess those who believe they own and control it, it can warp their understandings, so that any word which begins as a referent quickly slips into some*sign* more uncomfortable: the name 'woman' dematerialises in this word-warp and reforms as the signifier 'woman', which in turn lo[o]ses its shape in an acceptance of what 'woman' signifies . . . she is 'a tabula rasa, a lack, a negation, an absence'.[17] Women are spelt in spaces, in the absences between the letters: ▌▌▌ 'M'. ▌▌ ▌▌▌ 'E'. ▌▌▌▌▌ 'N'. ▌▌▌▌▌▌▌.

The Spells That Come 'Out of O'

The poets in *SP/ELLES* acknowledge the pain of trying to make themselves heard, let alone understood, in a language which has excluded them. For them, writing as a woman is an alienating process, they are like immigrants in a new land failing to grasp the meaning of the signs which will lead them home. Marlatt exhumes those fragile strands that have silenced women, bound their tongues within the crippling bands of propriety:

> although there are stories about her, versions of history that
> are versions of her, & though she comes in many guises
> she is not a person, she is what we come through to &
> and what we come out of, ground & source, the space
> after the colon, the pause (between the words) of all pos
> sible relation. ('long after The Brown Day of Bride', *SP*,
> p. 70)

The earth-mother power Marlatt discovers while she runs her tongue through the organic developments of language, emits the faint mustiness of a diachronic elementalism, which then lingers in the voicing of her text:

> that bears us in
> this *kiel*, to *ku-*, to, a hollow space or place, enclosing
> object, round object, a lump. mound in the surrounding
> sea of grass. *ku-,kunte*, to wave-breaking womb . . . .
>
> (*SP*, p. 69)

The mummified body of the brown bride becomes an icon which legitimates absence as presence . . . its womb becomes the female space, the dark space from which all women may create/write their way into language. Because of her/she/elle, women who write may weave a different herstory, one in which absence is power, where the night belongs to them.

Brossard indicates the same traces of exclusion, but with a bitter recognition of the DISadvantages for women . . . a disadvantage which she experiences personally:

> As for myself, my poetic is essentially to make space for the unthought. As a woman, I am left with a language that has either erased or marginalized women as subjects. Therefore in my poetic I perform what is necessary to make space for women's subjectivity and plurally, to make space for a positive image of women. This task engages me to question language.[18]

Brossard exists in the present, on a synchronic plane of awareness which acknowledges the inheritance of a silent 'space', but which is determined 'to make space' for female subjectivity. This absence is there to be filled:

> my continent of spaces of reason and
> (of love) like a history of space
> where we can speak concretely
> about allegiance and caresses in silence
> a form of reverberation
>
> (*SP*, p. 31)

Reason and love colour in areas of vacancy. The concrete voice, solid/hard/strong, builds the structures of fealty and loyalty . . . these are the bridges which TRANSverse the divide between identities, between lovers.[19] The sexual love between women, the 'caresses in silence', are not dependent upon the DISpossessed women, the worn-out garments of nothingness handed down from woman to woman . . . the skilful needlewoman making something out of nothing, the seamstress weaving spaces of absence. Brossard's 'history' is there to be filled, to exist in 'the radical/ effect of light in broad daylight/ today' (*SP*, p. 33), to spell out clear material action for the present. The politics of lesbianism and feminism coalesce in the pursuit of change through linguistic revolution. If women have been marginalised by language, then language will have to be TRANSformed, will have to be used in experimental forms, will have to emerge from a history of spaces – the escape from O.

O U T   O F

O

The placard, this particular banner is taken from the first line of Tostevin's poem 'Gyno-Text' (*Color of Her Speech*). This is a poem to be visualised – speak it, tongue its shape and it DISintegrates, fragmented apart by an attempt at definition:

> Out of Oh
> Out of nought
> Out of zero
> Out of nil
> Out of nothing, out of absence, out of space,
>   out of time.

But on the page, the black circle/the white sphere, is an open shape . . . open to meaning, to a meaning which opens out to the last line of the poem: '<u>vagin</u>'/'<u>vagir</u>'/'<u>enfin</u>' (vagina/the cry of a baby/finally). O as orifice, as the entrance to the womb, from which emerge the inarticulate cry of life and the closing silence of death. Like Marlatt, Tostevin equates a feminine space with the female body, but there is no comfort in the sense of bodily continuity, only a bleak recognition that the O of language is a nothingness which cannot be filled, a void of despair . . . the 'O, O, O, O, O' of Lear's tragedy.[20] So, *enfin*, Tostevin unlays the course, lays bare the body of facts: that the passage through the vaginal O, the entry into language means Only One thing – the *renversée* of the source into the wordless pre/postlinguistic cry which foreTELLS the cessation of breath, the stilling of the tongue. There is no way OUT OF O.

Interstice

How is it possible to weave together the writers of the text (the collection/my essay)? Three so far and already their use of 'space' is entirely different from one another's. How is it possible to entwine the horrific invasion of Tostevin's orality:

> you said: let's see
> how deep down your throat I can thrust
>
> (*SP*, p. 99)

with the organic eroticism of Marlatt's explorations:

> its smell, its answering touch to my tongue. fondant,
> font, found, all that melts, pours.
>
> (*SP*, p. 73)

with Brossard's self-conscious manipulation of her *langue*:

> *My continent* in this hour she now has
> all my saliva, since, at your place, I've
> forgotten the text i wanted before your
> reading eyes which have watched centuries
> of hallucinations, of skin, pass, the noise/
> detonation. (ma*) it's a space/anhypothesis
> *ma – Japanese term for space.
>
> (*SP*, p. 31)

with a fourth, random, example – Warland's insistent radicalised voice:

> this text is full of holes
> mouth cunt ears urethra
> nostrils anus eyes
> infinite constellation of pores.
>
> (*SP*, p. 117)

The use of the mouth, the oral 'O', multiplies in its usage on this One page: the raped orifice, the caressing tongue, the lubrication of language and one more bodily puncture. O appears to be so simple; it circles around and offers to bind those within and those without, it is the fossilized ammonite on the cover of *SP/ELLES*, it is a symbol for woman (not wom*e*n) – an unchanging and unending metaphor for the feminine subject – and Judith Fitzgerald's collection pays 'lip'service to what could be mistaken for its inner self. The tonguing of the poets . . . caressing, probing, playing, stirring the bodily depths of O. Then deserting her. Leaving her high and dry, shrivelled into more of an ellipse, a deflated form which cannot sustain:

> the impossibility of definition
> the emphasis upon active process
> the broken identities
> the TRANSient nature of language
> the concrete spaces to be filled . . .

■■■■■■■■■■■■■■■■■■

Interstice

How is it possible to gather the strands of heterogeneous text[ure]s together to make a collection of *SP/ELLES?* A perpetual/self-perpetuating question . . . one which emerges from our INSIDE desire to alphabetise/to order/to fix/to chronologise/to SPELL out accord from DISaccord. To spell out an arrangement from a DISarrangement. To spell out an assembly from a DISassembly. Instead of looking for answers, for a way to neatly classify the poets (Allison, Black, Brossard, Cotnoir, Dupré), look at why the question is asked, and – further – why the questioning of the question is possible. Others have asked/are asking these questions.

Postmodernism – Linda Hutcheon deftly demonstrates how Western, especially Canadian, readers have lost their faith in the certainties of the past, in their metanarratives of existence:

> There has been a general (and perhaps healthy) turning
> from the expectation of sure and single meaning to a
> recognition of the value of difference and multiplicity,
> a turning from passive trust in system to an accept-
> ance of responsibility for the fact that art and theory
> are both actively 'signifying' practices – in other words,
> that it is we who both make and make sense of our
> culture.[21]

'Disspelling' participates in this 'turning from the expectation of sure and single meaning' . . . language is the mesh upon which postmodernism may embroider itself, may articulate its own identity. Yet there is an optimism here, a sort of vigorous summer-camp attitude – 'eat up all your difference and multiplicity and you will grow up to be big and strong' – which is exactly what is belied by Hutcheon's autobiographical account of her introduction into an academic discourse:

I tried to 'situate' myself for my students, as Foucault and later Edward Said and Catherine Belsey urged. This was especially necessary because I taught (among other things) Canadian literature, which at that time was not in the least canonical or even secure as part of the curriculum of many Canadian universities. And what I specifically taught was the literature written by women.[22]

What Hutcheon unravels from her own past is an alienation that was uncomfortable, a positioning of her own subjectivity in a marginal area because: she was Canadian, a woman, 'working-class', from an Italian family. But especially because, she had the 'privilege' of a liberal, humanist education – as Hutcheon points out, 'I cannot even articulate this today without some irony' (although . . . she attributes this to her own 'lack', rather than adopting Brossard's combative style).

Feminism – Catherine Belsey explicates postmodernism in similar terms to Hutcheon's, and then proceeds to link it to the current multiplicities evident in feminism:

> The postmodern is precisely the condition of the most recent flowering of feminist analysis, that feminism and postmodernism share a scepticism which is both epistemological and political . . . The plurality of the postmodern . . . discredits supremacism on the part of any single group. It celebrates difference of all kinds, but divorces difference from power. Postmodernism is in all these senses the ally of feminism.[23]

Again, there is the powerful optimism that women have found the answer to the unspoken question of where and when and why not now and how much longer will feminism signify conflict? Difference becomes a cause for celebration . . . hang out the flags of multiplicity, there's been a cessation of hostilities.

Interestingly, Belsey's essay provides another, fainter, echo of Hutcheon's in a short passage describing her education in the fifties when she:

> experienced fantasies of myself as an earth-mother, working at a trestle table to produce apple pies that would gratify hordes of rosy-cheeked and smiling children. Mercifully, in my case it is at the same time to have been sent to a girls' school that firmly regarded such notions as unmitigated nonsense, and to a women's college where it had apparently never occurred to anyone that a rational human being could think of higher education as the prerogative of men.[24]

Undoubtedly, for Belsey, her school and college days were happy. But perhaps this British system – in which the only way women could be educated to a higher level was where they were segregated from men (not to mention the patriarchal hierarchy of the single-sex colleges in Cambridge) – is not so far removed from the prejudices uncovered by Hutcheon. Perhaps there is an air of privilege, or perhaps Belsey re-works her experience for the sake of her argument, but the political awareness resides firmly with Hutcheon.

■■■■■■■■■■■■■■■■■■■

Interstice

How is it possible to value and celebrate difference when the past/pres-ent of experience DISmembers identity?
   DIS: a split in the linguistic self – Black's 'mi cry buckets of wata'. DIS: deprivation, being on the out[side] of [in] – Marlatt's 'all the ways the walls say no'. DIS: the darkness which foretells silence – Tostevin's 'small hook in the flesh'.DIS: trust the ease of plurality. Tear off the literary/academic plaster of K.N.O.W.L.E.D.G.E. from the skin-texts of women poets/critics (especially from those doubly removed from C.O.R.R.E.C.T. canonicity by their Canadian/postcolonial identity), and uncover the autobiographical wounds, the unhealing traces of violence written upon the self.
Brossard:
   In the days when I thought like a man, I had simple ideas . . . (the circle quickly closed on the little academic who contested for her brothers an inheritance to which she herself would never be entitled) . . . I have a score to settle with Knowledge because it terrorizes me from the moment it forces me to school, that is, forces me to learn more about the master's fantasies than about knowledge itself.[25]
Marlatt:
   It wasn't sharing but difference in a multiplicity of ways i felt first as a child in Malay where i was taught the King's (it was then) English . . . i had become embarrassed by the language i spoke . . . this i, fraught with inner difference, cannot simply graph those inner differences onto others. A recognition of real differences of life experience, privilege and accessibility to the centre is essential here.[26]

■■■■■■■■■■■■■■■■■■■

Interstice

The poetry in *SP/ELLES* is important because it acknowledges its ancestry in the alphabeticisation of experience, and at the same time teaches us how to DISSPELL patriarchal language. Have we reached the point, then, when it is no longer possible, necessary, or even desirable, to answer the question posed at the beginning of this essay? When the question itself becomes redundant?

Perhaps that point will be experienced as the Utopian dissolving of all barriers, but the systems of meaning have not disintegrated – yet. And for all our postmodern posturings, the inability to understand an unknown code remains unnerving.

Notes

1. *Orthographier*: the French verb for the discipline of spelling; I could have chosen *écrire* or *épeler*, meaning to spell in writing as well as verbally, which would result in a shift of signification to a more casual, less *academic*, base. While not denying the possibilities of these translations, the challenge to authoritative language made by Canadian women poets suggests the first interpretation to be more productive.

2. The quotation comes from the Introduction to *SP/ELLES. Poetry by Canadian Women*, ed. Judith Fitzgerald (Windsor, Ontario: Black Moss Press, 1986), p. 8. All future references to this text will be made in the essay itself.

3. The issues mentioned here, including the feminist journal *Tessera*, will be discussed below.

4. I am using the Kristevan notion of 'semiotic'; see 'Revolution in Poetic Language' in Julia Kristeva, *The Kristeva Reader*, ed. Toril Moi (Oxford: Basil Blackwell, 1986), pp. 89–136.

5. Nicole Brossard, 'Poetic Politics' in *The Politics of Poetic Form*, ed. Charles Bernstein (New York: Roof Books, 1990), p. 86.

6. Linda Hutcheon, *The Canadian Postmodern* (Oxford: Oxford University Press, 1988), p. 19.

7. My understanding of 'Trans'-culturalism has been influenced by Janice Kulyk Keefer's discussions of this phenomenon in Canada, in her paper at the BACS conference at Leeds ('Differences and Community: Canada and Europe in 1992', 2–6 April 1992).

8. The term of 'father' was given to Chaucer soon after his death, implying that he was an originator of ENGLISH POETRY. This particular expression comes from Thomas Hoccleve, 'An Aged Man Addresses the Poet' in *Chaucer: The Critical Heritage*, ed. Derek Brewer (London: Routledge, 1978), Vol. 1, p. 63.

9. Geoffrey Chaucer, 'The House of Fame', ll.2075–80, in *The Works of Geoffrey Chaucer*, ed. F. N. Robinson (London: Oxford University Press, 1957), p. 301.

10. *Tessera* was founded in 1981 after the Dialogue conference; it is a feminist journal which aims at bridging the divide between innovative creative and theoretical writing. Brossard, Marlatt and Tostevin have all contributed to the journal. Further information may be obtained from the

Department of English, Simon Fraser University, Burnaby, B.C., V5A 1S6, Canada.

11. All the quotations in this paragraph come from Fitzgerald's Introduction: *SP*, pp. 10-1.
12. Brossard, *op. cit.* (1990), p. 77.
13. Susan Gubar discusses the notion of the blank page, women's use of this trope and their act of writing imaged as an act of the body in '"The Blank Page" and the Issues of Female Creativity' in *The New Feminist Criticism*, ed. Elaine Showalter (London: Virago, 1986), p. 296.
14. Lola Lemire Tostevin, *The Color of Her Speech* (Toronto: The Coach House Press, 1982).
15. Margaret Atwood, *Surfacing* (New York: Popular Library, 1976).
16. Hutcheon, *op. cit.*, p. 143.
17. Gubar, *op. cit.*, pp. 305-6.
18. Brossard, *op. cit.* (1990), p. 81.
19. The poem in *SP/ELLES* is taken from a book entitled *Lovhers*, trans. Barbara Godard (Montreal: Guernica, 1986; first published in French, Montreal: Editions Quinze, 1980).
20. Lear's final line has been the cause of editorial dispute: the Oxford editors, Stanley Wells and Gary Taylor provide both Folio and Quarto versions in *William Shakespeare. The Complete Works* (Oxford: Clarendon Press, 1986).
21. Hutcheon, *op. cit.*, p. 23.
22. Hutcheon, 'The Particular Meets the Universal' in *Language in Her Eye*, eds. Libby Scheier, Sarah Sheard and Eleanor Wachtel (Toronto: Coach House Press, 1990), pp. 149-50.
23. Catherine Belsey, 'Afterword' in *The Matter of Difference*, ed. Valerie Wayne (Hemel Hempstead: Harvester Wheatsheaf, 1991), p. 262.
24. Ibid., pp. 259-60.
25. Nicole Brossard, 'Turning Platform' in *The Aerial Letter*, trans. Marlene Wildeman (Toronto: The Women's Press, 1988; first published in French, Montreal: Les Editions du remue-menage, 1985), pp. 37-51; the quotations are taken from pp. 37-9.
26. Marlatt, 'Difference (em)bracing' in *Language in Her Eye*, op. cit., pp. 188-93.

6

The Improprieties of Janette Turner Hospital: Strategic Punning in *Borderline* and *Charades*

Alistair Stead

> The universe, I hold, is no charade,
> No acted pun, unriddled by a word
> George Eliot: *A College Breakfast-Party* (1874)[1]

> *I myself.* What a riddle that is. Where, in the
> grab bag of costumes and masks, does the self hide out?
> *The Last Magician* (1992)[2]

I

The first impropriety: as a teacher of literatures in English but with no specialism in Canadian writing, I may not be in my proper place in this volume. I shall take heart, nevertheless, from my sense that fascinating migrants, borderers and hybrids are not unique to Canadian culture, and that my semi-detached critical stance may be perceived to be in tune with Janette Turner Hospital's inventive fictions of displacement, crowded as they are with statements like 'We all find ourselves in places we never expected to be in',[3] and 'Nothing can be counted on to stay in its proper place'.[4] The second impropriety: Hospital herself may be considered out of place as the subject of study in this collection. Is she properly Canadian? She would appear to border on that state: an Australian-born and –educated novelist and short-story writer, she has been a teacher and writer-in-residence in the United States, Australia and Canada (which has furnished the settings for several works), and now divides her year between Australia, Boston and Canada. On the evidence of this career and her literary reception (awards, nominations for prizes, reviews, assignment to critical context), she still tends to straddle a North American/Australian boundary, and her responses to enquiries about her self-perceived national identity as a writer have so far been deliberately evasive or charmingly inclusive ('a hybrid').[5] A 'dislocatee' (as she coins it in her dedication to the story collection *Dislocations*)[6] and something of a 'global nomad', like the father of the protagonist of *Charades* (p. 25), she seems improperly constrained by any regional classification; yet she might still be assimilated to the terms of a peculiarly Canadian literary-cultural criticism. So, 'ex-centric' in Linda Hutcheon's use of it to signify a postmodern privileger of the oppressed and disregarded margins,[7] or in Barbara Godard's more specific use in application to the Canadian woman writer deploying the decentering ironies of the colonised.[8] Her inclusion in the Canadian fold could be urged, in a very general way, since the culture's identity has so often been seen as synonymous with the postmodern, the multicultural, or variously doubled discourses. Furthermore, the novel which secured her reputation in many countries was *Border-line*,[9] which in its title, action, and crucial Canada-US border setting, would seem to harmonise curiously with a classic essay by Marshall McLuhan on the identity issue, 'Canada: the Borderline Case'.[10] But, if multiple borderlines and divided lineages have not apparently made Hospital overanxious about the construction of a distinctive, maybe distinctly indistinct, Canadian selfhood, more attention should be paid to the proposition that Canadian and Australian literatures are currently convergent in the creative revisionism of their post-colonial discourses, challenging the tenets of both essentialist nationalism and unconsidered multi-culturalism. Her concerns as a novelist are broadly sympathetic to such deconstructive manoeuvrings and, more strikingly, in her crossover and composite history and her role in the mediation of 'one culture (or subculture) to another',[11] she may be thought to epitomise 'borderblur', not as soft-focus denial of difference but as intelligent and eloquent probing and problematising of divisions within and between the worlds with which she is familiar. Her major fictions are conspicuously hazy hybrids, perpetually evading clear generic classification: *Borderline* grafts Borgesian metaphysical speculation onto a political thriller which is also a psychological romance; *Charades* mixes witty feminist revision of oriental and medieval storytelling with a romantic quest for personal and cultural roots imbricated with bold conjectures about the correlation of quantum physics and human behaviour; and *The Last Magician* ambitiously compounds murder mystery, elegy, and cinematically Expressionist satire on class divisions in modern Australia.

The main object of this essay, however, is to study the operations of the pun in the later novels of Hospital: *Borderline, Charades,* and *The Last Magician* with particular reference to punning on proper names. The pun, which exploits the interplay of similar sounds and

dissimilar meanings, is a favoured borderblur device, the proper vehicle for exploring improprieties, transgressions of borderlines and
boundaries of every kind. Hospital's passion for puns, it should be
emphasised, is hardly isolated or deviant in the context of contemporary writing. After that unprecedented 'explosion of puns in serious
literature' which David Hayman has associated with Modernism,[12]
the indulgence in word-play by postmodern fiction has been widespread, plethoric, almost required, particularly under pressure from
poststructuralism's promotion of the self-reflexive linguistic over the
referential dimension to texts. Hospital's work belongs, then, not
only with the slippery languages and formal dislocations of Canadian
writers like Robert Kroetsch and Daphne Marlatt, but with the oc-
casional, sometimes habitual playfulness of Thomas Pynchon and
Salman Rushdie, Christine Brooke-Rose and Michèle Roberts, which
has fun with the pun as it problematises the relations between real
and fictional worlds and engages the reader in strenuous semantic
production.

Although my title-topic of 'improprieties' is to be interpreted in
largely formal terms, it would be hard to divorce study of these from
their manifest thematic correlatives and motivators in the texts, where
proper/improper distinctions are regularly drawn and frequently sig-
nalled by repetition of these very terms or their cognates. The most
clamorous announcement of the theme appears in the title and polemic
of a minor, ironically pseudonymous book, a Greenean entertainment
called *A Very Proper Death*. It is Hospital's most 'proper' novel to
date, the kind of 'well-written but structurally conventional and traditionally realistic suspense novel' which she did not want to produce
in *Borderline*,[13] and it even has a British butler who, in a manner of
speaking, 'did it'. Nevertheless, the book, though comparatively stable
generically, is fiercely critical of virtually all the pejorative significances
of the proper in the socio-political sphere. The proper/improper distinction may be developed into a conceptual interplay, some kind of
dialectic, but there is no missing the locally vivid and cumulatively
forceful aggression toward aesthetic, cultural and social proprieties.
The proper is, romantically, the token of limit, a stultifying deference
to imposed decorum whether in small or portentous forms. Disruptive Charade, heroine of *Charades*, criticises a little girl's drawings
for being too neat, like the mind of the scientific rationalist she takes
her lover to be; she 'keeps all color neatly within its boundaries, and
this is ominous' (C, pp. 31–2). More menacingly, the murderously
repressed, dogmatic judge Robinson Gray in *The Last Magician* insists on adherence to laws 'straight and true' (*LM*, p. 266) as railway
lines. Significantly, by an implicit interlingual or macaronic pun, both
instances are contextually associated with *propre*: 'Everything's clean'

(*C*, p. 32), Charade protests and Gray's son is keeping a file on him and other 'Mr Cleans' (*LM*, p. 260). The proper is recurrently associated in Hospital's novels, from *The Ivory Swing* (1982) to *The Last Magician*, with a deathly bourgeois respectability, the authoritarian propensities of the propertied and ruling classes, an anxious social conformism, an insular enslavement by rule, convention and good taste; and, as a woman, she is constantly alive to the terrible damage done to girls by their 'proper' upbringings in all the worlds which she has imaginatively explored – Australia, South India and North America.

II

I will, in what follows, focus on the pervasive paronomasia of her complexly organised and thematically layered fictions, conscious that in word-play itself both puns and metaphors are potentially involved and that the pun, although it works distinctively through the single signifier with two (or more) meanings, may have the revelatory power of metaphor in 'the producing of a new semantic pertinence by means of an impertinent attribution'.[14] More particularly, I wish to address the way in which the novelist's naming of important characters constitutes and excites a kind of word-play. Such puns on proper names, are a species of impertinence, but they may serve a more important function, as structural allusions, parodic intertextual cross-references that sustain a valued impropriety by equivocating about determinate identifications, whether of fictional agents, mimetic illusions, or the genres to which books might be assigned. It would be disingenuous, or rather conventionally intemperate, to regard the pun as self-evidently or wholly improper. Recent students of the device tend to grant it a double status, as intrinsic to language and yet subversive of it. In poststructuralist terms, it is taken as 'paradigm for the play of language' testifying to polysemic copiousness and mutability of meaning, but as a fine excess, 'Puns present the disquieting spectacle of the functioning of language where boundaries – between sounds, between sound and letter, between meanings – count for less than one might imagine and where supposedly discrete meanings threaten to sink into fluid subterranean signifieds too indefinable to call concepts . . .'[15] The boundaries may seem to be dialectically necessary, and the notion of punning's tastelessness, indecency, and anarchic challenge, persist both in popular and more scholarly traditions, as in Dr Johnson's declarations that the quibble was an affront to 'reason, propriety and truth'. Quibble-quick Hospital may need to register the prejudice, then proceed to overleap it, and in her boldly designed and generically ambiguous work, traces of deference to good taste in these affairs

are to be found functioning conspicuously as foils to her stylistic
bravura.

In their later fictions, punning performance by a character on the
proper (their own, often enough) name, moves to centre stage. In these
novels most narration and focalisation is given over almost entirely to
transparent punsters (Jean-Marc in *Borderline,* Charade and Koenig
in *Charades*), who possess an intense double awareness of themselves
and others as legible texts as well as mysterious psyches. Charade, for
example, pores over 'editions' of her adoptive aunt and mother in *K:
the Variorum Edition* and *The B-Text* (titles to parts II and IV), while
Jean-Marc, composing his 'gospel according to Jean-Marc' (*B*, p. 189),
textualises himself by subdued but percurrent punning on his name –
marks, markers, marked, remarks, unremarkable, even Marquez –
and distributing across the book those synonyms of marks (as signs
or traces, borders or boundaries) which incarnate its major thematics.
At first glance, this word-play may be read as manifest propriety,
legitimising the quibbling game by referring it to the characters, osten-
tatiously self-dramatising word-jugglers and puzzlers; mimetic illusion
seems in place. Yet their accommodation to a conventional realism
may be compromised. As in Shakespeare, punning may occasionally
be an act of character (from a court fool to a satirical wit like Hamlet) but is more frequently, in Jonathan Culler's words, 'a structural
connecting device that delineates action and explores the world'.[16]
Flagrant punning on the proper name – Gaunt, Hotspur, Oldcastle,
say, in the Histories – may have a comparable macrostructural function to that of Hospital's name-plays. Transgressive in their wholesale
invention and mimicry of others' perspectives and their metafictionist
punditry, her self-conscious narrators are patently interpretable as the
rhetorical strategy of an implied author. The device is laid bare when
Jean-Marc admits, in chapter 22 of *Borderline,* that his narration is a
species of Shakespearean drag (he enacts Felicity) and, extratextually,
Hospital points out the ironic re-gendering of Jean-Marc as, in fact,
the discursive construct of a woman.[17] The interplay of proper and
improper continues: Jean-Marc, the self-confessed impersonator, still
insists, ' . . . there *is* a Felicity' (*B*, p. 192), and the story solicits a sympathetic engagement with his puzzlings as well as appreciation of the
joke of his dreamed-up and awfully convenient status. With this habit
of punning so nearly universal within and across these fictions, narrators and characters can only be regarded as equivocal, now substantive,
now textual, according to the context contrived and the reader's constructive responsiveness. Puns on proper names, then, far fetched and
frivolous as they might appear in some of their more extravagantly
ludic manifestations, tend to foster another suspicion of the proper,
understood as the unitary, self-identified, bounded. Nicknames may

signal this fissile and dissolvent function – Felicity as Fliss (German *fluss* for flux) and Lucy as Luce (loose, *LM*, p. 138) – but extended play on the proper name may do more: Koenig (German for king) is dispersed across *Charades* in a set of regal variations (in The Kynges Tale, King Tide, King Sun, King Oak, kingfisher, Kingston, even corduroy!) and so conjoined and blurred with Koenig's double Nicholas Truman as Nicholas II (as if the Tsar). Comparable representations of the self as bifurcated or diffused appear across the major fictions; they take on some of the patterning of Jungian conceptions of personality[18] and often associate with the language of vision and dream such overlappings and blurrings of discrete identity.[19]

In *Charades* the etymological pun is one of the ways in which the macrostructural function of the play on proper names may be discovered. Convinced that 'words do not have immutable meanings . . . they mutate as they cross borders, they curve through time . . . ',[20] Hospital sometimes gives form to her suspicion of the illusorily fixed identity of the proper, as it applies to words, through etymology, scarcely distinguishable from the pun in its semantic play on the acoustic accidents of language, and so releases the energies of the improper. Dubious as etymology may seem as a science, it may have, whether 'correct' or 'folk' in form, its supple literary uses, helping to subvert, as Attridge has argued, any conventional treatment of words as 'solid, simple wholes (representing solid, simple concepts)'.[21] In this respect, Hospital's fictions frequently operate on a constructive principle that has strong affinities with the evolution of the plots of allegorical narratives, according to Maureen Quilligan's account of them as unfolding 'investigations into the literal truth inherent in individual words, considered in the context of their whole histories as words' and deriving from a cardinal pun.[22] An exemplary case would be Spenser's scrutiny of error (*error*, Latin for 'wandering') in Book 1 of *The Faerie Queene*. As Patricia Parker's studies in Spencer and Ariosto confirm, this is 'a romance pun'[23] and, in a broad sense, all Hospital's major fiction may be seen to pivot on the same word, for all her wandering and eccentric heroines, from Juliet in *The Ivory Swing* (1982) to Lucy in *The Last Magician*, are the creatures of romance. Both Juliet and Charade are specifically called 'erratic' (*IS*, p. 169; *C*, p. 21) and Charade, to clinch the matter, advertises the etymological ploy when she defends herself from her professor's charge of 'brilliant but erratic' by retrieving 'the pristine and original sense' of the word (a neutral 'wandering'), but then proceeds to accept the extension to the meaning, positively embracing the notion of 'the meandering mistake-making self' (*C*, p. 22).

Like the Canadian novelist Robert Kroetsch, Hospital finds etymology one of those 'storymaking things' that tempt 'toward the quest for origins', but like him, too, she turns from any commitment to a myth of origins and lays stress on 'recovery of energy in a word'.[24] For, although Charade goes on to identify with the erratic genius of Captain Cook who discovers Australia by an unforeseen and round-about route, and knits herself into the history, or is it invention, of her nation, the quest for her origins, as the foundation of her selfhood, is filled with ironical reflections on mistaken identities and the divided or disseminated derivation: seeking an elusive putative father abroad, she will be led back home to a mad, alienated mother, self-identified with the old English exile *The Wayfarer*; looking for a single, singular origin in European parentage, she will find it strangely doubled and obscure back in Queensland. Alerted to the etymological interpreta-tion in this text, the reader might then respond to various signals that invite speculation on the 'weird name' of the heroine (C, p. 30) in this context. 'Charade' is pertinently of obscure origin (according to the *Oxford English Dictionary*) derived from a romance word signifying 'to chatter' or 'to gossip', hence 'a long talk', or (according to Skeat's *Etymological Dictionary*) 'idle talk'. This certainly suits the apparently disorganised loquacity of Charade as narrator, most particularly as the frenetically speculative and intrusive interlocutor of Koenig in the framing scenes of the book. Skeat goes further in deriving the word from the Spanish *charrada*, the speech or action of a clown (*charro*: 'a clown or peasant'), an association which would foreground the heroine's roots in a working-class home in the Tamborine Rainforest as well as her sometimes gauche 'mistake-making self' in her earnest search for a convergence of physical and metaphysical truths. Con-sonant with this 'radical' interpretation of her character would be the sense attached to the comparatively recent extended use of 'cha-rade' as travesty, 'something easily seen to be foolish', '*As in Paris talks are a bloody charade, Prime Minister says*' (C, p. 7), which is evoked significantly when she is attempting to explain the source of her name in Bea's (her adoptive mother's) gutsy indignation at her involvement in the farce of having to mother the child of Nicholas and Verity: 'What kind of a charade is this?'; '(that's what this is, all right, a bloody charade)' (C, pp. 73, 270). Yet the principal sense of 'charade' is a riddle or a word game (probably originating in France), in which the word or phrase to be guessed is enigmatically described or, from the nineteenth century on, acted out (with or without dia-logue), syllable by syllable, or as a whole. Victorian charades, it is worth remembering, 'accustomed people to breaking words down and considering their homonyms or multiple meanings'.[25] The punning procedures of such games would alone make us reluctant to accept that the etymological pun has fixed the identity rather than opening it up to stranger possibilities. If Charade indulges in 'long talk' it need not be 'idle', mere gossip; it is, substantially, a bookish student's eager effort to relate the theories of quantum physics to human behaviour and belief and an arduous struggle to find herself in a world of shams, paradoxes, alternative versions of the truth.[26] In so far as Charade's name and situation conjure up the famed storyteller of the *Arabian Nights*, the nearly homonymic Shahrazad (better known as Sheherazade), we have a pun that is plainly structural – Charade dons the oriental mask and plays a game, both erotic and heuristic, with the M.I.T. physicist Koenig, equivalent of the despotic Shah (Persion for king) who is tantalised by constantly interrupted stories – but is also revisionary, converting 'erratic', 'idle' protracted talk into her (partially) triumphant and therapeutic manipulation of the overweening male, and an effectively devious progress to her desired end.[27]

III

Hospital has felt on the pulses the truth of Lacan's conception of the pun, as a homonymic convergence 'based on a non-identity which is initially mistaken for identity',[28] when, ludicrously mistaken for a medical centre by Boston callers who had been confused by the misplacement of her (husband's) name in the local directory, she had to yell down the phone: 'No, no, no, this is a *name* not a *place*. I am a person.'[29] Mistaking identity is a common occurrence in her intricate fictional patterns of coincidence and synchronicity, and misidentification may be underlined with a pun, as in *Charades* when Kay pivotally mistakes Koenig for her niece's absent father, Nicholas, and goes to bed with him (King = Nicholas II). '"Who was I supposed to be?"', asks Koenig, when he has at Kay's prompting taken the part of 'Nicholas' in her fantasy-fulfilling re-play of her earlier romance (C, p. 180). It is as if he had been playing in unscripted charades, enacting a pun, for the name a character bears may be a kind of act or masquerade, presented as a play on words. This acted pun is George Eliot's succint definition of the charade as I have quoted it in my first epigraph. Taking my cue from the title of the novel in which the Kay-Koenig game appears, I have found it suggestive to look at Hospital's fictions as extended and complicated enactments of key puns that invite the reader to speculate on the role play and identities behind the masks of the leading characters' proper names.

Even in *Charades*, it should be stressed, Hospital makes no literal reproduction of the popular word game. Direct representations, usually composing symbolic scenes of great hermeneutic interest figure in many novels in English.[30] But *Charades*, like Hospital's other fictions, offers only suggestive analogues, such as the puzzle pictures of the

Old Volcano's paintings (B, ch.39) or Charlie Chang's photocollages (LM, Book 3, ch.2), and pervasive metaphors of theatrical performance, since narrators and characters are busily engaged in play-acting, masquerade, or posing, and 'riddles, games, puzzles, conundrums' (LM, p. 57), which constantly casts them as encoders or decoders of enigmatic appearances.

Now, in the traditional charades, the proper name was usually enigmatically enacted (in puns) and the withheld name provoked by guessing. In Hospital's ludic fictions the proper name itself is given and prompts the quest.[31] Characters are the namesakes or nearly homonymic doubles of well-known originals; set within the context of whirling word-play and semantic shiftiness, they secrete allusions to potential identities, possible roles. Characters are names acted out, 'speaking names' as one of Robert Kroetsch's critics has called characters encapsulated in their names.[32] In charade-like fictions, however, they speak in riddles, as it were, not in propria persona, and identification is elusive, only come at by the slippery ambages of the pun. The name is then no longer, strictly speaking, proper (literal or denotative), supposed badge of a unique identity, but rendered questionable in the borrowing (connotative), a persona or mask whose fit is to be tested by the audience. Thus masked characters may be self-dramatising, playing with names and hiding behind them, like Charade, self-translated as Enigma (C, p. 226), or Jean-Marc Seymour (See-more), progressing from being 'stage manager' to donning all the characters' 'masks' and remembering 'the view from their eyes' (B, pp. 178, 191, 193); or, they may be overdetermined creatures of multiple and doubtful designation, virtually silent enigmatic objects of others' constructions, like La Desconocida in Borderline (La Magdalena/Dolores Marquez/La Salvadora) and Verity in Charades (Acier/Ashkenazy/De l'Anneau/Delaney/Sleeping Beauty).

Charades isolate a word for perplexing performance, and Hospital's strategy depends on making the proper names functionally strange. Their homonyms (or near-homonyms) are like the postmodern titles of Umberto Eco's prescription: they 'must muddle the reader's ideas not regiment them'.[33] Yet, although Hospital may share Charlie Chang's belief in the 'ancient and unassailable knowledge' that 'Names have potency' (LM, p. 77), the punning potential of the proper names may seem, often enough, unapparent at first glance, where names like Gus and Felicity, Katherine and Nicholas, Lucy and Gabriel, seem the plausible appellations of the conventional realist novel. Like the pun in general, the name only becomes semantically charged when a context has been contrived that will allow the reader to produce more than one meaning for it, as when we discover that Gus is a guise for the detested Augustine and the sainted namesake can only be sensibly evoked and brooded upon where the dense web of circumstantial signifiers (notably, Carthage) cooperate to this end. Hospital rarely deploys the patently unreal, comically hyperbolic cartoon names so widespread in experimental postwar American novels whose attention-grabbing onomastic masquerade seems bent on demonstrating 'the arbitrary significance of labels'.[34] The penchant is for allegorical names (Dolores and Felicity, Hunter and Seymour; Charade and Enigma, Verity and Truman) or names slightly alienated by translation into another tongue (Jean-Marc; Koenig; Delaney), or for exotic soubriquets (La Salvadora; the Ashcan) and innocent-seeming diminutives opening up the names to play (Fliss; Nick). Names at home in the metonymic system of the naturalistic narrative are most forcefully relocated in the metaphoric design of these postmodern texts when they are openly framed as enigmas like the already cited La Desconocida and Verity; or the dislocation of the character, the latently intertextual resource, is made salient by direct comment on out-of-placeness in the modernist myth-minded tradition of Joyce. So, Koenig on Charade, 'Weird name' (p. 30), or a garage attendant on Gus Kelly, 'Augustine. Jesus. Don't often come across a name like that. Not in here anyways. Bet no one forgets it' (p. 272). The last speaker draws a distinction between acceptabilities on different sides of the Canadian-US border, but in Hospital's cross-culturally sensitive texts, where the critique of intolerance toward difference and a solidarity with hybrid and blurred identity are passionately presented, the displaced names may resonate with socio-political alienation. So the Australian Verity Delaney, who deliberately adopts or re-assumes the Jewish family name of Ashkenazy out of solidarity with victims of the Holocaust, is either faintly disbelieved (C, p. 172) or jeeringly nicknamed 'The Ashcan' for her Pom-like pretentiousness (C, p. 61).[35]

IV

Fictional charades from earlier literary texts solicited the reader's willingness to probe the interplay of identity and difference, the compatibility of performer and the part, and presumed some intertextual competence in the guessing. Hospital's charades obviously engage us in exploration of Barthes' 'stereographic space' of intertextuality in similar ways. Encrypting prototypes or archetypes in the proper names, set within a network of paratextual and intratextual insinuations, she makes of these acted puns a kind of structural allusion, even a generic marker.[36] Her practise in this is comparable to that of contemporaries like Rushdie or Pynchon and, in the examples under examination, similarly sponsors a reading of their intertextuality as parody. To understand Hospital's intertextual space as parodic is of some importance to my case. One of the most effective ways of foregrounding this space in postmodernist fiction, according to Brian McHale, is to borrow characters from another text, but he draws attention to the difficulty in applying Umberto Eco's distinction between a 'transworld identity', where the essential properties of the prototype are carried over into the new text (as is usually the case with 'Cordelia' in the many versions of *King Lear*), and mere homonymity, where only the names are identical.[37] (What do we make of 'Cordelia' in Edward Bond's *Lear*, for instance?) In Hospital's fiction, however, intertextuality through homonymic character is wholly parodic, the figures having undergone a significant deformation in transit; like puns, they will stand revealed as cases of mistaken identity. It would be unfortunate, however, if 'deformation' bore implications of the 'ludicrous' rather than the 'ludic'. Parody need not connote travesty, a deriding or demeaning of a previous text. Linda Hutcheon's Bakhtinian revision of the term, stressing its dialogical and hybrid character, is an enabling one in this context. To Hutcheon parody is 'repetition with critical distance', which marks difference rather than similarity, but, although difference/distance is the *raison d'être* of the device, her etymologising of parody (*parodia*) as inclusively 'countersong' and 'side-song' brings out to what extent it is pliable, putting its contrastive function in play with its potential for demonstrating accord.[38]

The title of *Charades*, alluding at once to the protagonist's proper name and the improper game in which she is involved, is a blatantly structural pun, and at the same time undermines our faith in strict generic classification: the grammatical ambiguity, pun-filled, allows us to think via the plural noun of travesties, fictionalised word games, a myriad guises and selves converging on the proper name Charade, and via the singular noun, with the possessive apostrophe restored, of what properly belongs to Charade, her history. The heroine's name, like parody, repeats and re-interprets the past, and its propriety in these circumstances is tested by the story. The parodic distance in Hospital's revision of the situation in the frame of *Thousand and One Nights* may be considered a feminist 'herstory', where both storytelling and lovemaking are entered into quite voluntarily, and are both broken off by Charade as she returns to Queensland in search, now, of a mother rather than a father. Her full name, Charade Ryan (Ryan is her adoptive father's name), is patterned on the king's name, Shahryar, and hints at her casting of Koenig as a father-surrogate. The Shah, Hospital has alleged, has been turned from 'an obnoxious chauvinistic womanising murderer into a charming settled married man and father of three',[39] but her account hardly conveys the parodic remodelling's complexity – the pain of Koenig's estrangement from his wife and Moonie son, his failure to marry his enchantress and have children by her, his suspension between desire and renunciation at the deliberately open ending. Most striking is the way this Shah is given a story to tell himself, as part of the humanisation of the prototype, to match Charade's versions of her childhood and the stories of Kay and Bea, but also to deepen the resemblance to Nicholas, another teller of tales.[40] The mock-Chaucerian 'Kynge's Tale' intended as his counterblast to Kay's account of their entanglement, is corrected by Charade to 'The Physician's Tale' as the nearest equivalent to 'The Physicist's' (C, p. 202). Yet there is more than a hint here that the scientific theorisings with which the text is peppered are themselves physicist's tales, metaphoric, stochastic, useful fictions, and that the alternative and equally valid versions of reality which Charade and the rest narrate (instead of the ultimately concluded oriental fables of the adopted text) are also incomplete, their enigmas unsolved.

Hospital's parody is primarily that 'serious, reverential' kind that Linda Hutcheon attributes to the Eliot of *The Waste Land*, more homage than thumbed nose.[41] This is particularly apparent in *Borderline* and *The Last Magician* for which Dante's *Divine Comedy* is a creative resource. Both re-enact unmockingly Dante's sublimated love for Beatrice in a basic psychological configuration ('three people searching for elusive and idealised love-objects') set in those infernal and purgatorial regions which have long symbolised for writers the modern sense of disorientation and moral confusion.[42] In *Borderline* Jean-Marc first announces his calque on Dante as he modulates from Felicity lost 'in the dark world' to 'all in the dark wood together' (B, p. 171). Lucy, too, conjures up that *selva oscura* but arguably makes serious parody of Dante too thumpingly explicit, especially by opening *The Last Magician* with a performance/translation of the first line of the *Inferno*. Nevertheless, we are plainly stimulated to read these texts as, among other things, variations of an allegorical vision of a psychological-cum-spiritual quest. What will concern us here, however, are two interrelated issues: how Dante's double role, as retrospectively recording poet-seer and suffering, questing pilgrim, is distributed to and performed by distinct and riddlingly-named characters in *Borderline*, and how that affects our sense of generic indeterminacy.

The title of *Borderline* inducts us into blurrings of such clear-cut divisions of labour. Jean-Marc Seymour narrates, mostly after the fact and guessingly, a situation in which Gus (Augustine) Kelly reluctantly participates and, afflicted by fear and guilt, undergoes a conversion in his transit from 'hell' (B, pp. 240, 226), through purgatorial visions of

types of Beatrice (Felicity, p. 29, Dolores, p. 170), to his end in purgatorial flames. But we are allowed to see how Gus's epiphanies are
shaped by the conjecturing dreamer-artist, who has been 'putting on
the masks of Gus, of Dante, of all the flounderers in dark woods' (B,
p. 191) just as we appreciate the irony at young Seymour's expense
that he is compelled to modify his narrative designs as he proceeds,
gropingly, to a crisis in his own affairs (attachment to Gus's daughter and re-attachment to the estranged older Seymour). Seymour is, of
course, an indicative pun: see-more (prophet, visionary, artist), seemer
(trader in dreams, portentous appearances), and seamer (borderer,
joiner). Both 'Dantes' are more than 'borderline cases' (B, p. 250),
equivocal functions; each is, what Jean-Marc artfully designates Gus,
'a borderline saint' (B, p. 283). Nowhere does Jean-Marc identify Gus
with St Augustine directly; but proper name puns are almost direction
enough in another test-by-story naming. The philandering salesman's
distaste for the Christian name given to him by his pious Catholic
mother establishes parodic distance from a figure whose conversion
from *eros* to *agape* he apparently re-enacts, as he repents his infidelities and commits himself to helping an illegal immigrant across the
border. His long-suffering wife is Therese, near-namesake of that St
Teresa of Avila who was so ardent a follower of Augustine that she
names no other author in her autobiography.[43] The crucial scene in his
transformation, threshold of his fatal rescue-effort, is Carthage, New
York State (B, p. 270), evoking the memorable opening of the *Confessions*, Book III, which the older Seymour will later use as caption
to his pictorial transfiguration of Gus as 'tragic clown': 'To Carthage
then I came' (B, p. 286). Now this *nomen* as *omen* in Augustine may
act as more of a structural pun than at first appears; for, notwithstand-
ing that the Saint figures only fleetingly, among the enthroned blessed
spirits, in the Comedy (*Paradiso*, canto XXXII), it has recently been
maintained that the *Confessions* were decisive in Dante's modelling of
his masterpiece on conversion narrative, where events of the *pilgrim*'s
life only become meaningful in the light of the *poet*'s retrospection.[44]
Furthermore, in a text rife with religious puns ('catholically', 'miracu-
lous', 'grace') 'confession' – 'confessing' – 'confessional' forms a cla-
mant cluster that implicates not only Augustine but others, most
notably the supposedly detached metanarrator whose book becomes,
in one light, another (borderline) *Confessions*: 'I have a confession to
make' (B, p. 282).

  Unlike Gus, Jean-Marc has not consciously tried to evade the possible fatality in the name's sainted inscriptions, yet his name, a riddling
translation, is unmistakably *en travesti*, conducive to further levels of
parody and generic indeterminacy. Englished, his forename conflates
the first and last Evangelists, St Mark and St John, as Hospital attests:

Jean-Marc, then, is deliberately named for two of the Gospel writers who, from fragments, similarly try to put together the truth of what happened. The entire book is his jigsaw puzzle.[45] His groping, conjectural, and semi-detached mediation of events is the formal correlative of the author's 'bemused and mystified' state in the process of writing.[46] Up to a point, the comparison with the two gospels, considered as twins, holds: they combine a certain reticence, terseness, tolerance of perplexing gaps and discontinuities with an impression of subtle, systematic connectedness as they (at a remove from the material circumstances in which it manifested itself) address the mystery of Christ's identity. Each, like *Borderline*, opens strikingly with a kind of prologue or overture of themes and figures (Mark I: 1–13; John I: 1–18) but, where Mark emphasises Jesus's ministry, John makes enigmatic play with the ambiguities of the Word (*Logos*). This more lyrical approach to the theological mystery of incarnation makes a better match with *Borderline* whose first short chapter weaves its tantalising proper names into an incantatory pattern of crucial motifs ('borders', 'in the ordinary course of events'). Yet although John's gospel may be plausibly presented by Frank Kermode as the work of a 'protonovelist' writing 'narrative of remarkable variety, subtlety and freedom',[47] Mark's (and Kermode's representation of it in his Harvard Lectures of 1977–8 as the paradigm of the way narrative generates interpretations through gaps and riddles provoking coherence-seeking constructions and encouraging initiates, our approved interpreters, to privilege spiritual over carnal significances) seems the more influential model.[48] Perhaps the most interesting feature of Mark's proto-modernist text is its strange stopping-short of total revelation of the risen Christ, since it breaks off abruptly as Mary Magdalen and the other women are dumbstruck by the empty tomb: 'for they were afraid'. The fact that dubious material is usually added to the gospel to give more weight to the Resurrection yields a parallel with *Borderline*'s double ending, with the evidence for Felicity's tragic death followed by her consolatory quasi-resurrection in Jean-Marc's conjectures that she is doing voluntary work in El Salvador and will soon be in touch. A closer look at the narrator's name might make this sense of accord seem more doubtful. 'The gospel according to Jean-Marc' (*B*, p. 189) contains after all a self-mocking pun.[49] For 'John Mark', messily involved with Felicity, and Old Volcano, Kathleen and her father, it is hard to tell any absolute 'gospel truth'. Making discoveries as he writes, he comes to appreciate that he must transcend both the Gospel, that abandonment of dubiously literal chronicling for the reaching after essential truths, and 'the gospel of trivia' (*B*, p. 67), the merely formal realism of the novel. Yet the tempering of the facts may entail that the 'template' of his temperament imposes its distorted meaning on the world.

(*B*, p. 171) The evangelists, on the contrary, remain obscure, fleshless scribes, whose aesthetic choices appear to be either doctrinally dictated or deeply enigmatic. What kind of a gospel is this book? No true report on the life, death and resurrection of Jesus Christ from 'the official biographer, the final authority' (*B*, p. 256), it still shows its characters enacting a little *imitatio Christi*. Martyrdoms and resurrections are insinuated, though all may be borderline cases: Felicity dies aged 33, Dolores is a woman of sorrows, Gus is driven to self-sacrifice, even the Old Volcano becomes in his art, the rising sun/Son (*B*, p. 219). If 'good news' there be, it is in part his intuitional paintings and the reconciliation with his son which they help bring about. That leaves the tragic residue of human losses, and the flinching from them, to give us pause.

V

In conclusion, I return briefly to my first epigraph drawn from George Eliot's Platonic dialogue in verse, published in 1874, halfway between *Middlemarch* and *Daniel Deronda*. The quoted lines come from a speech of Laertes, one of the six friends whom Hamlet has gathered together at a breakfast symposium in the English Wittenburg. 'Ardent, rash, radical', Laertes objects violently to Osric's gaudily figurative denigration of philosophy, denouncing any argument by analogy as simply play on words, a charade. Since Eliot sets up a dramatic, inconclusive debate, it is doubtful where her sympathies lie, more doubtful still if we relate it to those potent unstable compounds of her late great poetic novels, where realist and idealist positions co-exist, metonymic and metaphoric modes interinanimate each other, and exploration of moral and metaphysical truths may be advanced through devices like the riddle (*Middlemarch*, ch. 60) and the charade (*Daniel Deronda*, ch. 6), the very strategies suspected by Laertes. Hospital's fictions, indisputably less massive, ambitious, accessible perhaps, still play a similar double game: they too insist – in the violence and violations inflicted on Felicity and Hester in *Borderline*, on Verity and Rachel in *Charades*, that 'pain is solely pain', but Laertes puts it like that in a poem that notably borrows the dramatis personae of *Hamlet* for a play-ful parody. Both writers seem to agree, moreover, that the world might be a charade (at least in the troubled perceptions of the characters) not easily unriddled by a word, a *single* word, but riddled with disorienting – maybe re-orienting – word-play, manifold meanings, ambiguous discourse, which demands a corresponsive improper form. Hospital's late twentieth-century modes may seem more structurally irregular, more susceptible to Laertes-like strictures on preciously embroidered intertextual effects,[50] more averse to reaching 'the decrypting, unriddling, enigma-solving moment'.[51] But, strange virtuoso hybrids as they are, with their panoply of puns as heuristic probes, they may still stand in that line, which Valentine Cunningham traces back to Eliot, of:

> self-reflecting, cryptic, riddling fictions, a set of puzzles to readers, about puzzled characters compelled constantly to behave as readers and presented with a world, other people, life, as a rebarbative set of shockingly difficult textualities.[52]

Notes

1. *George Eliot: Collected Poems*, ed. Lucien Jenkins (London: SKOOB Books, 1989), p. 162.
2. Janette Turner Hospital, *The Last Magician* (London: Virago, 1992), p. 56. The following abbreviations for the titles of Hospital's novels will be used: *IS* (*The Ivory Swing*), *TTP* (*The Tiger in the Tiger Pit*), *B* (*Borderline*), *C* (*Charades*), *AVPD* (*A Very Proper Death*), *LM* (*The Last Magician*).
3. Alex Juniper (Janette Turner Hospital), *A Very Proper Death* (Ringwood, Victoria: Penguin Books Australia, 1990), p. 134.
4. Janette Turner Hospital, *Charades* (Toronto, Ontario: McClelland and Stewart, 1989), p. 5. All subsequent page references are to this edition and included in the text.
5. 'Janette Turner Hospital' (Interview) in *Writers in Action: The Writer's Choice Evenings*, ed. George Turcotte (Sydney: Currency Press,1990), p. 75.
6. Janette Turner Hospital, *Dislocations* (Toronto: McClelland and Stewart, 1986).
7. *A Poetics of Postmodernism: History, Theory, Fiction* (New York and London: Routledge, 1988), p. 12.
8. 'Ex-centriques, Eccentric, Avant-Garde' in *Room of One's Own*, 8, no.4 (1984), p. 57.
9. Janette Turner Hospital, *Borderline* (Sydney and London: Hodder and Stoughton, 1985). All subsequent page references are to this edition and included in the text.
10. *The Canadian Imagination: Dimensions of a Literary Culture* , ed. David Staines (Cambridge, Mass.: Harvard University Press, 1977), pp. 226–248. McLuhan's Canada is 'a land of multiple borderlines, psychic, social and geographical' (p. 244).
11. 'Janette Turner Hospital' in *Contemporary Novelists*, ed. Lesley Henderson (Chicago and London: St. James's Press, 1991), p. 455. Hospital's comment.
12. *Re-Forming the Narrative* (Ithaca and London: Cornell University Press, 1987), p. 194.
13. Janette Turner Hospital, 'Letter to a New York Editor' in *Meanjin Quarterly*, 47 (1988), p. 560.

14. Paul Ricoeur, *Time and Narrative*, 3 Vols, trans. Kathleen McLaughlin and David Pellauer (Chicago: University of Chicago Press, 1984–88), I, p.ix.

15. Jonathan Culler, 'The Call of the Phoneme: Introduction', *On Puns: The Foundation of Letters* , ed. Jonathan Culler (Oxford: Blackwell, 1988), pp. 5, 3. Other notable exponents of the pun are Walter Redfern, (*Puns* , Oxford: Basil Blackwell, 1984) and Derek Attridge (*Peculiar Language: Literature as Difference, from the Renaissance to James Joyce*, Ithaca: Cornell University Press, 1988).

16. Culler, p. 8.

17. 'Letter to a New York Agent', *op. cit.*, p. 563. 'But J-M doesn't see the joke that the reader sees: someone else (and a woman at that) is dreaming Jean-Marc.'

18. Hospital admits that her 'constant theme' is the 'shadow self', all of the novels (up to *Charades*) having featured 'a bifurcated woman' (e.g. Felicity and Dolores as obverse sides of the same coin): *Writers in Action*, *op. cit.*, p. 85. Elsewhere she writes of Jean-Marc's awareness of the 'mythic, or Jungian' dimension to his material: 'Letter to a New York Agent', *op. cit.*, p. 562. Her reconciliation of science and religion in *Charades* is also indebted to the Jungian holism of *The Tao of Physics* by Fritjof Capra, and a Jungian approach to her work would be appropriate.

19. Hospital has more than once exploited the ontological conundrum of Chuan Tzu (about a man dreaming of a butterfly, doubtful on waking up whether he was a butterfly dreaming of a man), cited in the 'essential' epigraph to *Borderline*, probably originally found in Borge's 'A New Refutation of Time' and echoed in the use she makes of 'The Circular Ruins' (*B*, pp. 286–7), and re-told once more by Charlie Chang (*LM*, pp. 20-21).

20. Quoted by Helen Daniel, 'Introduction' to *Borderline* (London: Virago Press, 1990), pp.[1–2].

21. Derek Attridge *op. cit.*, p. 123. See also Jean Paulhan, *La Preuve par l'etymologie* (Cognac: Le temps qu'il fait, 1988, originally published in 1953) for magisterial exposure of the abuse of etymology.

22. Maureen Quilligan, *The Language of Allegory: Defining the Genre* (Ithaca and London: Cornell University Press, 1979), p. 33.

23. Patricia Parker, *Inescapable Romance: Studies in the Poetics of a Mode* Princeton, N.J.: Princeton University Press, 1979), ch. 1 and 2.

24. *Labyrinths of Voice: Conversations with Robert Kroetsch*, ed. Shirley Neumann and Robert Wilson (Edmonton: NeWest Press, 1982), pp. 148–9.

25. Sue Lonoff, *Wilkie Collins and his Victorian Readers* (New York: AMS, 1982), p. 136.

26. Charades revolves around extensive exposition of the implications of Heisenberg's Uncertainty Principle and its corollaries: observation creates reality; all perception lacks precision; ours is a duplex world of potentials and actualities; in the quantum world of potentials, contradiction and paradox reign. Charade, perplexed by this, finds some solace in the precedent of the thirteenth-century Averroists' Double Truth (what is

true in philosophy can be false in theology and vice versa) (*C*, p. 26). It is this context-dependent truth which may have its rhetorical counterpart in metaphor and the pun.

27. Apart from the homonymic convergence of the principals' names, an elaborately contrived linguistic context sustains the playful comparison with the *Thousand and One Nights* through echoings of the title phrase, with Part and Chapter headings making allusions to Nights and Tales, and characteristic locutions (Pouff! Shazam, open sesame, *And with that . . . she vanished like camphor*). But Charade's name functions similarly to Oedipa's in *The Crying of Lot 49*, as Chris Hall sees it, the very name signifying 'the postmodern tendency to subvert and re-work genre simultaneously', *op. cit.*, p. 67. The slight deformation in the names presages some failure to keep to the script.

28. Francoise Meltzer's account of Lacanian theory in *On Puns*, ed. Jonathan Culler, *op. cit.*, p. 162.

29. *Writers in Action, op. cit.*, p. 77.

30. Examples, from Charlotte Brontë's *Jane Eyre* (1847, ch. 18) and Thackeray's *Vanity Fair* (1848, ch. 51) to Alison Lurie's *Foreign Relations* (1984, ch. 4) and *Prospero's Daughter* by the Canadian writer Constance Beresford-Howe (1988, ch.1), are all attended by feelings of unease and impropriety.

31. In real life charades, as in canonical fictional representations, it might be a place name (Bridewell in *Jane Eyre*); more often it is the name of a noted person (Agamemnon in *Vanity Fair*, Rip Van Winkle in *Ulysses*, 'Nausicaa').

32. *Labyrinths of Voice, op. cit.*, p. 189. Robert Wilson draws Kroetsch's attention to W. F. H. Nicolaisen's 'Ordering the Chaos: Name Strategies in Robert Kroetsch's Novels' in *Essays on Canadian Writing*, II (Summer 1978), pp. 55–65.

33. *Reflections on 'The Name of the Rose'* (London: Secker and Warburg, 1989), p. 3.

34. David Seed, 'Naming and Identity in Modern American Fiction' in *Dutch Quarterly Review of Anglo-American Letters*, 20 (1990–92), p. 136.

35. Compare the fate of Chinese-Australian Charlie Chang in *The Last Magician* who has to suffer loss of his ancestral name and translation into the racist 'Charlie Chink' (*LM*, pp. 77, pp. 167-8).

36. Chris Hall, '"Behind the Hieroglyphic Streets"': Pynchon's Oedipa Maas and the Dialectic of Reading' in *Critique*, 33, no. 1 (Fall 1991), pp. 63–77. See p. 67 and compare David Seed, *op. cit.*, pp. 130-31.

37. Brian McHale, *Postmodernist Fiction* (London: Methuen, 1987), pp. 35–6, 56–7. He cites Umberto Eco, 'Lector in Fabula: pragmatic strategy in a metanarrative' in *The Role of the Reader: Explorations in the Semiotics of Texts* (Bloomington and London: Indiana University Press, 1979).

38. Linda Hutcheon, *A Theory of Parody: The Teachings of Twentieth-Century Art Forms* (New York and London: Methuen, 1985), pp. 6, 32.

39. *Writers in Action, op. cit.*, p. 74.

40. Nicholas, ambiguous narrative authority, has the aspect of the kind of oriental storyteller who produced *The Arabian Nights*: 'he told the same story over and over again, a thousand versions . . . the same story under different names, set in different countries' (C, p. 235). 'A compulsive liar' (p. 231), he appears to be identified by Koenig's researches as a trickster (he may have authored papers on its figure in medieval French *fabliaux*, one of which was presented at the Queen's University in Kingston, Canada, pp. 289–90). He may have invented Charade (fathered her and given her that gamesome name), may be author of the whole shebang! Except that he has had 'the assistance of a certain lady', herself a medievalist who has taught at Queen's and might not be able to resist the toponymic pun.

41. *A Theory of Parody, op. cit.*, p. 98.

42. Hospital writes that her narrator, Jean-Marc, is 'perfectly aware that when he is writing about Gus in the dark wood, climbing the mountain toward the vision of Dolores, he is also parodying Dante (the dark wood, the inferno, the vision of Beatrice in a chariot at the top of the Purgatorial mountain)'. 'Letter to a New York Agent', *op. cit.*, p. 562. Her short story, 'The Dark Wood', in *Dislocations* centres on a dying woman called Beatrice. In *The Last Magician* Lucy and Charlie share Dantean roles, but Charlie as film maker is more like Jean-Marc as narrator: 'So Charlie (in his film Charlie's Inferno) was Dante, speaking in code and turning history into allegory' (*LM*, p. 64).

43. John Freccero, 'Autobiography and Narrative' in *Reconstructing Individualism* , ed. Thomas C. Heller and others (Stanford: California Stanford University, 1986), p. 18.

44. John Freccero, *Dante: The Poetics of Conversion*, ed. Rachel Jacoff (Cambridge, Mass.: Harvard University Press, 1986), ch. 1. The essays were published between 1959 and 1984.

45. *Writers in action, op. cit.*, p. 72. But both Mark and John have at different times been identified with the 'John, whose surname was Mark' in Acts 12: 12, 25, so Hospital's hybrid has appropriately disputed and murky origins.

46. 'Letter to a New York Agent', *op. cit.*, p. 561.

47. 'John' in *A Literary Guide to the Bible, op. cit.*, pp. 454, 452

48. *The Genesis of Secrecy: On the Interpretation of Narrative* (Cambridge, Mass.: Harvard University Press, 1979). See ch. III 'The Man in the Mackintosh, Boy in the Shirt': 'The story moves erratically, and not always forward; one thing follows another for no very evident reason. A good deal of the story seems concerned with failure to understand the story' (p. 69).

49. Not just on Jean-Marc and his Gospel, but possibly on the proprietorial 'according to': French for the (French-named) piano tuner is *l'accordeur*'.

50. The evident cleverness, the air of in-joking, may give ammunition to critics of her overdoings. When Felicity sees Dolores in the refrigerated meat van and thinks of Perugino's *La Magdalena*, it seems too neat that the van is Beckett's (Samuel Beckett used an allusion to a Perugino Magdalene to help characterise his Ruby in *More Pricks than Kicks*). Is the

choice of Lucy's ur-name Lucia influenced by the location of the University of Queensland Press (St Lucia) which has published *Charades* and *Isobars* in Australia?

51. Valentine Cunningham, *In the Reading Gaol, op. cit.*, p. 299. The whole of the discussion of George Eliot's *Middlemarch* in 'A Sort of Practical Rebus' has proved illuminating (pp. 297–319).

52. Ibid, p. 303.

7

Reconstructing *The Ledger:*
Canadian History in
the Poetry of Robert Kroetsch

Lee Spinks

I wish to begin with a reflection on the ambivalent status of Canadian cultural discourse. Writing in 1974 in a special 'Canadian issue' of the journal *Boundary 2*, Kroetsch comments:

> The Canadian writer's peculiar predicament is that he works with a language, within a literature, that appears to be authentically his own, and not a borrowing. But just as there was in the Latin word a concealed Greek experience, so there is in the Canadian word a concealed other experience, sometimes British, sometimes American.
>
> In recent years the tension between this appearance of being just like someone else and the demands of authenticity has become intolerable – both to individuals and to the society. In recent Canadian fiction the major writers resolve the paradox – the painful tension between appearance and authenticity – by the radical process of demythologising the systems that threaten to define them. Or, more comprehensively, they uninvent the world.[1]

This passage, with its meditation upon the questions of 'otherness', 'appearance' and 'authenticity', demarcates several areas of concern that will come to interest us. In particular, it highlights the problematic nature of historical representation within postcolonial cultures. By focusing upon the 'concealed other experience' within the Canadian word, Kroetsch acknowledges the curious interstate occupied by the Canadian imagination as it strives to express its own historical experience within the language of another culture or alien discursive regime. Paradoxically, Kroetsch argues, the only means of asserting a recognisably 'Canadian' identity is by means of that 'British' or 'American' language that has historically represented Canada as other to its own traditions or modes of self-reflection. For Kroetsch, attempting to rehabilitate lost or forgotten narratives of Canadian history, this experience of 'otherness' is forcibly inscribed in the language he uses by its unavoidable collusion with the representational systems that formerly circumscribed the expression of Canadian experience. As the movement in his rhetoric from 'authenticity' to 'the radical process of demythologising the systems that threaten to define us' demonstrates, the ambivalence or doubleness of postcolonial discourse has its attendant benefits, since it suggests that all discursive positions are unstable and liable to revision, and extends the possibility of a quite other relationship between Canadian subjectivity and the 'mandarin language' of the former imperial powers.

This sense of the alterity of the Canadian position haunts Kroetsch's writing from its earliest moments. His published work over the last three decades represents a form of double writing in which the search for a specifically Canadian discourse of place, history and origin coincides with the recognition that such a discourse can never escape contamination by the history of representation that formerly defined its parameters and set it into play. Thus his prose fiction, which commences, appropriately enough, with the narcissistic experience of estrangement from an 'authentic' self in *But We Are Exiles*, dramatises the tensions between experience and representation through a series of double plots. One has only to think of the struggle between Madham and Sadness for control of Canadian cultural history in *Gone Indian*, the collision of patriarchal and counter-patriarchal discourses in *Badlands*, and the dialectic between oral and graphic sensibilities in *What The Crow Said* to detect Kroetsch's sense that postcolonial history exhibits a series of primary tensions between identity and placelessness, centrality and excentricity, and between language and silence.

The doubleness of these plots originates in Kroetsch's desire to hold together in a single space both hegemonic and marginalised narratives of Canadian history. The importance to these three novels of the binary relationship between a representative of cultural order (Demeter, Madham, William Dawe) and a marginalised 'other' that contests its position within the discourse, locates the dichotomy between 'same' and 'other' within the basic structure of meaning of Kroetsch's fiction. As the narratives of Jeremy Sadness, Anna Dawe and Vera Lang ironise and qualify the 'official' cultural records of Mark Madham, William Dawe and Gus Liebhaber, the excluded histories of the Amerindian heritage, feminist struggle and the rural community are reinscribed into the documents of Canadian life. Through this process of juxtaposition and narratorial revision, Kroetsch creates an adversarial form that transforms his experience of history as otherness into a series of *other* histories which are subsequently reincorporated into the narrative of Canadian self-discovery.

My reading of the first phase of Kroetsch's poetry – the period that encompasses the transition from 'Stone Hammer Poem' in the late 1960s to *The Ledger* in the early 1970s – seeks to identify three positions in Kroetsch's work consonant with this progression. First, I propose that the liberating moment in Kroetsch's poetics comes with his decision to reinscribe the experience of alterity within the process of signification itself. Next, I want to urge that this artistic move is contemporaneous with Kroetsch's elaboration, in poems, novels and critical articles, of an explicitly Derridean approach to language, history and subjectivity. And, third, I take the position that both of these developments are predicated upon Kroetsch's failure to sustain a phenomenological poetics of history, place and identity in 'Stone Hammer Poem'.

'Stone Hammer Poem' dramatises the search for a phenomenological poetics that would identify a necessary connection between place, history and the intentional subject. The poem reproduces, in its rhythms and cadences, the foraging movement of the intelligence as it searches for its identity among the leavings of history. It takes as its subject an archaeological relic – a stone hammer found by Kroetsch's grandfather – and examines it as an historical index of the relationship between the postcolonial subject and the landscape that sustains it. The fact that the poem is concerned with an archaeological fragment is instructive because 'archaeology' represents for Kroetsch a critical as well as an historical practice. By the physical act of entering the ground, the archaeologist identifies a stratum of Canadian history uncontaminated by the binary codes of imperial discourse. The archaeological fragment therefore constitutes a point of historical origin prior to the experience of difference and otherness instituted by the ludic play of language. The archaeological poetics of origin that Kroetsch adumbrates in 'Stone Hammer Poem' necessarily admit an implicit distinction between conscious experience of the land and the medium by which that experience is related. By privileging the integrity of individual conscious experience over the 'impure' semantic associations of a 'British' or 'American' language in this way, Kroetsch attempts to circumvent the problem of writing in colonial space by means of a direct engagement between the intending consciousness and the unwritten history of the Canadian past.

Kroetsch's search for an unmediated discourse of the object is predicated in 'Stone Hammer Poem' upon a wholesale repression of the referential potential of language. This entailment becomes clear from the opening lines:

This stone
become a hammer
of stone, this maul

is the colour
of bone (no,
bone is the colour
of this stone maul).

Here we encounter an extreme nervousness concerning the syntactic relation between nouns, verbs and prepositions. The movement of this passage is curiously circular: it revises and qualifies an assertion that would usually be taken as a statement of simple fact. The poem spends seven lines seeking a plausible order between 'maul', 'colour' and 'bone'. The reason, I think, for Kroetsch's extreme nervousness about the bounds of reference is that he adopts the position that any attempt to describe his home place in a borrowed language necessarily reintroduces the distinction between identity and alterity that 'Stone Hammer Poem' works so hard to suppress. Words, especially english words, become a troublesome opacity that reintroduce a covert history and metaphorics from another time and place. By contrast, the stone becomes a symbol of a pre-linguistic origin of meaning unmarked by ambiguity or the binary codes of colonial rhetoric.

The problem, of course, is that Kroetsch's position is based upon a naive theory of language. It assumes that linguistic meaning is produced not by the diacritical movement of signs but by a direct unmediated relationship between consciousness and the world around it. Words become mere tokens which embody a 'meaning' that they effortlessly bring to plenitude. What is interesting about 'Stone Hammer Poem' is that Kroetsch's meditation upon the character of colonial history dramatises the transition in his thought from an immanent to a structural theory of language. We watch as Kroetsch's effort to develop a discourse of Canadian history that makes no discursive gesture beyond the object of its attention gradually founders as he becomes aware of the referential overdetermination of the linguistic sign. And, as the following passage demonstrates, he begins to use the resistance of language to fixed points of semantic resolution to disorder the structures of historical classification.

It is a stone
old as the last
Ice Age, the
retreating/ the
recreating ice,

the retreating
buffalo, the
retreating Indians.

The attempt, in these lines, to determine the hammer's historical
origins is frustrated by the diacritical tension operating between separate units of language. The stanza's portrait of declension, loss and
abandonment represented by 'the retreating / buffalo, the / retreating
Indians' is compromised by the abundant possibilities of the unwritten suggested by the image of 'recreating ice'. The difference between
'retreating' and 'recreating' is only a letter, but the fact of this
difference, produced by the irreducible phonic play between two denotative signs, articulates a space outside established historical and
textual structures. Meanwhile Kroetsch's acknowledgement of the in-
eradicably *textual* character of human experience emerges with his
representation of the hammer as a 'paperweight' – a term that signifies
both its present physical function and the act of deferral ('paper-
wait') that produces meaning by the temporal dislocation of referents
across the space of the printed page. Eventually the space between
the textual and the historical is eliminated as the poem becomes
'shaped/ like the stone/ hammer' itself. Fittingly, then, the hammer
is last pictured lying on the poet's desk, occasion and symbol for
a poem that traverses the field of Canadian history, opening up its
latent possibilities in time to the disorderings and reconstitutions of
language.

Kroetsch's poetry of the 1970s continues to exploit the discrepancy
between ordered structures of historical representation and the textual
production of meaning. His work from this period is 'postmodern' to
the extent that it asserts the provisionality of historical discourse and
interrogates the idea of a point of 'origin' from which to date the evolution of Canadian historical identity. One of the defining features of
this verse is its 'intertextuality' – its ability to inhabit a particular textual
world (the ledger of a nineteenth-century community, for example, or
the details of a seed catalogue) while occupying a critical space outside those discourses that constitute the world under discussion. With
the juxtaposition of 'poetic' language and accountancy notation, or
horticultural classification and the tall-tale, a breach is made in the uni-
form surface of historical representation through which marginalised
or repressed narratives of cultural experience can be rehabilitated and
brought back into the public sphere. Such an emphasis on discursive heterogeneity, and its concomitant disruption of teleological and
foundational myths of origin, retains a peculiar resonance for a culture positioned as 'other' to American and European meta-narratives
of historical identity.

Kroetsch's subversion of unitary or 'closed' narratives of historical order is coterminous with his appropriation, in the 1970s, of the discourse of Derridean 'deconstruction'. Derrida's thought is important to Kroetsch because it radicalises Husserlian phenomenology. Husserlian phenomenology attempts to provide a personal ground for experience in consciousness, and it served as the basis for the phenomenological poetics of immanence that Kroetsch articulated in the first half of 'Stone Hammer Poem'. Derrida's critique of Husserlian thought revises the relationship between signification and experience, positing the sign as anterior to consciousness. The sign therefore becomes the first stage in the production of knowledge. Since the written sign is a typographic 'presence' that 'stands in' for the absence of what is meant, the relocation of history and knowledge within the movement of signification institutes an originary difference between being and meaning. Consequently the 'origin' of history produced by the self-presence of thought to itself is displaced into the 'non-origin' of language generated by the ceaseless circulation of signs.

The concept of signification as a 'non-origin' that originates meaning and history interests Kroetsch because it offers a metaphoric 'translation' of the colonial experience of history. Seen from the perspective of colonial culture, history has no authentic 'origin' because it is comprised of discourses of self-identification represented to the colonial subject in the language, and from the perspective, of another culture. But Derrida's deconstructive displacement of 'history' and 'meaning' into the process of signification not only subverts the very idea of 'origin' – it assigns a positive value to those discourses of history and identity that exceed the representational space of Western Metaphysics. Canadian history, in which the colonialist word has been applied to the colonial subject, is one such force. This disjunction between language and experience prompts Kroetsch to embrace the deconstructive turn in order to open up the question of historical representation itself.

Derrida's insistence upon the textualisation of historical origin becomes the animating impulse of *The Ledger*. Kroetsch's poem, which offers an elliptical record of a provincial Ontario community in the middle of the last century, asks us to reconstruct the pioneer experience from a series of textual fragments. Consequently *The Ledger* is a poem written about Canadian history that inspects the ways in which that history has been written. This imbrication of the historical in the textual is more easily approached if we explore the metaphoric suggestiveness of the poem's title. Thus the 'Ledger' is both the book of record in which Kroetsch's grandfather noted his financial transactions and the larger historical record of which *The Ledger* forms a part. The idea of a 'balanced' account imparted by the trading ledger is significant since Kroetsch's poem juxtaposes marginalised or repressed narratives of historical experience with more established versions of the acts of settlement on which modern Canadian identity is based. Kroetsch's characterisation of *The Ledger* as the 'book of final entry' is therefore accurate on two counts: it retrieves the rhythms of Bruce County existence for historical attention while exploring the series of exclusions on which official records of that experience depend.

Kroetsch subverts established narratives of the pioneer experience in several ways. In particular, *The Ledger* problematises glib appropriations of its historical data through its dislocated columnar structure. Kroetsch's poem, like the Bruce County ledger, is 'a book of columns' built out of vertical and horizontal slats of language. Working in the same spirit as the postmodern poetics of David Antin and Tom Raworth, Kroetsch impedes the sequential logic of reading by redistributing narrative units across the space of the printed page. As any reader of *The Ledger* will testify, the spatial syntax of Kroetsch's technique often imposes no necessary order between vertical or horizontal modes of reading. The poem asks us instead to put together a version of the historical record for ourselves. As such, *The Ledger* becomes formally mimetic of the construction of a home place seen as the struggle of contending versions of Canadian history for a position of discursive hegemony.

Numerous examples from *The Ledger* of the productive tension generated between different columns of language could be cited. Kroetsch frequently exploits the oppositional structure of the text to yoke together incommensurate accounts within a single moment of critical attention. This *collagiste* tendency of *The Ledger* is most effective where it counterpoints different orders or registers of historical discourse. Hence Father Holzer's urbane praise for 'the climate of the region' is challenged by a ritualistic account of the cost of human settlement that ironically appropriates the antiphonal rhythm of the Christian litany. 'To raise a barn', it reminds us, we must 'cut down a forest'; while 'To raise oats and hay' we must 'burn the soil'. Later, in a darker passage, the bathing of young children in 'the clean, the original mud' is contaminated by the maiming of Joe Hauck who was 'never the same / after that water wheel tried lifting him / up to heaven'.

Ultimately *The Ledger* lays claim to our attention in the correspondence it creates between textual inscription and historical 'presence'. The poverty of the accountbook's details, which elide human and economic worth in the columns of credit and debit, represents in symbolic form a comment upon the impoverishment of those lives for which the Canadian historical record can provide no account. In this way the

communal identity of the provincial homestead is shown to be constituted by a process of social and linguistic exclusion from the grand
narrative of historical self-discovery. In one of the most moving sections of the poem, we see this process of exclusion and marginalisation
explicitly at work, as the affirmations of mercantilist progress and the
numbed response of the immigrant settler are brought together within
the unforgiving ratchet of profit and loss:

> '. . . a specimen of the self-made men who have made
> Canada what it is, and of which no section has brought forth
> more or better representatives than the County of Bruce.
> Mr Miller was never an office-seeker, but devoted himself
> strictly and energetically to the pursuit of his private busi-
> ness, and on his death was the owner of a very large and
> valuable property . . . '

Shaping the trees.
Pushing up daisies.

Have another glass, John.
Ja, Ja. What the hell.

What's the matter, John?
My bones ache.

Take a day off, John.
No time.

Here the monosyllables of John, the harried worker, suggest that
those who are isolated by language are outside historical representation: effaced, occluded, unremembered. Appropriately, John has 'no
time': the 'alien' strain of his expression can find no place within historical narratives of provincial experience. Kroetsch extends this thought
with the grim reminder that if linguistic competence underpins cultural
identity and social authority, those denied their share of a common
idiom are uniquely vulnerable. Consequently Kroetsch's recollection
that 'Gottlieb Haag's only son / grew up to be the first man / hanged
for murder / in the County of Bruce', plays on the lexical similarity of
'Haag' and 'hanged' to show that for those outside the confirmatory
structures of language etymology can become destiny and words can
kill.

By demonstrating that language both inscribes and marginalises
cultural identity, *The Ledger* becomes a poetic exploration of what
Dominick LaCapra has referred to as 'a recontextualisation of culture
in terms of collective discourses'.[2] In its refusal to separate historical

value from the textual work in which it is inscribed, Kroetsch's poem insists that questions of meaning and identity are historically determined by their position within the representational systems that define them. Concomitantly, the hegemony of individual discourses of identity, place and origin – the teleology of commercial profit, say, or the eschatology of Christian moralism – become postscripts to specific acts of interpretation implicit in the construction of 'Canada' itself. Consequently the disruptive movement of the sign, which problematises the relation between the discourses of history, political economy, theology and semiotics, works to resituate 'history' and 'identity' back within the registers of political choice.

Enjoining us to 'see the confusion again/ the chaos again' out of which history springs, Kroetsch asks us to see that 'history' is a textual field constructed by a series of repressions and exclusions. It is not an open field of interpretation: some meanings, like some political and social choices, are simply unavailable at a specific historical conjuncture. He dramatises this perception by fissuring the representational surface of *The Ledger* into six versions of the word 'ledger' itself: it is defined as, amongst other things, a piece of timber, a permanent resident, a millstone and a tombstone. These six definitions function less as organising metaphors for the poem than as examples of the semantic displacement that gives the poem its meanings. As these etymological roots show, words fall in and out of use, accrue meanings, become obsolete. But for Kroetsch, this is simultaneously a process of historical loss and an opportunity for textual and historical reinscription as new stories become available in the wake of new forms of historical experience. Conjoining the obsolete definition of 'ledger' as 'resident' and its active function as 'the book of final entry', *The Ledger* becomes, in its final form, 'a book that lies permanently in some place'. Here the two interpretations of 'lie' offered by this definition – permanent residence and semantic duplicity – combine to suggest the permanent duplicity on which *The Ledger* rests its account. This simultaneous movement of identity and difference shakes the representational structures that conflate the meaning of history with the history of meaning and opens a space for an other history to be articulated in the interstices of the historical text.

And this is where *The Ledger* leaves us, caught between historical possibilities and suspended between different interpretations. By asking us, in its closing moments, to 'marry the terror' Kroetsch calls for a *transformational* reading of Canadian historical discourse that exploits the radical alterity of language to reinscribe the otherness of an unrepresented historical experience. Holding to the double register of deconstructive poetics, which simultaneously records and overturns unitary or 'metaphysical' conceptions of history, Kroetsch's radical suggestion is that the 'concealed other experience' within the Canadian word is the history of Canada itself. Only by rethinking identity and deconstructing established narratives of history can postcolonial culture move beyond what Kroetsch has referred to as the 'authorized text'[3] of colonialist representation and risk the 'nightmare and the welcome dream of Babel'[4] that displaces Canada from an historical 'origin' it never really knew.

Notes

1. Robert Kroetsch, 'Unhiding The Hidden' in *The Lovely Treachery of Words* (Toronto: Oxford University Press, 1989), p. 58.
2. Dominick LaCapra, *History and Criticism* (Ithaca: Cornell University Press, 1985), p. 46.
3. Robert Kroetsch, 'Disunity as Unity: A Canadian Strategy' in *The Lovely Treachery of Words* (Toronto: Oxford University Press, 1989), p. 32.
4. Robert Kroetsch, 'Beyond Nationalism: A Prologue' in *The Lovely Treachery of Words* (Toronto: Oxford University Press, 1989), p. 71.

8

Mapping and Masking:
The Migrant Experience in
Michael Ondaatje's *In the Skin of a Lion*

Susan Spearey

In the Skin of a Lion marks a shift in Michael Ondaatje's writing insofar as it approximates more closely than any of his previous publications to conventional conceptions of the novel. Earlier books such as *The Collected Works of Billy the Kid, Coming Through Slaughter*, and *Running in the Family* offer the reader an assortment of fragmented – and yet nonetheless clearly related – stories, verbal snapshots, reminiscences, personal testimonies and historical reconstructions. These textual fragments are presented by disparate voices in a variety of tones, registers and generic formats and are interspersed, variously, with newspaper clippings, photographs, maps and poems. By way of contrast *In the Skin of a Lion* takes the more traditional form of a series of interconnected plots and subplots articulated by an omnipresent – but significantly not omniscient – narrator. In this paper, I will endeavour to demonstrate that Ondaatje's adoption of this seemingly more coherent and less unconventional mode of presentation should not be taken to signal an abandonment of experimentation with form. On the contrary, through his revised techniques of (re)presenting source materials, and through his pronounced concern with spatial dimension as an arena for resistance and transformation, Ondaatje pushes back the frontiers of form that have been delimited by his earlier textual experiments.

A brief glance at the patterns of intertextuality within the novel will give some indication of the directions in which Ondaatje's formal experimentation could lead. *In the Skin of a Lion* draws on and reworks a number of sources and traditions that span a varied range of concerns and historical situations. These include the ancient Babylonian legend, *The Epic of Gilgamesh*, from which Ondaatje derives the title of the book; turn-of-the-century socialist polemical novels, such as Upton Sinclair's *The Jungle*; early Canadian 'landscape' fiction and poetry which focuses on the relationship between the settler and the wilds of the harsh and seemingly inhospitable adopted land; and Kipling's story, 'The Bridge Builders', from the 1914 collection *A Day's Work*, which is refashioned by Ondaatje in his chapter, 'The Bridge', and removed from its setting on the Ganges to Toronto's Don Valley. Through these allusions and revisions Ondaatje commemorates and extols the enactment of heroic deeds while questioning the conventions of epic narration, and its suitability for a contemporary context. He draws attention to the 'alternative' histories of the immigrant and labourer, while exposing the constraints of the political and social agendas advanced by polemical writers such as Sinclair. His exploration of the relationship between landscapes and their inhabitants departs from earlier writings in this tradition insofar as Ondaatje does not document the individual's taming of, or coming to terms with, a wilderness that is at once external and internal, alien and familiar. Rather, he traces the ongoing *transformations* of landscapes and individuals as he explores their influences upon one another. Similarly, the ideological underpinnings and points of focus of Kipling's story are radically dislocated as it is reinscribed in *In the Skin of a Lion*. Ondaatje's invocations of these earlier texts and his enlistment and reworking of existing traditions and generic conventions can be read on one level as a project of reclamation. More importantly, I would argue, these strategies can also be seen to illustrate a point that is suggested by the novel's second epigraph, 'Never again will a single story be told as though it were the only one': that a profusion of narrative renderings are inherent in any story.

Ondaatje has continued to base his fictions on characters and records retrieved from the archives, and on stories which these findings have brought to light. He has just as consistently and carefully incorporated a diverse range of media into his writing, in no way privileging one over another, but constantly drawing attention to both the strengths and weaknesses, the possibilities and limitations of each. In the case of *In the Skin of a Lion* a list of such media would include archival records, personal photographs and mementoes, dramatic scripts for both radio and theatre, lyrics of popular songs, films, atlases, newspaper clippings, letters, tall tales, blueprints and even dreams.[1] For the first time, however, the majority of the primary documents upon which he draws are not presented directly to the reader. Instead these same materials, which are no less abundant, are either referred to or described within the text by one of the characters or by the narrator. This narrative mediation between primary texts and the reader means that Ondaatje's sources are not merely held up as documentary evidence in and of themselves which the reader is invited to read 'straight' or alternatively, against the grain. Rather, the circumstances of their production are foregrounded, as is the manner in which their producers and receivers make use of the medium in question. By exploring the parameters within which each form of cultural production operates aesthetically and ideologically, Ondaatje offers the reader a model for reading (and perhaps also a set of criteria for evaluating) *In the Skin of a Lion.*

Because of the description of, or reference to, primary materials within the narrative – as opposed to their direct citation – *In the Skin of a Lion*, unlike Ondaatje's earlier texts, does not 'jolt' the reader into active engagement with the various voices encountered in the text. Instead he or she is lured into the role of searcher, a role which de-mands the ongoing pursuit and exploration of the boundaries which delimit the novel's textual and even geographic worlds, all of which exist in a state of perpetual flux. Ondaatje does acknowledge his own shaping of a guiding or organisational principle in the novel through the narrator's assertion that 'The first sentence of every novel should be: "Trust me, this will take time, but there is order here, very faint, very human".'[2] This statement, however, is qualified by the lines from Conrad's letters that Alice whispers to Patrick: 'I have taught you that the sky in all its zones is mortal . . . Let me now re-emphasize the extreme looseness of the structure of all objects' (p. 135). Although the author inevitably pulls together disparate texts and in this novel often takes the further step of providing descriptions of certain cultural artefacts, room for negotiation is deliberately left within the novel's structure.

Migration and Metamorphosis

The tropes of migration and metamorphosis insistently recur in the novel as Ondaatje explores textual, ideological, geopolitical and spatial boundaries, and as he investigates the multifarious and shifting subject positions occupied by the migrant. Indeed, movement and transfor-mation feature prominently not only as thematic concerns but also as structural devices. The girl who 'gathers' the story and the man who 'picks up and brings together [its] various corners' are literally in transit from Toronto to Marmora, while we as readers move with them, forward through the narrative and through the night, backward for retrieval of hidden histories, and laterally across space in an attempt to grasp the simultaneity of events and lives that are here 'touch[ed] . . . into words' (p. 1).[3] The story that the driver and passenger piece together somehow transforms into the account of an omnipresent ob-server, and it is in this form that the narrative reaches us, awaiting the further transformations engendered by our readings. Likewise, accounts of migration abound throughout the novel and include Nicholas Temelcoff's harrowing passage from Macedonia to Canadian shores; Patrick's voyage from hinterland to metropolis followed by his repeated journeys between various peripheries and correspond-ing centres; Ambrose Small's mysterious disappearance underground and subsequent calculated movements about the province; the equally strategic manoeuvres of Cato in his efforts to fortify union organisa-tion while avoiding the reprisals threatened by company authorities; and Caravaggio's numerous and clandestine odysseys (p. 157). No less abundant are images of metamorphosis – of 'break[ing] through . . . chrysalis into language', of shedding (or donning) skins, of the emergence of entirely new identities or states of being, of the transformation of landscapes both urban and rural.

What is significant over and above the implications of these images and tropes for a poetics which is deeply engaged in movement and transformation is Ondaatje's pronounced concern with spatial dimen-sion, to which I have already alluded. This focus points to the more radical formal revisions suggested in a text which could otherwise be viewed as merely another endeavour to rewrite history, to stake claims for those disenfranchised by dominant or existing narratives. The man-ner in which the ambiguities of subject position and the interplay of spatial and historical consciousness inform the treatment of migra-tion and metamorphosis needs to be explored. Again, Ondaatje's own multiple subject positions – as post-colonial, as a male from a pri-vileged Ceylonese Burgher background, as a migrant, as a Canadian citizen and as a Toronto writer working within the academy – place him in an interesting situation from which to address such issues and examine the implications of wearing a succession of skins. In a review of some of his early poetry J. E. Chamberlin observes:

> Ondaatje is in a curious position as a poet, but a position that is close to that of other contemporary poets writing out of sit-uations that define essentially colonial predicaments, where language or audience or the identity and role of the poet are indeterminate . . . Canada offers Ondaatje a geography, but no inheritance; Sri Lanka offers him a family history, but no tradition, no way of passing things on; the English language offers him both an inheritance and a history, but no time and place.[4]

In the Skin of a Lion seems to me to provide Ondaatje's re-sponse to Chamberlin's remarks. By alluding to and reappropriating received stories, traditions and generic conventions, Ondaatje stakes his claim to a cross-cultural inheritance and pieces together an alter-native literary tradition that answers to his most pressing concerns as a migrant writer. Similarly he shapes connections with old worlds and new, situating himself in relation to their various geographies and histories. The text also explores the transformative powers of language and, in so doing, offers numerous strategies for passing things on.

Over the course of his career then, Ondaatje has consistently foregrounded his concern with movement and transformation, especially as these pertain to artistic production and reception. But as I have observed, in *In the Skin of a Lion*, these actions or impulses or occurrences are not merely traced out within historical trajectories. Here Ondaatje's deployment of the tropes of migration and metamorphosis points to a deliberate spatialisation – as opposed to, or more accurately, in addition to, an historicisation – of the investigation of social structures and relations of power. While history and the manner in which events are related in temporal terms provides a focus for many of the questions raised by the novel, we are not presented with an account of its linear or cumulative progression. Nor does Ondaatje's engagement with the plight of the worker necessarily involve the advocacy of a teleological Marxist vision which projects the inevitable downfall of that 'bare-knuckle capitalism' (p. 57) exemplified by Ambrose Small. Many instances of the appalling exploitation of immigrant labourers are exposed in the novel's pages. However, unlike the works of Upton Sinclair and his fellow early twentieth-century 'muckrakers' which share similar themes and concerns, *In the Skin of a Lion* espouses no explicit political or ideological agenda which would harness it to a framework privileging linear historical time. Nor does Ondaatje posit historical continuity as a given condition. Rather, the text stays true to Patrick's demand that ideology be made human, less rigid. *In the Skin of a Lion* invites its readers, writer and characters, each in different ways playing the role of searcher, to trace out and negotiate – and often to explode – the boundaries of the structures within which they work and exist. In its exposure of the pretence to objectivity implicit in official histories and of the bias and artifice that go into their construction, the novel does not merely offer up an alternative, and by implication, more viable version. Instead it questions the ascendancy of historical time consciousness itself.

Crucial to such a questioning is an examination of the assumptions commonly held about time and space and their mutual relations. Edward Soja begins his study of postmodern geographies with a quotation from Michel Foucault which is highly instructive as it exposes the beliefs which typically underpin theoretical views of time and space:

> Did it start with Bergson or before? Space was treated as the dead, the fixed, the undialectical, the immobile. Time, on the contrary, was richness, fecundity, life, dialectic.[5]

In a later statement also quoted by Soja, Foucault elaborates on this observation, gesturing towards the possibilities which arise when such assumptions are called into question:

The great obsession of the nineteenth century was, as we know, history: with its themes of development and of suspension, of crisis and cycle, themes of the ever-accumulating past, with its great preponderance of dead men and the menacing glaciation of the world . . . The present epoch will perhaps be above all the epoch of space. We are in the epoch of simultaneity: we are in the epoch of juxtaposition, the epoch of the near and far, of the side-by-side, of the dispersed. We are at a moment, I believe, when our experience of the world is less that of a long life developing through time than of a network that connects points and intersects with its own skein. One could perhaps say that certain ideological conflicts animating present-day polemics oppose the pious descendants of time and the determined inhabitants of space.[6]

By positing space as more than a mere backdrop upon which historical progression is enacted, Foucault offers the possibility of conceiving time and space in a dialectical relationship, as forces which temper without determining or dominating one another. Such a conceptual revision has far-reaching implications not the least of which is the reformulation in aesthetic terms of the possibilities offered by the novel, and in ontological terms a reassessment of the significance of shifting subject positions. *In the Skin of a Lion* plays out an exploration of the dynamics of space in relation to time, examining the implications of such play for poetics and politics alike.

Perhaps the first clue to the rejection of a purely historically-based reinscription of Toronto's past within the novel can be found in the previously mentioned epigraph taken from John Berger: 'Never again will a single story be told as though it were the only one'. This statement undermines the notion of a linear and totalising account of events by pointing to their simultaneity and the reductive nature of confining narrative to a story*line*. In *The Look of Things* Berger expands on this point, revealing in the process the boundaries or limitations of historical accounts which privilege time over space:

We hear a lot about the crisis of the modern novel. What this involves, fundamentally, is a change in the mode of narration. It is scarcely any longer possible to tell a straight story sequentially unfolding in time. And this is because we are too aware of what is continually traversing the storyline laterally. That is to say, instead of being aware of a point as an infinitely small part of a straight line, we are aware of it

as an infinitely small part of an infinite number of lines, as
the centre of a star of lines. Such awareness is the result of
our constantly having to take into account the simultaneity
and extension of events and possibilities.[7]

Although *In the Skin of a Lion* constantly delves into the past, it does
so without positing a definitive sequence of events awaiting discovery
and in fact obstructs such discovery in several ways.

First, its juxtaposition of varied and diverse stories continually
unseats the reader's expectations, so that he or she is never sure what
direction the narrative will take next. The 'Little Seeds' of the first
chapter are not the symbols of growth and development that the opening scenes might lead the reader to expect – seeds from which mighty
oaks inevitably grow – rather they are seeds of dynamite from which
'abrupt lessons' are learned and by way of which the unexpected unfolds. Second, different schemas of temporality are evidenced in the
text. For example the narration is circular, bringing the reader back to
the motor journey with which the novel opens, and certain moments
of epiphany such as the nun's fall from the bridge, or Patrick's intervention in Alice's performance, or Alice's death, provide evidence of
synchronic time, in which great significance is concentrated into a
passing instant. Third, gaps and room for omissions are insistently
left in the stories recounted. This tactic is evidenced, for example, by
the obscurity in which Alice's past is shrouded, by the absence of ex-
planation as to how her friendship with Nicholas Temelcoff comes
to develop after their initial and anonymous encounter on the bridge
and by the lack of an exact explication of the circumstances surrounding Patrick's release by Commissioner Harris. Such omissions gesture
towards a proliferation of narratives and narrators surrounding each
character and event. This is reinforced by the fourth method through
which linear narrative is undermined as a result of characters being
presented in spatially contingent positions without any indication of
their awareness of each other, or of the ways in which they will come to
influence one another. Caravaggio tars the road leading to the bridge,
Temelcoff works in its piers below, Harris stands by assessing its development and Alice wanders past its barriers. Although it could be
argued that the presence of each in this scene is determined by timing,
the spatial contingency of the characters will in turn affect the course of
their unfolding histories. Michael Greenstein also notes of the narrative
structure of the novel that '[i]nterception and interruption character-
ize two ways of proceeding through Ondaatje's text: narrative pushes
the reader forward while lyrical imagery turns around on itself'.[8] The
latter move, he goes on to suggest, involves a typically postmodernist
self-reflexivity, constantly drawing attention to the boundaries within
which writer, reader and character alike are operating.

These strategies which render narration discontinuous or disjointed on the one hand, and self-reflexive on the other, are reinforced by the manner in which the characters are presented. None is portrayed as being essentially linked to, or determined by his or her respective origins, which by and large remain obscure. Rather, within the narrative each has a point of beginning which underscores the relation of that character to the stories mapped out in the text. These textual beginnings are shown to be arbitrary or constructed and in no way deterministic. Moreover, each is succeeded by a series of instances of beginning again as the framework within which the character in question operates is altered or adjusted, either by his or her own actions or through the workings of external forces. Patrick's story, for example, opens with his boyhood in Depot Creek and recommences with his move to the city. His relationship with Alice provides another starting point and he begins yet again upon his release from prison as he takes up Alice's cause. In the novel's final pages his reunion with Clara signals a further point of departure.

The recurrence of beginnings also highlights the absence of those many openings left out by the narrative. The skins that each character wears can be seen as manifestations of various personalities and subject positions rather than as disguises which conceal an essential and predetermined character. Alice in particular is described as 'remain[ing] sourceless, like those statues of men with wrapped heads who symbolize undiscovered rivers' (p. 74), and Patrick is mesmerised as much by the lacunae of her past as by the apparent disjunctions of her present existence, which undercut notions of linear progression and integrity of character (p. 74). He wonders,

> How can she who had torn his heart out at the waterworks with her art lie now like a human in his arms? Or stand catatonic in front of bananas on Eastern Avenue deciding which bunch to buy . . . [H]e can never conceive how she leaps from her true self to her other true self. It is a flight he knows nothing about . . . In the midst of his love for Alice, in the midst of lovemaking even, he watches her face waiting for her to be translated into this war bride or that queen or shopgirl, half expecting metamorphosis as they kiss. Annunciation. The eye would go first, and as he draws back he will be in another country, another century, his arms around a stranger. (pp. 152–3)

Even Clara, who is much less elusive about her personal history, nonetheless reveals herself like all good actresses through the manifestation of a series of masks and voices. Patrick uncovers neither a sequential history nor a cohesive set of traits, but 'keeps finding and losing parts of her' (p. 79), and is himself – and here Ondaatje employs a striking spatial image – caught 'within the complex architecture of her past' (p. 66). The glimpses of Patrick's own boyhood that the reader is afforded are also selective and reveal nothing of his origins, for example, the circumstances of his family's arrival in Depot Creek or the whereabouts of his mother.

In his realisation that human beings can no more be reduced to essences than stories can be reduced to linear and fixed narratives, Patrick is able to realign the structures which have thus far shaped his world:

> His own life was no longer a single story but part of a mural, which was a falling together of accomplices. Patrick saw a wondrous night web – all of these fragments of a human order, something ungoverned by the family he was born into or the headlines of the day. A nun on a bridge, a daredevil who was unable to sleep without a drink, a boy watching a fire from his bed at night, an actress who ran away with a millionaire – the detritus and chaos of the age was realigned. (p. 145)

Here, Ondaatje succinctly articulates a poetics of migrancy. Patrick recognises the various roles that he plays in each story and is therefore able purposefully to negotiate the parameters of the structures in which he exists.

Questions of Agency

Ondaatje, then, uses spatialised images which demand intricate mapping and continual realignment rather than definitive linear plotting. He thereby provides a model for a more open reading of texts and history. However questions of agency need to be addressed. How is such realignment orchestrated and by whom? Clearly migration can be seen as either imposed, an act of flight, or voluntary and strategic, an act of will. Similarly, metamorphoses and the wearing of different skins can be enforced – the tannery workers, for example, have of necessity to sport the coloured skins of the dyes with which they are working – or tactical, as in the cases of Alice and Caravaggio who deliberately don disguises or assume alternative names and personas. Two important and related considerations influence Ondaatje's treatment of agency within the novel's many contested territories. The first is the relationship between process and progress and the second is the links between the knowledge of space and power.

Process, whether artistic or otherwise, is not necessarily tied up with progress or development, both of which imply continuity and improvement. It is concerned, rather, with exploration and the ongoing negotiation of all the possibilities presented by any statement or action or ideal. Notions of progress can be closely linked to the assertion and regulation of authority from a given centre of power which constitutes a frequently-evidenced form of agency in the novel. For instance the technologies which enable the mass production and distribution of leather goods and beef, timber and water, are endorsed by the economically-empowered elite of Ontario through whom the introduction of tanneries, slaughterhouses, lumber camps and sanitation systems is effected. It is interesting to note that Victorian notions of progressivism posit a unilateral process of 'advance'. This fails to take account of the detrimental effects of 'progress' on certain communities or the legitimacy of their efforts to voice opposition. Quite evidently the artistic, historical and ideological processes evidenced within *In the Skin of a Lion* involve ongoing engagement with various communities, without any determined end for such interchange being proposed. This is not to say that the agency of the proponents of 'progress' is any less pronounced; Ondaatje does not deny its influence but offers possibilities for its contestation. In other words agency does not result solely from efforts to build or to bridge, but can just as easily derive from the more open-ended enterprises of searching or dismantling. This observation may help to shed light on Ondaatje's by now familiar fascination with the trope of explosion.

In Ondaatje's text the knowledge of space is implicitly equated with the exercise of power within its bounds. Once again the examination of space – whether textual, geopolitical or otherwise – as contested territory highlights the various ways in which agency can be manifested. Patrick's blindfolded memorisation of his hotel room is a way of controlling the space that he and Clara share and of asserting himself against 'the power of his unseen enemy', Ambrose Small. At first his mastery seems inviolable:

> He positions Clara on the bed and tells her not to move. Then he takes off into the room – at first using his hands for security then ignoring them, just throwing his body within an inch of the window swooping his head down parallel to shelves while he rushes across the room in straight lines, in curves, as if he has the mechanism of a bat in his human blood. He leaps across the bed delighted at her shriek. He is magnificent. He is perfect, she thinks. (p. 80)

However, once his mastery becomes oppressive, an overt bid to detain and possess her, Clara lowers herself to the floor and stops her ears. Her unexpected movement thwarts Patrick's designs and leaves them both stunned and physically hurt. In not allowing for any movement save his own, Patrick learns an 'abrupt lesson' about the control of space.

Caravaggio is much more tentative in his similar spatial 'pelmanism'. Although he has 'trained as a thief in unlit rooms', rearranging

furniture, putting everything back in its place, mentally measuring the
size of objects in relation to windows, doors and other escape routes, he
has 'a sense of the world which [is] limited to what existed for twenty
feet around him' (p. 189). Caravaggio not only takes detailed note of
the physical features that surround him at any given moment, he is
also constantly aware of the possible encroachment of others into the
spaces he occupies, and of the consequent improvisation which could
be required of him. When out in the open this awareness is even more
marked. As he escapes from prison,

> Landscape for Caravaggio was never calm. A tree bend-
> ing with difficulty, a flower thrashed by the wind, a
> cloud turning black, a cone falling – everything moved
> anguished at separate speeds. When he ran he saw it all.
> The eye splintering into fifteen sentries, watching every
> approach. (p. 183)

In his intimate knowledge of space Caravaggio recognises the play of
various forces, is nervously attuned to their potential proliferation, and
to the array of possible effects on him. Only by acknowledging and/or
confronting these forces can he exercise power within – and not over –
a given space.

Elizabeth, the woman Patrick encounters in the Garden of the Blind,
is less defensive than Caravaggio about intrusion into the space she
knows so intimately, but the 'precise antennae' (p. 168) of her senses
of hearing and smell alert her to the presence of sighted visitors in the
garden. She welcomes Patrick and shares with him her understanding
of sounds and scents which provide her with a map of, and alert her to
changes within, the garden. Through these passages Ondaatje not only
offers the reader alternative ways of knowing and understanding the
spatial dimension but also draws attention to the negotiation of spatial
boundaries, which is most successfully carried out when allowance is
made for the presence of multiple agents of change.

Greenstein argues that the annihilation of such boundaries is con-
sonant with the novel's 'levelling of hierarchies in class and culture',
pointing out that

> Painting the tin roof of the Kingston Penitentiary blue . . .
> Patrick and Caravaggio become uncertain of clear bounda-
> ries so that the painted painter becomes indistinguishable
> from the sky. Through this metamorphosis the prisoner gains
> his freedom and comments, "Demarcation . . . That is all we
> need to remember". (p. 179)

And the reader remembers these instructions when Caravaggio later
makes Patrick invisible in preparation for dynamiting the tunnel. "De-
marcation" (p. 228), Caravaggio repeats, and we get the sense that
it means the opposite – an effacement of all distinctions in air or

water, fire or earth, four elements for a dynamics of making and destroying.[9]

I would add to this argument the observation that knowledge or recognition of boundaries and the forces that operate within them is an essential precondition of their effacement or to pushing back their limits. Intangible boundaries can be precarious. Ondaatje's vision of order is one of constant reformulation, one that depends on the diversity of individuals and communities in any given space, and that involves the dialectical play of powers within and between the boundaries dividing these groups.

In the process of such dialectical play, as in migration and metamorphosis, the disorientation caused by shifting parameters enables reorientation, reformulation. Existence in liminal areas where contexts or frameworks of order become unclear allows for their revision as Temelcoff learns English and his translation dreams strangely alter the aspect and character of objects as familiar as trees, animals and human beings, alerting him to the transformative power of his new vocabulary, a power which allied to his gift of storytelling he will later use to reshape the past.

In a second instance, Alice loses her sense of direction and falls from the bridge, an accident which leads to the reshaping of her existing world. Suddenly she finds herself unveiled, speechless, in a state of slight shock, sitting for the first time alone with a drinking man. However, as she explores the Ohrida Lake Restaurant, seeing in it the recreation of a Balkan courtyard, she arrives at an understanding of the multiple significations of its surfaces and borders:

> Leaning forward, she laid her face on the cold zinc, the chill there even past midnight. . . . The zinc was the edge of another country. Its memory of a day's glasses. The spill and the wiping cloth. She put her ear against the grey ocean of it. Confessional. Tabula Rasa. (p. 39)

She then steps out into the night taking on the parrot's name and a new identity, later to emerge as the political activist whose mission is the reshaping of social structures.

A third example of such moments of transformation is Patrick's intervention in Alice's performance and life as he mistakes her staged cry of desperation for those of the actual immigrants by whom he is surrounded. Here Patrick confuses active performance and passive victimisation as well as the 'dangerous new country of the stage' (p. 116) with that in which the lives of the immigrants are played out. Backstage where all that 'had been theatrical seemed locked within metamorphosis', Patrick observes that he is himself moving like a puppet and is unable to discern whether those he encounters are composed of flesh or wood. This disorientation reveals to him the nebulous nature of the border between art and life, as well as the urgency and possibility of acting, politically.

Jonathan Raban examines the transformative potential to be found in such moments of disorientation in a context which is pertinent to *In the Skin of a Lion*, that of urban existence. *Soft City* commences with the proposition that the feeling of being 'jetshocked' or alienated within familiar surroundings, or of feeling a stranger to oneself, provides the ideal opportunity to reshape the urban environment in which one exists:

> For at moments like this, the city goes soft; it awaits the imprint of an identity. For better or for worse it invites you to remake it, to consolidate it into a shape you can live in. You, too. Decide who you are, and the city will again assume a fixed form around you. Decide what it is, and your own identity will be revealed, like a position on a map fixed by triangulation. Cities, unlike villages and small towns, are plastic by nature. We mould them in our images: they, in their turn, shape us by the resistance they offer when we try to impose our own personal form on them.[10]

Similarly, the constant reshaping and reformulation of Toronto is perhaps the most striking manner in which Ondaatje spatialises his account of the building of the city and demonstrates the significance of migration and metamorphosis.

As Patrick arrives at Union Station for the first time, he regards the city 'as though it were land after years at sea' (p. 53), an established, secure and firm foundation upon which to build his life. This initial certainty, almost immediately undermined as he finds himself an alien to the many immigrants among whom he lives and works, is sharply contrasted with the view of a fellow immigrant reluctant to leave the 'safe zone' of the station fearing that 'one step away was the quicksand of the new world' (p. 54). Toronto offers neither a solid base nor a deliquescing formlessness, rather it is continuously mapped out and pieced together by its inhabitants as they move in and around its limits, and at the same time it shapes them. As Patrick and Alice look out towards Lake Ontario the narrator observes, '[t]he vista was Upper America, a New World. Landscape changed nothing but it brought rest, altered character as gradually as water on a stone' (p. 126). Toronto both realigns itself to and resists the forms that are imposed upon it. It is no accident that the city assumes almost human proportions; it too is a character that wears many skins, acts and is acted upon.

Commissioner Harris acknowledges the human qualities that Toronto must necessarily possess, but understands character in a way utterly at odds with that posited elsewhere in the novel. He is perhaps the most emphatic proponent of 'progress' in *In the Skin of a Lion*

and in his view, change entails growth and continuity rather than
migration and metamorphosis. Harris sees the need to create and protect organs which control and regulate circulation, such as the Bloor
Street Viaduct with its trestles conveying motor vehicles, water, railway traffic and pedestrians between the East and the centre, and the
waterworks which circulates water from Lake Ontario to the farthest
reaches of the metropolis and is in many ways its lifeline. The Viaduct
is his first project to reach fruition and he watches over it obsessively,
likening his relationship with it to that of a parent, albeit an over-
protective one. When he witnesses the fall of the nun he reflects that
'[t]his was his first child and it had already become a murderer' (p. 31).
In spite of his recognition of the city and its 'organs' as vital, Harris
remains true to his role of over-protective 'parent' in his refusal to admit to any development which departs from his own plans. He quotes
Baudelaire to his critics – '[t]he form of a city changes faster than
the heart of a mortal' (p. 109), but desires only those changes which
evolve 'naturally' from the conditions of continuity he has imposed
and regulated.

Through his ambitious dreams to control space and his perseverance
in forcing his plans through various stages of administrative sanction,
Harris attempts to physically impose his vision of Toronto upon the
city. The fixed grid which for him delineates the existing city is both
mapped and understood as a rigid structure through which space is
enclosed and hierarchised. Harris's attempts to elaborate on this structure are based upon two assumptions. First, that the relationship of
continuity and organic growth referred to above links his blueprints
for a future Toronto to a mental map of the existing city and, second,
that this mental map reflects an uncontested and *a priori* reality. But
as Graham Huggan notes, 'the reality represented mimetically by the
map not only conforms to a particular version of the world but to a
version which is specifically designed to empower its makers'.[11] The
city as Harris envisions it presupposes the ascendancy of the Establishment and takes for granted an exploitable labour market and the
various apparatuses for recording its history, stabilising its structures
and ensuring its continuity.

Harris has no knowledge of the 'clandestine lives' of the bridge or
waterworks – of the procession of labourers commemorating the dead,
whose ceremony pre-empts his own official christening of the viaduct,
or of the political meetings and performances of the immigrant popu-
lation in the unfinished waterworks. He therefore has no idea of the
transformative power of such gestures and the ways the city resists
the form he imposes on it. Patrick reveals to him the instability of his
own position, his marginality within the Establishment, and in so doing suggests the need to reassess subject position constantly and call

into question the fixed order upon which such assertive formulation is based.

In contrast to Harris, Hana views the city as both vital and protean, and pieces it together accordingly. Patrick looks on with wonder as she maps out the Toronto that is her own: '[he] wanted the city Hana had constructed for herself – the places she brought together and held as if on the delicate thread of her curiosity' (p. 138). The flexibility implicit in her gesture is reflected in the manner the immigrants shape and are shaped by their new environs. Locations such as the Ohrida Lake Restaurant and the Balkan Cafe recreate the landscapes and sites of Europe, but are linked together with other locations which answer to the needs and celebrate the rituals of the New World – places such as the steam baths where the labourers retreat after a week's toils, theatres in which English is learned, cinemas, market places and illicit venues for meetings following Police Chief Draper's prohibition of public gatherings conducted in any language other than English.

Ondaatje's presentation of the city and its history as being in constant metamorphosis reveals the value and potential of migration and movement and, at the same time, eliminates the determinism inherent in more linear conceptions of geographies and subject positions. By echoing this flexibility and dialectical play in the novel's characterisation and narrative structure, Ondaatje convincingly meets the criteria he sets for his art: the detritus and chaos of the age is indeed realigned. And in rendering novelistic space a conglomeration of multiple and by no means mutually-exclusive contested territories, *In the Skin of a Lion* affords post-colonial writing an aesthetics with possibilities greatly exceeding the recuperation of 'lost ground'.

Notes

1. For an extended discussion of Ondaatje's use of photographic, cinematographic and theatrical texts in *In the Skin of a Lion*, see my chapter, 'Michael Ondaatje: Prodigality and Genealogy' in *Translating Worlds: A Study of Post-colonial Migrant Writing*, with particular reference to V.S. Naipaul, Bharati Mukherjee, Michael Ondaatje and Salman Rushdie, PhD thesis, University of Leeds, 1993.
2. Michael Ondaatje, *In the Skin of a Lion* (London: Picador, 1988; first published 1987), p. 146. All subsequent page references are to this edition and included in the body of the text.
3. Here I borrow a phrase coined by Ondaatje in *Running in the Family* (London: Picador, 1984; first published 1982), p. 22.
4. J.E. Chamberlin, 'Let there be commerce between us: the poetry of Michael Ondaatje' in *Spider Blues*, ed. Sam Solecki (Montreal: Véhicule Press, 1985), p. 41.

5. Michel Foucault, 'Questions of Geography' in *Power/Knowledge: Selected Interviews and other writings 1972–1977*, ed. and trans. Colin Gordon (Brighton: Harvester, 1980), pp. 63–77, cited in Edward Soja, *Postmodern Geographies: The Reassertion of Space in Critical Social Theory* (London and New York: Verso, 1989), p. 10.

6. Michel Foucault, 'Of Other Spaces', trans. Jay Miskowiec in *diacritics*, Vol 16 (1986), p. 22, cited in Soja, p. 10.

7. John Berger, *The Look of Things* (New York: Viking Press, 1974), p. 40, cited in Soja, p. 22.

8. Michael Greenstein, 'Ondaatje's Metamorphoses: "In the Skin of a Lion"' in *Canadian Literature*, 126 (Autumn 1990), p. 123.

9. Greenstein, p. 119.

10. Jonathan Raban, *Soft City* (London: Hamish Hamilton, 1974), pp. 1-2.

11. Graham Huggan, 'Decolonizing the Map; Post-Colonialism, Post-Structuralism and the Cartographic Connection' in *Past the Last Post: Theorizing the Post-Colonial and the Postmodern*, eds. Ian Adam and Helen Tiffin (London: Harvester, 1991), p. 127.

9

Lost Body: Reading
Marlene Nourbese Philip's
Looking for Livingstone

David Richards

I

Homi Bhabha, in a typically post-structuralist turn, reverses the Enlightenment dialectic of self and other by insisting that 'the question of identity can never be seen "beyond representation"',[1] in that it is representation which constructs identity, not the other way round. Bhabha defines the historical construction of identity, nonetheless, in a familiar Kantian fashion as 'two . . . traditions in the discourse of identity': ' . . . the philosophical tradition of identity as the process of self-reflection in the mirror of (human) nature: and the anthropological view of the difference of human identity as located in the division of Nature/Culture'.[2]

Bhabha envisions the subject emerging from a conjunction of two correlative intellectual convictions: the post-Enlightenment, critical philosophy of epistemologies of the individual, where the self achieves consciousness and definition by its *location* as the focus of an assemblage of antinomies of analytic and synthetic propositions, and an 'anthropological' discourse, the goal of which is to *locate* identity in the structural matrix of social roles. The degree to which this has truly been anthropology's historical endeavour, in particular, is perhaps a question for another time and place,[3] but there is, at least, a sense of recognition of Bhabha's broadly-based and loosely-defined evocation of the history of the construction of identity found in the double locations of the self as both *persona* and *individual* (in Marcel Mauss's terminology).[4] But that joining of the traditions of the public and the private, the 'anthropological' and the 'philosophical', which Bhabha offers as the uniquely powerful artifice of the Western episteme is, of course, precisely what is deconstructed in Bhabha's post-structuralist, deconstructive turn. Remove that embrace of the persona and the individual, and the subject becomes 'depersonalised, dislocated' . . . 'an incalculable object, quite literally, difficult to place. The demands of authority cannot unify its message nor simply identify its subjects'.[5] Panopticon 'authority', is met by the gaze of 'the evil eye, that seeks to outstare linear history and turn its progressive dream into nightmarish chaos':[6] the gaze of those denied a presence – 'philosophical' or 'anthropological' – except in the misrepresentations of their 'philosophical' and 'anthropological' identities.

Bhabha's deconstruction of the discourses of identity replaces these notions of a plenitudinous subject with an 'incalculable', an 'unrepresentable' subject which 'returns as a persistent questioning of the frame, the space of representation, where the image – missing person, invisible eye, oriental stereotype – is confronted with its difference, its Other'.[7] Whereas the artifice works to produce a rapprochement between the philosophical sense of selfhood and the anthropological notion of the person to make an ethnographic representation which confirms and perpetuates the Western episteme by extending its power to represent *even these others*, Bhabha sees identification, subjectivity and representation as the markers of imperialism's designation of its subject peoples. For Bhabha, others make their otherness felt, not by an adherence to the rapprochement of individual and persona, but by the alternate strategy by which those rules of representation must be utterly denied, systematically subverted, cancelled or erased from representation: the fabricated nature of identity must be marked by the hide and seek of erasure. Only by denying representation – both 'philosophical' and 'anthropological' – can the postcolonial be truly represented. This postcolonial self is a field of negative definitions cancelling the doubleness of 'identity' by inhabiting the double negative of 'not being not there'. In this location – this 'dislocation' – the postcolonial subject becomes opaque, 'incalculable', emptied of 'content', but recognised because 'empty'. The postcolonial subject emerges as a shadow figure, 'tethered' to the more substantial presence of an erroneous Western subjectivity.[8]

The ascetic stricture which this 'empty' postcolonial subject connotes contrasts with the libidinal discharge which flows from the 'full' subject of the conjoined anthropological and philosophical notions of selfhood, yet this is a false dichotomy which replicates the very essentialism and manichean antinomies which Bhabha would seem to wish to subvert. Philosophy/anthropology's 'full' and Bhabha's 'empty' subjects are both, in their different ways, improvisations on the same themes of the manichean economy of the self: alternating states of limitation and excess, celibacy and promiscuity, by which the individual or social organism regulates its health. Bhabha's reconstruction of Fanon's psychology of colonialism depicts the postcolonial self as a product of the historical intervention of imperialism as a denial of the enabling features of humanity: language, law, civil society, culture. The urge for conquest represents a desire for the subjugation of otherness to bring it within the surveillance of the imperial self. The coloniser substitutes an image of dominance and imperial power for the colonised sense of other; the colonised self looks at the world and sees a reflection of imperial power which has replaced an enabling sense of otherness. The colonial condition prevents, therefore, the formation of workable forms of social and cultural life by creating psychological dependence on substituted colonial domination. In all of this, Bhabha appears to insist upon a recognition of the historical fact of colonisation as the determining feature of postcolonial, but this preliminary insistence upon history rapidly gives way to an admitted sense of 'historylessness' in the postcolonial world of the 'incalculable subject'.[9] It is not so much that history is another strategy of hegemonic representation, nor that the historical achievement of independence from empire removes the colonialists' distorting mirror to return the subjected peoples to their rightful sense of identity, but that the colonial rupture has made, in Fanon's phrase, 'a constellation of delirium' which enacts and re-enacts a tragic cycle from which no recuperation is possible and which renders the colonial subject silent, invisible and unformed, since language, law, civil society, culture consist of the replicated divisions of colonial identity. If, Bhabha writes,

> the [colonial] subject of desire is never simply a Myself, then the Other is never simply an *It-self*, a font of identity, truth or mis-recognition . . . [M]an as his alienated image, not Self and Other but the 'Otherness' of the Self inscribed in the perverse palimpsest of colonial identity.[10]

Bhabha inserts the misrepresented, forgotten or omitted historical presence which reminds us that we read not primitive *Genesis* but postcolonial 'apocalypse', not the sovereign individual but the subject person. Paradoxically, this is done by denying the possibility of representation and of history. What seems to begin, therefore, as the insistence upon the historical situation of the native subject reinscribed as a postcolonial subject, finds its terminus in the erasure of that history except as a denial of its enunciation. To deconstruct the problem as one of a textual conflict between unrepresentable 'real' and untenable 'written' identities and to counter the nightmare of history with an evasion or denial of history is not to attempt to deal with the *effects* of that history. What is gained in the creation of, what Bhabha evocatively calls, 'the secret art of invisibleness'[11] is an awareness of those who lie outside representation. What is lost is the perception of the anthropological 'persona': an identity of social roles, obligations, connections, contexts and histories.

In many respects, Bhabha's writings would seem the absolute antipathy of anthropology, in particular. Whereas anthropology's exotic subjects are made in order to flood the eye with their outlandish colours, Bhabha's postcolonials are invisible to representation. For anthropology even to begin its work, it must predicate the existence of a subject rooted in a matrix of social and cultural formations and, in addition, those culturally-specific formations must share some common elements with formations from other cultures for anthropological representations to assume a common ground of signification and meaning. In his deconstruction of the tropes of identity, Bhabha displaces the anthropological subject with the image of a dislocated postcolonial subject who is invisible to and 'contentless' to anthropology. Such a subject is compelled to represent him/herself paradoxically as an 'absent presence' in representation, an ellipsis. Bhabha denies anthropology's masses, the 'field full of folk' which is so integral to anthropology's panopticon ambition. Anthropology is blind to Bhabha's postcolonial subject, preferring to reinscribe his/her presence as native, primitive, authentic. Bhabha counters anthropology's insistence upon a rooted plenitudinous subject of analysis with a dislocated 'invisible' or representationally 'empty' identity.

The key term is dislocation. Anthropology's textualisations insist, above all, on the evocation of a locale. The others are indistinguishable from the place, *their* place: they grow out of and exist only in a place which is not *here*. They are overwhelmingly *there*, and their 'reality' is enforced by their massed presence as an undeniable, incontrovertible fact. The postcolonial subject's radical challenge to cultural representation begins fundamentally in the denial of a sense of place. The panopticon vision withers if there is not a landscape to survey, if there is no 'there' to be in, no 'there' to see. A sense of place is the first denial in the writings of dislocated postcolonial writers.

Homi Bhabha's theoretical formulation of the postcolonial subject is radically antithetical to the spirit of anthropological representations. But it is more than just anthropology which stands to lose from these acts of denial.

> Without anthropology neither modern poetry nor modern art would be what it is today, for anthropology has given modern artists the mood of distance and estrangement from their own familiar traditions, and, by enriching and relativizing the storehouse of knowledge, symbols, and odd and diverse facts out of which poets or artists fashion

their work, has enabled their exploitation of the archaic, the exotic, the primitive, the primordial, the universality of myth and symbols, and the relativity of language and thought.[12]

The denial of a sense of place to the dislocated unwinds the sense of an identity – 'philosophical' or 'anthropological' – which is constructed upon the foundations of cultural misrepresentations and concludes ultimately with a questioning of the 'art forms' within which all of this is articulated . The postcolonial, in Bhabha's formation, expresses identity by repudiating identity, represents by renouncing representation, makes art by disclaiming art: which returns us to the art of the postcolonial – what may this 'secret art of invisibleness' look like?

As a way of broaching that question – of framing that question (*pace* Bhabha) – before this essay moves on to its main subject, consider this object. Kane Kwei is a Ghanaian carpenter who specialises in coffins which in their shapes and colours reflect the occupations or lifestyles of his clients. A gardener will be laid to rest in a giant onion or cocoa-pod, a traveller in a jumbo jet with detachable wings, a wealthy businessman in this Mercedes Benz-shaped Coffin. These objects, wonderfully extravagant, are nonetheless intended to fulfill a functional purpose as receptacles for the dead.

Kane Kwei, 'Mercedes Benz-shaped Coffin'

Or at least, that last statement is true in Ghana. In Europe and North America, since the Mercedes Benz-shaped Coffin's display at the 'Magiciens de la Terre' exhibition in Paris in 1989, Kane Kwei has become an artist whose work (often half-size) is much sought by private collectors and museums. His work has been described as surrealist, an iconoclastic marriage of consumer durables and cults of the dead, a blurring of the real and the simulation, a postmodern pastiche which makes no distinction between natural objects and European manufactured goods, a 'wry critique' of modernity. There are comparisons with Claes Oldenburg.[13]

In the strict terms of post-Enlightenment cultural relativism, of course, objects have in themselves no meanings other than those which a culture – any culture – creates for them and a dislocated object such as this will inevitably accrue to itself diverse, contradictory or paradoxical significations. This coffin is both singular and familiar. The coffin's dislocation has transformed a functional object into a postmodern artwork. But it is not only that transfiguration I wish to address. Another dislocation has taken place – something is not in its place. Surely, what is most striking about this object is a certain absence? an absent object of display? The absence of a body – the lost body.

Kane Kwei's coffin seems graphically to conjure the dilemma of cultural representation. The full coffin of Kane's *carpentry* – with its owner in place – speaks of the full subject: of descriptive plenitude, location, function, presence, community. The empty coffin of Kane's *artistry* connotes an empty subject: the abode of the now-invisible African body is occupied by a pastiche of postmodern discourses, by an absent incalculable object – the 'secret art of invisibleness'. From that dislocation and denial descend myriad further questionings of the frames of identity: of race, of gender, of art, of language.

II

Marlene Nourbese Philip's dislocations, personal and ancestral migrations, lead from Africa to the Caribbean to Toronto. In *Looking for Livingstone: an Odyssey of Silence*, Philip has extended and resituated her poetic analysis of language, which she began in *She Tries Her Tongue* where she drew heavily on nineteenth-century philological discourse, more overtly in an adjacent domain of exploration and colonisation. As an inversion of the genre of the male quest narrative the text replicates and subverts many of the themes which have their textual origin in the chivalric romance as the text's narrator searches in Africa for the 'blatant beast' of colonial darkness.

The object of her search is David Livingstone, the missionary, ex-
plorer, ethnographer and (for Philip's narrator) the archetypal figure
of sexual and cultural oppression. But Livingstone is also the missionary of the heresy of the Word; of language as an agent of
oppression. He appears, unbidden, in the narrator's dreams as the
explicit phallogocentric demon of linguistic, sexual and racial difference:

> HE – LIVINGSTONE – AND I COPULATE LIKE TWO
> BEASTS – HE RIDES ME – HIS WORD SLIPPING IN AND
> OUT OF THE WET MOIST SPACES OF MY SILENCE –
> I TAKE HIS WORD – STRONG AND THRUSTING –
> THAT WILL NOT REST, WILL NOT BE DENIED IN
> ITS SEARCH TO FILL EVERY CREVICE OF MY SI-
> LENCE[14]

From this subconscious encounter with the demon unfolds a reality of
catastrophic suffering enacted upon the body of the African. Rapacious
white words underpin a history of witch-burnings, colonial conquests
and the 'transplanting' and dislocation of peoples which destroyed the
ordinary course of the things of cultural possession. The litany would
seem endlessly predatory upon those who have no power, no history,
no memory, no language. The 'body' is lost but what remains is the
empty husk of a humanity ravaged by imperial words: a theme which
Philip broached also in *She Tries Her Tongue; Her Silence Softly
Breaks*:

> This
> disfigurement   this
>   dis
> memberment
>   this
>   verbal crippling
>   this
> absence of voice
>   that
> wouldnotcould   not
> sing[15]

But in the dream, Philip assigns to Livingstone the status of a 'succu-
bus' which, in demonology, is invariably female and by this simple act
of inversion the victim redirects the language of the demonised female
against its inventor, while simultaneously pronouncing her 'absence of
voice'. Philip's complaint against language is filled with such moments
of simultaneously articulating a presence through the representation
of absence.

Philip assigns a linguistic provenance to a myth of the origins of unequal differences and fractured black female identities. In the beginning, Philip writes:

> God first created silence: whole indivisible, complete. All creatures – man, woman, beast, insect, bird and fish – lived happily together within this silence, until one day man and woman lay down together and between them created the first word. This displeased God deeply and in anger she shook out her bag of words over the world, sprinkling and showering her creation with them. Her word store rained down upon all creatures, shattering forever the whole that once was silence. God cursed the world with words and forever after it would be a struggle for man and woman to return to the original silence. They were condemned to words while knowing the superior quality of silence. (p. 11)

Philip's exploration of the relationships between language, 'race' and femininity rededicates the myth of genesis to reflect a paradise lost through sexual-linguistic 'first sin'. In the beginning was, not the 'male' word, but the silence of a female deity, a prelinguistic eden. But sexual difference, having engendered a gendered language, rapidly devolves to a system of racial difference as 'mounted armies of words . . . colonise the many and various silences of the peoples round about, spreading and infecting with word where before there was silence' (p. 12).

'Remove a thing – a person – from its source,' Philip writes, 'from where it belongs naturally and it will lose meaning – our silence has lost its meaning' (p. 58). The text's narrator is therefore engaged in a double quest, for Livingstone but also for the essential quality of Africa, its 'silence', as a counter to a language indelibly tainted by imperial phallogocentrism. The narrator encounters in her Swiftian travels a number of peoples each bearing a name which is an anagram of Silence – the Ecnelis, Lenseci and so on – who have perfected various ways of dealing with language and silence.

What is being enunciated in this articulation of a presence through the representation of absence is a state of *lack* of enunciation. This seemingly paradoxical sentence is only paradoxical if silence is seen as the antithesis of speech. The demonic Livingstone's main error, his heresy given the scriptural qualities of Philip's text, is to assume that identity can *only* be ascribed to the speaking subject: that only language makes presence and that that which cannot be said is, in the manichean economy of identity, an index of the 'empty subject'. The 'empty subject' for Livingstone is black and female, to be 'filled', sexually and verbally, by the plenitudinous white male. But for Philip, speech is *contiguous* to silence since what is said only indicates what is unsaid: language proves the existence of silence. Silence is imminent in enunciation proclaiming the potential for a 'future biblical with anticipation', as if the depredations, colonialism's erasing of identities, creates (inadvertently) the latent potential for the construction of new identities in the present and future.

Claire Harris writes that 'the only effective creative responses, faced with the abomination [of black history], are surrealism and fact'.[16] For Harris, black women's exclusion from presence, their lack of status as enunciating subjects, would seem to compel them to embrace the oxymoron of 'factual surrealism'. Language and narrative are reformed – deformed – into strange combinations: a kind of baroque narrative architecture as language is made to sprout magic realist cupolas, contradictions of styles which gesture to contradictory states of identity.

Philip pursues an alternative course when she writes about 'a new house of language' in the essay 'Making the House our Own: Colonized Language and the Civil War of Words'.[17] She combines architectural and medical imagery and she speaks of, as Harris describes it, 'detoxifying the English Language'. She proposes that black women writers work upon the structure / body of language until the 'equation between the image and the word [is] balanced again'. And, in *Looking for Livingstone*, that 'The word does not belong to you – it was owned and whored by others long, long, before you set out'; 'My words were not really mine – bought, sold, owned and stolen as they were by others.' Language is untrustworthy, predicated as it is upon the Livingstonian premise that language inscribes the 'unspeakable' nature of the black woman (pp. 43, 52, 43).

Philip's 'cure' is radical. She desires to recuperate the literary by a millenarian purging, an emptying out and a scrubbing clean of the language. Central to this ambition is a challenging of metaphor:

> Tongue-tied   rests
> in the 'is like' of simile
> defies the is   (p. 22)

Such writings have a simple ambition to demystify or confront the racist encodings of the 'white words' by reconstructing the 'bridge/ between speech and magic' and achieving the '*is*', in a perfectly expressive minimalist poetics.

In *Looking for Livingstone* the narrator is placed in a verbal sweat house where her body 'sweats' words. Ultimately, she has only three words left, 'root words', which refuse to be shed: 'Birth' 'Death' and 'Silence'. Philip's interest in root words, the essential qualities of purged language, lies in the opposite direction to Harris's surrealism and factuality and to the 'philosophical/anthropological' construction of identity Bhabha alluded to. Philip's alternative to metaphor is a colourless and abstract representation more consonant with the refined 'silence' of prelapsarian existence. A pristine language that passively and virtuously lies beyond pollution. Paradoxically, language is only tolerable when it approaches the condition of silence.

The prospect of 'unspeaking' language, Philip's narrator's purification of language, acts as an anchor for a dislocated identity as the lingusitic/'racial' paradigm is sweated down to its essentials to discover the lost body within the bloated false body of language. Language in this condition is barely language at all since it approaches the 'nonlinguistic language' which St. Augustine described as the language of Heaven, where 'we will be able to *see* our thoughts'.[18] But in *distilling* language there is a danger that language may also be *stilled* to a language without etymology, a language denied the defining characteristics of language: no accent, no dialect, no syntax, no grammar. Language without system; language as atomic particles; language without difference. It is also a language without rhetoric or currency, conceived of as a purified nomenclature. Philip's 'root words', a poetics purged of structure, are valued as *objects*; abstract monoliths between which blow the winds of silence. The main function of such a language is to gesture to that which separates words: silence. She writes:

> There *were* two separate strands or threads – word *and* silence – each as important as the other. To weave anything I first had to make the separation . . . (p. 54).

> Word
> and Silence
> balance in contradiction
> Silence and Word
> harmony of opposites
> double planets
> condemned
> to together
>
> (p. 34)

> It is the coarsest of currencies, you know – the word – crass and clumsy as a way of communication; a second cousin, and a poor one at that, of silence. (p. 72)

Lyotard (and Harpham after Lyotard) describes a tendency in modern art in which 'the image is both fetishized and discredited in the name

of the unrepresentable'.[19] Philip takes this manichean antinomy, between the unrepresentable 'true' subject which language cannot utter
and the material but 'false' representation which language makes available, to its extreme and radical conclusion. The word is objectified,
'fetishized and discredited' by Philip in the name of the unrepresentable
silence. Increasingly, in *Looking for Livingstone*, Philip turns away
from language towards the purer form of silence:

>   Silence
>   Trappist
>   Celibate
>   seeking
>   The absolute
>   in Virgin
>   Whole

(p. 56)

This is an enigma which extends much further even than Bhabha's
elliptical identities seeking enunciation in the denial of enunciation:
wordless words, the pure form of the formless, an identity which speaks
without speech, an articulate silence. Silence for Philip is 'the off-limits
of the imagination' (p. 22) which means that nothing the reader reads
is *it*; the subject of this text lies outside the limits of textuality. Outside
discourse.

In her state of dislocation and exile from the Africa of her origins,
beset by the Livingstonian demon, plagued by the swarms of rapacious
white words, and set upon the task of purification and enunciation,
Philip's narrator becomes like an ascetic experiencing an extreme *acedia*. From seclusion and exile from the world of language as social
exchange comes *acedia*, temptation and the struggle with demons,
conversion and, finally, the written 'biography' of the struggle for
enunciation of this purified self. The process by which enunciation is
achieved is to endure a condition in which she becomes, in Geoffrey
Galt Harpham description of the ascetic impulse, 'dead to the world
and recuperable only through textuality'.[20]

Philip suppresses the turmoil of colonial language by designating
manichean boundaries in silence, purification and 'absence'. Again
an inversion works to designate as demonic, not the anthropologist's
habitual abode of chaos, Africa, but the place of her migration, the
cities of North America, the new heart of darkness. Yet the text brings
the reader back repeatedly to, as Philip puts it, 'the true discovery'
which is 'just me, me and more me' (p. 62). *Looking for Livingstone*
is Philip's achievement of 'complete narratability'[21] and the insistent
egocentrism raises an interesting prospect: as silence, the subject of the
text, becomes increasingly situated in an extra-textual off-limits, the

'real' subject, identity, takes its place. The poem documents an identity trying to achieve enunciation through that which cannot be made a substantial textual presence.

The structuring form of *Looking for Livingstone* is the epic journey or quest for the source of silence, but as the source cannot be represented, the familiar identity tropes of the epic quest fill that void with the language of self discovery.

> Every cell within me released its ancient and collective wisdom. No longer was body separate from mind and spirit. (p. 42).

The two objects of the quest are finally discovered simultaneously: the narrator confronts Livingstone and, after a lengthy exchange, she 'surrenders to the silence within'. The surrender seems like a simulacrum of death in that the speaking subject embraces eremitic silence, not the world of speaking/living beings:

> The traveller seeks
>   contentment
> in silence
>   containment
> of press of circle upon circle
> that cleanses
>   the pollute
>   the profane in word
> to confine within small
>   large
>
>   (p. 39)

The metamorphosis from speech to silence is not accomplished without a considerable sense of loss since the price of self-fashioning is to come to resolution through the relinquishing of desire. The double quest, then, of the epic motif, can be seen to have two destinations: one metaphysical, the other ascetic. The destination of Philip's metaphysics is to evoke the wondrous ellipsis of silence; her asceticism purifies the language of enunciation to its minimal, emaciated limit.[22]

The poem's meaning, undiscoverable in what it says (but only discoverable in what it says) is communicated directly to its reader through, but in spite of, language. Its goal is unmediated communication; 'Might I,' Philip asks in *She Tries Her Tongue*, 'Like Philomela . . . sing / continue / over / into pure utterance?' (p. 98).

Not without cost. The 'unspeakable' self is necessarily diminished in its metaphysical 'vitality' by being transformed into discourse. Furthermore, language cannot be 'distilled' to the ascetic values of Philip's root words. It remains, as Bakhtin writes, 'populated – overpopulated with the intentions of others'.[23] Much the same can be said for the self since it too is 'overpopulated with the intentions of others' and does not achieve the status of a 'root word' without some diminution: the loss of a social presence or 'persona'. One consequence of this reformulated identity is the re-presentation of an essentialist version of, as Philip puts it, 'silent' Africa (p. 70). To prove the existence of the chauvinist intentions of language, a prelinguisitic and 'historyless' Africanité must be assumed to act as foil and victim. But can other African voices become audible in this poem? or must they be drowned out by the silence so that Philomela can sing?

Philip may claim that her quest has led to the union of body and mind to produce a healed identity, but it is achieved only by erecting a different antimony in its place: the text ends with a 'surrender to the silence within' as the 'body' of a written identity contains a 'soul' of silence. Philip reconstructs the *homo duplex*, not in the enlightenment conjunction of the double locations of the self as both anthropological persona and philosophical individual, but as a dislocated ascetic black woman. In attempting to remake a vision of a unified and holistic identity in which the outer world of social intercourse is relinquished in favour of an inner world of spiritual purity, Philip reinvents the *double régime* afresh but nonetheless as a recapitulation of the ancient manichean tropes of spiritual and bodily interiors.

Philip is driven by an evangelical sense of empowerment of the voice of black women and in an important sense her 'secret art of invisibleness' radically deconstructs modes of representation by evoking a sense of the absence of postcolonial identities in representation. Her art is to make a literature of loss – to recover the lost body. But paradoxically, given this ambition, Philip's 'silence' documents a postcolonial world without 'ethnography', without access to representation, without an ethnotext. Philip attempts to recuperate from that loss an equally paradoxical 'silent voice'. Her fictional Africans (the Lenseci and others) exist *as fictions* without actuality, without history, as polemical and linguistic ciphers, and without the host of practices which constitute the fabric of social experience. There is, of course, no obligation on Philip to elaborate an ethnography for her creations, indeed, there is every reason why she should not since it is those misrepresentations which she holds responsible for the condition of lacking 'an objectifying confrontation with otherness'.[24] For Philip cultural representation carries with it the taint of Livingstonian language and power and the triumphalism of the text occurs when the narrator seems to repossess herself, recovering the lost body of colonial misrepresentations and expelling the demonic presence of Livingstone, but only by the same kind of purification, objectification and 'fetischizing' of the self to which language was subjected. The narrator turns herself – as a displaced subject experiencing the world – into an object of display to herself –

an observing subject immune to experience.[25] The 'real' subject becomes articulate, that much is true since she is, at the end, able to crush Livingstone with a series of devastating arguments. But that articulate being only comes about by secluding itself to become an object like language. This self is a 'root word'. Philip's narrator achieves the substantial, irreducible status of a noun in its distilled/stilled form, purged of public and private differences, purged of its currency in a world of social exchanges. The lost body of the self/language is recovered only to be revealed as what it truly always was – a corpse, dead to the world.

Notes

The title of this essay is taken from Aimé Césaire's collection of poems *Corps Perdu/Lost Body*, translated by Smith and Eshleman, (New York: G. Braziller, 1986).

1. Homi K. Bhabha, 'Interrogating Identity', *ICA Documents*, 6, 1987, p. 6.
2. Bhabha, 'Interrogating Identity', p. 5.
3. I have tried to discuss the nature of cultural representations in anthropology more fully in *Masks of Difference: Cultural Representations in Literature, Anthropology and Art* (Cambridge: Cambridge University Press, 1994). See 'Third Eye/Evil Eye', Chapter 7, which contains a fuller version of the essay reproduced here.
4. Marcel Mauss, 'A Category of the Human Mind: the Notion of the Person; the Notion of the Self', translated by W. D. Halls in Martin Carrithers, Steven Collins and Steven Lukes (eds.), *The Category of the Person* (Cambridge: Cambridge University Press, 1985).
5. Homi K. Bhabha, 'Foreword: Remembering Fanon', foreword to Frantz Fanon, *Black Skin, White Masks* [*Peau Noire, Masques Blancs*, 1952], translated by Charles Lam Markmann with a foreword by Homi K. Bhabha (London: Pluto Press, 1986), pp. xxii.
6. Bhabha, 'Interrogating Identity', p. 8.
7. Bhabha, 'Interrogating Identity', p. 5.
8. Bhabha, Foreword to *Black Skin, White Masks*, p .xiv.
9. The term 'historylessness' is Bhabha's own, see 'Interrogating Identity', p. 9.
10. Bhabha, Foreword to *Black Skin, White Masks*, pp.xviii, xiv-xv.
11. Bhabha, 'Interrogating Identity', p. 7.
12. S. A. Tyler, 'The Poetic Turn in Postmodern Anthropology: The Poetry of Paul Friedrich', *American Anthropologist*, 86:2 (1984), p. 329.
13. The photograph of Kane Kwei's 'Mercedes Benz-shaped Coffin' is from Susan Vogel, assisted by Ima Ebong (eds.), *Africa Explores: Twentieth Century African Art* (New York: Centre for African Studies, 1991), p. 110; see also Susan Vogel, 'New Functional Art: Future Traditions', for a discussion of the reception and 'use' of Kane Kwei's (and others') work, chapter ii, *op. cit.*, pp. 94–113.

14. Marlene Nourbese Philip, *Looking for Livingstone, An Odyssey of Silence* (Stratford, Ontario: Mercury Press, 1991), p. 25, all future citations given in the text.

15. Marlene Nourbese Philip, *She Tries Her Tongue; Her Silence Softly Breaks* (Charlottetown: Ragweed Press, 1989), p. 94, all future citations given in the text.

16. Claire Harris, 'Poets in Limbo', *A Mazing Space: Writing Canadian Women Writing*, edited by Smaro Kamboureli and Shirley Neumann (Edmonton: Longspoon Press, 1986), p. 124.

17. 'Making the House our Own: Colonized Language and the Civil War of Words', *Fuse*, 8:6, Spring 1985.

18. St. Augustine cited in Geoffrey Galt Harpham, *The Ascetic Imperative in Culture and Criticism* (Chicago: University of Chicago Press, 1987), p. 25 (my italics).

19. Harpham, p. 191.

20. Harpham, p. 73.

21. The phrase is Harpham's.

22. 'Metaphysics culminates in a state of wordless knowledge . . . Asceticism, by contrast, culminates not in the knowledge of essences but in self-transformation, accomplished through the agency of writing . . . ' Harpham, p. 92.

23. M. Bakhtin, *The Dialogic Imagination*, translated by C. Emerson and M. Holquist (Austin: University of Texas Press, 1981), p. 294, also cited by Harpham, p. 11.

24. Bhabha, Foreword to *Black Skin, White Masks*, p. xviii.

25. Harpham describes the moment of 'conversion' when the ascetic accomplishes a division in which 'the knowing self splits off from the being self, and observes it from a position magically free from being known, free from representation . . . far from uniting the self, [conversio] inculcates a sense of the otherness of the self.' Harpham, p. 98.

10

A Question of Form:
Phyllis Webb's *Water and Light: Ghazals and Anti Ghazals*

Shirley Chew

> In the beginning was the word,
> but was it followed by a question mark?
> (*Talking*, 1982)

Given Phyllis Webb's profound curiosity concerning the ways in which the question inhabits and governs our lives,[1] it comes as no surprise that questions should occupy a central place in *Water and Light: Ghazals and Anti Ghazals*, her sequence in five parts,[2] and among them, questions relating to poetry and poetic form.

> History and secrecy – that's what I said
> as a member of a panel whose topic was
>
> *Why Poetry?* And why not, I asked,
> my right brain humming sedition.
>
> Patrick insisted on games and the nature
> of games. Gary agreed with the seriousness
>
> and playfulness of that. And Tom, who
> started it all, was concerned about the
>
> alienation of the young, whom he loves.
> We were all uncomfortable and knew we were failures.
>
> The man from Iraq in the audience said,
> 'Where I come from when you fill out a job

application you begin by quoting poetry
and when you flirt you quote poetry

and when you marry poetry is all around you.
Why don't you speak of feelings!'

And when you die at the executioner's hands
(he did not say this though most of his family

was murdered) do you also quote poems, Amin?
Oh Allah. Why not?   (p. 55)

The answer to 'Why Poetry?', the poem suggests, may never be found
(and even if it were, what use would that be?) but just as various possibilities are tried out within the ground laid down by 'Why not?' – a
question twice repeated and mixing in different degrees belligerence,
defiance, good humour, resignation – so the search for answers runs
across the whole sequence. Interconnected with 'Why Poetry?', I wish
to suggest, is the more particular question 'Why ghazals?' and this essay
is an attempt to approach the first while engaging with the second.

Some of the answers – on the ghazal's provenance and distinguishing
features, for example – lie outside the sequence and are briefly summarised below. Others, more inward to Webb's creative temperament
and aims, must emerge, as I shall argue, from close scrutiny of the
text. The most popular of the classical forms of poetry to have origi-
nated from Persia, the ghazal found its way into northern India in the
course of successive waves of Muslim invasion and was there adopted
into Urdu poetry when Urdu started to develop as a literary language
in the eighteenth century.[3] By the beginning of the nineteenth century,
ghazals in Urdu as well as Persian were cultivated by poets and their
aristocratic patrons alike at the Mughal courts of Delhi and Lucknow.
A ghazal is made up of five or more couplets, each linked to the rest
in terms of the metre and a fixed pattern of rhyme, thus, aa, ba, ca,
da, ea, and so on to the final couplet conventionally inscribed with
the pen-name of the poet. At the same time, a principle of discreteness
is built into the form and thematically the couplets have the status of
independent units. 'Most ghazals are, so to speak, small collections
of little independent poems, and it is in scattered couplets in different ghazals that the poet says what he feels most deeply.'[4] Needless
to say, the reader/audience's appreciation of these 'scattered' couplets
will depend on his or her location within the ghazal tradition. In general, the distinctiveness of the genre, even among the more coherently
structured ghazals, is summed up in 'the classic description of "Orient
pearls at random strung"'.[5]

Pearls, roses, nightingales – images such as these are commonly associated with the form and its treatment of love, giving rise to the
complaint that the ghazal is more refined than sincere, more ornate
than meaningful, a convenient vehicle in other words for the duplicities
of a male-oriented society which forbade the use of alcohol and sang
of the delights of wine-drinking, enforced strict segregation of the
sexes and revelled in the exquisite pains and joys of extra-marital liai-
sons. Two important aspects of the genre are omitted however from
this view. First, the versatility of the form in the hands of its best
practitioners; and second, its ongoing vitality, in particular within
contemporary Urdu poetry. At once strict and open, elaborate and
cryptic, the paradoxical character of the ghazal has, over and above its
preoccupation with love, rendered it receptive to other and divergent
subjects, such as religion and politics. As in the Elizabethan sonnet
with which it is usually compared, the boundary between profane
and sacred love is often blurred in the ghazal, many of its images
and gestures lending themselves to a mystical as well as mundane
interpretation. Thus the poet's abject humility before the Beloved becomes a way of speaking of his human inadequacy before God; and
the eagerness with which the drinker turns to the *saki* who fills his
wine goblet corresponds to the disciple's feelings towards his spiritual
guide.

Likewise, as a vehicle for political themes, the ghazal has con-
duced to variety and depth, ranging from the haunting obliquities
of Ghalib, writing amid the violence of the Mutiny of 1857, to
the powerful dilemmas of Faiz in this century, torn between the
ideals of the private life and the brutal realities of the contemporary world, to the anger and resistance of Pakistani women today,
protesting against the oppressive institutions of a male-dominated
society. The tragic notes of Ishrat Aafreen's couplets quoted below
are underpinned by her ironic awareness that, as a ghazal poet,
she inhabits a form which has traditionally excluded her and yet it
is only through working from within the form that she can pen-
etrate the long history of male privilege and power with which it is
associated.

> Why do women keep their jewels locked in trunks
> To whom will they bequeath their legacy of grief?

> Those who were themselves worthy of worship
> Why do they clutch stones between jasmine ingertips?

> Those who remained hungry and barefooted
> Why do they never let their *chadurs* slip?

When tragedies strike behind a close door
Why do the walls often seem to know?[6]

When Phyllis Webb's *Sunday Water: Thirteen Anti Ghazals* first appeared as a volume on its own in 1982, the Preface points self-consciously to the contents as 'actually defying some of the traditional rules, constraints, and pleasures, laid down so long ago'. To this end, the far-fetched images, posturings, and male self-absorption are treated irreverently while the poet herself is incorporated as the writing presence and, since 'Writing is always speaking of a kind',[7] re-presented through a vivid play of voices – buoyant, witty, enigmatic, importunate, tender, sardonic.

> Drunken, amatory, illogical, stoned, mellifluous
> journey of the ten lines.
>
> The singer sings one couplet or two
> over and over to the Beloved who reigns
>
> On the throne of accidie, distant, alone,
> hearing, as if from a distance, a bell
>
> and not this stringy instrument scraping away,
> whining about love's ultimate perfection.
>
> Wait! Everything is waiting for a condition of grace:
> the string of the Sitar, this Gat, a distant bell,
>
> even the Beloved in her bored flesh. (p. 20)

As I shall go on to argue, Webb's experiments with the ghazal form are deft and subtle, and there is considerably more to interest the reader in *Sunday Water* than the matter of 'writing back'. Nevertheless, taking a cue from her statements in the Preface, critics have adopted this particular angle in reviews and essays published over the last ten years, that is, even after *Sunday Water* has been incorporated into the larger *Water and Light* as the first of its five parts. Examples include: 'Webb performs a feminist act of liberation, freeing the form from a male history and a male monopoly in practice'; and, more recently, '[Webb's] "anti ghazals" are . . . subversive of both traditional (and phallogocentric) lyricism and of the essentially masculist stance of the conventional ghazals of Hafiz and Ghalib', her 'great accomplishment' being to turn 'a terribly strict and conventional form in Urdu into a wholly open and questing one in English'.[8] These are, to say the least, astounding statements since for 'a feminist act of liberation', one must read 'white feminism', and for openness and freedom, the West. However while the questions they raise concerning the politics of 'post-colonial' criticism are crucial, they are beyond the scope of this essay. Here my express contention is that to insist upon the subversiveness of Webb's ghazals does less than justice to the imaginative explorations she has made into a form borrowed from a different cultural tradition, explorations moreover which tread a careful line between borrowing and appropriation and establish *Sunday Water* as only the beginning in a complex process of making and transforming which is *Water and Light*.

The problem for Webb, the writer of anti ghazals, presents itself at once in the opening poem of *Sunday Water* and, having set out to question the form, she finds it has, in its turn, questions to put to her.

> I watch the pile of cards grow.
> I semaphore for help (calling stone-dead John Thompson).
>
> A mist in the harbour. Hydrangea blooms turn pink.
> A game of badminton, *shuttlecock*, hitting at feathers!
>
> My family is the circumstance I cannot dance with.
> At Banff I danced in black, so crazy, the young man insisting.
>
> Four or five couplets trying to dance
> into Persia. Who dances in Persia now?
>
> A magic carpet, a prayer mat, red.
> A knocked off head of somebody on her broken knees.
>
> (p. 9)

Here is energy and activity, not the boredom of the Beloved. Here is the modern poet writing about her art, everyday surroundings, personal history, revolution, injustice, in other words, subjects very unlike the vapourings, for that is how they seem, of scented and lamp-lit rooms. The perspective is woman centred, it is Salt Spring Island centred, it is Canada centred. Granted all that, then how, being white, Canadian, middle-class, does the poet (or, anyone else for that matter) '*really* speak' the phrase 'Who dances in Persia now?'[9] With ruefulness, perhaps? Or severity? Or condescension? As Hulcoop remarks, a gulf lies between the ordinary existence Webb inhabits within 'the bourgeois security' of Salt Spring Island and 'the danger of daily life in revolutionary Iran'.[10] Is it the case that the ghazal is hedged about with boundaries which can only articulate otherness? If that is so, then how does one presume to subvert a form the roots and sensibilities of which lie outside the pale of one's experience?

Earlier in the essay I suggested that some of the answers regarding Webb's attraction to the ghazal must come from the sequence itself. To set *Sunday Water: Thirteen Anti Ghazals* next to *Water and Light: Ghazals and Anti Ghazals* is to note the distance Webb has traversed in her experiments with the ghazal in the space of two years and the more assured dynamics of the larger work. There is first the attendance upon two loci, the autonomous couplet and the evolving sequence. Webb has referred to herself as 'a minimalist producer' and also to her plan to write 'great long poems',[11] and it is possible that she found in a sequence of ghazals one way of reconciling these separate creative instincts. In that respect, the sequence is the 'documentary',[12] the narrative of 'factual, historical and imaginative material', the context, which the couplets of her ghazals inhabit and out of which they are read. Secondly, there is the interplay of two movements, a working against as well as *with* and *through* the ghazal form. For example, after 'Sunday Water', Webb is less inclined to treat the couplet as a self-contained unit. On the other hand, the breaks between couplets are often made integral to a ghazal's meaning.

These structural features – the two loci, the counter movements – are apparent even in the framing of the sequence. The title, two sets of opposites held in balance, is followed by an acknowledgement made to Aijaz Ahmad's *Ghazals of Ghalib: Versions from the Urdu*,[13] then a Contents page in which five of Ghalib's couplets, each taken from a different ghazal, are used to mirror the five section headings of the sequence, Webb's terseness ('Frivolities') contrasting happily with Ghalib's fluency ('Now Ghalib, these verses are idle amusement. / Clearly nothing is gained by such a performance'). Finally, an epigraph, a ghazal itself of five couplets, invokes Krishna, the god in his erotic aspect, who invites the cowherds' wives to leave their husbands' beds and dance with him in the moonlight; and Shiva, Lord of the Dance, whose dancing brings into existence the world of time and, in time, destroys it.[14] The playful correspondences and contrasts in these opening pages are a lively prelude to the rest of the work. Thus if 'Sunday Water' is located in the landscape of Salt Spring Island, the fifth section, entitled 'Middle Distance', looks beyond the familiar West Coast environment towards India. If 'stone-dead John Thompson'[15] is the Canadian antecedent invoked in 'Sunday Water', then the presiding spirit of *Water and Light* is Ghalib. And it is with an address to this gifted and enigmatic figure in what is possibly the most beautiful of Webb's ghazals here that the sequence ends.

The couplets reproduced below provide an example of the complex criss-crossings of *Water and Light*. On one level, it is Webb speaking of her own creativity, a habit of waiting for words 'that arrive unbidden to lead me into poems',[16] and enacting a highly individual process of feeling and listening her way to sense and shape.

> The pull, this way and that, ultimately into the pull
> of the pen across the page.
>
> Sniffing for poems, the forward memory
> of hand beyond the grasp.
>
> Not grasping, not at all. *Reaching* is
> different – can't touch that sun.
>
> Too hot. That star. This cross-eyed
> vision. Days and nights, sun, moon – the up-there claptrap.
>
> (p. 18)

The poet's restive state[17] is projected in the half comic images of the writer as excited dog, straining at the leash as it picks up the scent; and of the pen and the writing hand assuming a will of their own. 'Hand' is also handwriting though the words when they appear elude the understanding ('grasp') of the poet who holds ('grasps') the pen. Weak at 'grasping', the poet begins to have doubts about the word, in particular its sense of taking things by force and out of greed. As a preferred alternative, there is 'reaching' which, as well as picking up on 'hand' and 'touch', implies effort and struggle before understanding or contact can be achieved. Even then, the likelihood of disappointment cannot be ruled out – 'can't touch that sun'.

The activity of words calling up words produces a concentration of localised meanings and intensities. At the same time, it leads away from the couplets, the words becoming part of an intricate pattern of symbols and allusions in the sequence. Thus the interchanges of 'hand', 'grasp', 'reach', 'touch', reverberate with echoes from the works of earlier poets, for example, Tennyson and Browning. There are the visionary pronouncements,

> And out of darkness came the hands
> That reach through nature, molding men. (*In Memoriam*)
>
> Ah, but a man's reach should exceed his grasp,
> Or what's a heaven for? ('Andrea del Sarto')

and also the notes of loss and doubt so that the 'hand' of Arthur Hallam hovers over the triumphal close of *In Memoriam*, and the low-keyed perfection of Andrea del Sarto's own paintings speaks poignantly for an alternative aesthetics to the flawed but sublime works of Rafael. As if resisting such polarities, Webb's couplets move instead towards 'vision' of a more accommodating kind, not the 'up-there claptrap' but a manner of seeing which finds mystery and beauty and consolation in the qualities of dailiness:

> The women writers, their heads bent under the light,
> work late at their kitchen tables.   (p. 12)

> The eggs of Yahweh crack in the tight nest.
> Too big his bright wings. Too heavy his warm breast.[18]
>
>   (p. 14)

> Or should I save myself with long voyages
>
> interstellar longings
> where we might meet as pure event
>
> and I would say Mulberry tree, Catalpa,
> and you would say, simply, Phyllis.   (p. 45)

And also, as the excerpts above suggest, towards a poetry which is, in the words of Daphne Marlatt, 'shared ground through difference'.[19]

Before discussing the last ghazal in the sequence as reflecting that 'shared ground', I wish to say something about 'I Daniel', the third and middle section of *Water and Light*, in which Webb attempts to reach beyond the received text of the Book of Daniel, or the manifest history, and probe the cost in psychic terms of visionary absoluteness. The problems of Daniel are generally known among biblical scholars and, briefly, include the identity of Daniel himself (legendary or historical figure), the bilingual text (Hebrew and Aramaic), and the indeterminacies of the form (in particular, the generic shift midway from historical narrative to revelations).[20] However, given that a common approach to the interpretation of narrative[21] is 'the invention of a new narrative', these anomalies have lent themselves to fruitful reworkings by various writers, Webb's dramatic monologue among them.[22]

Her agile use of 'the feint'[23] in 'I Daniel' is epitomised in the 'doubled form'[24] of the title, taken from Chapter 7 of the Book. At once an affirmation of a unified self and a disavowal, it constitutes the border space in which a complex interplay of identities and roles is located. It links together the contemporary poet and the biblical figure and points up the distance between them. It assumes the stance of speaking out of the full consciousness of cultural identity as first person singular and prophet. At the same time, it denies that clarity of identification, pointing to the impossibility of distinguishing between the cluster of selves adhering to each of the terms – instrument of God, role model for the Jews in exile, servant of gentile kings, interpreter of dreams at the court, visionary, politician, survivor, victim, apocryphal figure. In its neat assertiveness the heading 'I Daniel' belies the presence of these tensions, contradictions and conflicts. The ghazals which follow show Webb at her most scrupulous in gauging and registering the balance of one brought close to breaking-point by crises of self-definition.

> But I Daniel was grieved
> and the vision of my head troubled me,
>
> and I do not want to keep
> the matter in my heart
>
> for the heart of the matter
> is something different.
>
> Neither do I want happiness
> without vision.
>
> I am apocryphal and received.
> I live now and in time past
>
> among all kinds of music – sackbut,
> cornet, flute, psaltery, harp, and dulcimer.
>
> You come bearing jobs and treachery and money,
>
> but I Daniel, servant to powers
> that pass all understanding,
>
> grieve into time, times, and the dividing of time. (p. 35)

Wonderfully terse, Webb's ghazals in 'I Daniel' pare down to where the border between voicing and silence becomes imperceptible. Rather than the 'astonishing leaps' associated with the form, the break between couplet and couplet is taut with the presence of the unsaid or half said. It is not easy to pin down Webb's technique but, generally speaking, line structure, syntax, words and their sounds are worked to release a mesh of intimations of meaning over and above what is stated. In the first two couplets of the opening ghazal reproduced above, 'and' may be read in each case as a loose connective or as interlinking Daniel's grief, his visionary powers, and the knowledge derived from these powers. Similarly 'the matter in my heart' seems to chime with 'the heart of the matter' and to be dissociated from it at the same time, while the objection to happiness without vision implies that it is not grief only which attends his visionary gifts. The ambiguities build up and in a variety of ways. In the fifth couplet, pulling against the structural sense created by balancing 'apocryphal'/'received', 'live now'/'in the past', the second line, 'I live now and in the past', tends to slip across the intervening space and attach itself to the enticement of 'all kinds of musick'. Finally, while the arrangement of the last four lines on the page sets Daniel apart from his enemies who come bearing bribes, 'but' effects a turn that leads back into the private condition of grief with which the ghazal began and not, as might have been expected, into the arena of public conduct.

Finally, between 'I Daniel was grieved' and 'grieve into time, times, and the dividing of time',[25] the relationship of speaker and grief has changed, its lines of interaction becoming twined in complicated ways through the workings of time. As well as being acted upon, Daniel is now the source of activity; and in contrast to his earlier aloofness, there is an acute and overwhelming involvement. Daniel grieves and is thereby made real, entering history ('time'); captive to grief, he is lifted out of history, a symbol through the ages ('times') until released at the ending ('dividing') of time. Grief gives definition to time – 'mourning three full weeks' (p. 37), and also empties time of meaning – 'the years of desolation' (p. 39). In its turn, it is subject to time as the agent of change and also to time as measure. With this latter meaning in mind, sorrow's long association with verse and music is to be heard behind 'Grieve into time, times, and the dividing of time'. The echoes range from Donne's certainty that 'Grief brought to numbers cannot be so fierce; / For he tames it, that fetters it in verse' ('The Triple Fool'), to Tennyson's indifferent view of 'measured language' as 'sad mechanic exercise, / Like dull narcotics, numbing pain' (*In Memoriam*), to Herbert's bleak recognition that, unlike the romantic lover, his 'rough sorrows' must exclude 'both measure, tune and time' ('Grief'), to Hopkins's excruciating sense of impasse in 'My cries heave, herdslong' ('No worst, there is none'). It is an association to which 'I Daniel' returns so that, through the poetry of the ghazals as well as the repeated allusions to the music of 'sackbut / cornet, flute, psaltery, harp, and dulcimer', the speaker's grief is at once sustained and tempered and sounded until it accrues, if no precise definition, then at least a series of possible interpretations.

The lure of beauty and power, the isolation, the years of servitude, the despair of the visionary faced with the loss of his powers – clearly, some of the anxieties and concerns lying close to Webb's own consciousness[26] have found their way into her interpretation of Daniel's grief and the sensitivity of the rendering. Furthermore, 'I Daniel' looks forward to her encounter with Ghalib at the close of the sequence. Like Daniel, Ghalib, the pen-name by which Mirza Asadullah Beg Khan is known, lived at the confluence of empires and of tremendous changes, in his case, the collapse of Mughal rule and the consolidation of British power in India, the imposition of English as the official language and the consequent decline of Persian, the advance of Western science and the inroads these made in traditional society. He too was deeply acquainted with grief, having experienced the bitter events of the Mutiny and the uncompromising force of the new invaders. Ghalib had little respect for the last of the Mughals, Bahadur Shah II, but any positive feelings he had for the British rapidly dwindled amid the brutal retaliations against Muslims and Hindus in the summer of 1857. Finally, he too understood the temptations of worldly goods and office, having lived for much of his life on the verge of poverty and known at first hand the vicissitudes of service at the Mughal court in Delhi. What chance for survival had poetry, let alone the poet, within such chaotic times? A deep sense of the precariousness of existence, and of his poetic calling, lies very close to the elegance of Ghalib's poetry. As in 'I Daniel', it is grief expressed through poetic indirection, understatement, wit, and the suggestiveness of symbols. For example, as explicated by Aijaz Ahmad, 'house' in the lines below is also the city of Delhi which, in the national failure to resist the British conquest, was crumbling like the poet's own house and the surrounding, similarly falling, provinces of India.[27]

> I have been shamed by my love's power to destroy.
> In this house the wish to build lives alone.
>
> Now Ghalib, these verses are idle amusements.
> Clearly nothing is gained by such a performance.

Unlike Daniel, however, Ghalib belonged to a specific history and culture, not the domain of legend and myth. Furthermore, he is only one of a number of literary figures of the age though certainly one of the most distinguished. Lastly, the poetry he excelled in, both the

Persian and the Urdu, the full and detailed correspondence of a life-
time, his prose writings – such as *Dastambu*, a diary of 1857, a
pro-British document intended for publication – all attest to a complex mind and personality, struggling to understand the times he lived
in as well as speak for it. Unlike Daniel, therefore, Ghalib's historicity
and 'alienness' means that he cannot be made a convenient vehicle
for Webb's opinions nor the symbolic representative of his society
and culture. Conceivably the only approach in trying to reach him is the
question, and so, 'Mirza Asadullah Beg Khan, who are you really?'
asks Webb in the last ghazal of *Water and Light*, some parts of which
are reproduced below.

> Ah Ghalib, you are drinking too much,
> your lines are becoming maudlin.
>
> . . . .
>
> Still, I love to study your graceful script,
> Urdu amorous, flowing across the page.
>
> There were nights I watched you dip your pen
> Into the old Persian too, inscribe 'Asad'
>
> with a youthful flourish. Remember Asad,
> Ghalib?
>
> . . . .
>
> Ah Ghalib, you are almost asleep,
> head on the table, hand flung out,
>
> upturned. In the blue and white jar
> a cherry branch, dark pink in moonlight –
>
> . . . .   (pp. 60-61)

Searching for answers, she is aware of her helplessness – the writing
she cannot read, the translations she has to rely on. Her sympathy and
admiration for him make themselves clear in the references to the poetry, the beautiful calligraphy, the music of his name (so many names),
his love of art (and also of 'women, politics, money, wine'). Nevertheless the distances between them are also important and, her voice
shifting from the mildly censorious to the inquisitive, to tenderness and
concern, she reminds him that she too is a seeker after beauty and a

maker of poems, some, such as the haikus as well as the ghazals she has written, quite unlike his work. The poem moves, back and forward, gracefully and tactfully, between her pressing curiosity and her recognition of his mystery, and not surprisingly, it is 'lines', 'script', 'pen', and finally the 'hand flung out, up-turned', which connect them, reaching across the intervening years and a world unimaginably changed since 1857, yet not so different after all. 'Why Poetry?' Why not, indeed.

Notes

1. Phyllis Webb, 'The Question as an Instrument of Torture', in *Talking* (Quebec: Quadrant Editions, 1982).
2. Phyllis Webb, *Water and Light: Ghazals and Anti Ghazals* (Toronto: Coach House Press, 1984). Page references are to this edition and included in the text of the essay. An earlier work, *Sunday Water: Thirteen Anti Ghazals* (Lantzville, BC: Island Writing Series, 1982), was incorporated into *Water and Light* as the first part of the sequence. The five parts are : 'Sunday Water', 'The Birds', 'I Daniel', 'Frivolities', 'Middle Distance'.
3. See D.J. Matthews, C. Shackle, Shahrukh Husain, *Urdu Literature* (London: Third World Foundation, 1985). The Urdu language is a hybrid of Persian, Sanskrit, and vernaculars such as Old Panjabi and a local variety of Old Hindi known as Khari Boli.
4. Ralph Russell, trans. and ed., *Hidden in the Lute: an Anthology of two centuries of Urdu Literature* (Manchester: Carcanet, 1995), p. 128. As Aijaz Ahmad tells us, poetics and performance have a bearing upon each other so that a poet of the ghazal form is represented by his best couplets, singers of ghazals often limit themselves to three or five couplets, and people who memorise or recite poetry, recite couplets, not entire ghazals. See Aijaz Ahmad, ed., 'Introduction', *Ghazals of Ghalib: Versions from the Urdu* (New York: Columbia University Press, 1971), p. xxvii.
5. Matthews, *et al*, p. 18.
6. These comprise the middle couplets of a ghazal taken from *We Sinful Women: Contemporary Urdu Feminist Poetry*, trans. and ed., Rukhsana Ahmad (London: The Women's Press, 1971), p. xxvii. Rukhsana Ahmad's 'Introduction' includes an account of the socio-political context of the poetry.
7. Phyllis Webb, Foreword, *Talking, op. cit.*, p. 8.
8. John Hulcoop, 'Webb's "Water and Light"', *Canadian Literature* 109 (Summer 1986), pp. 155; and Douglas Barbour, 'Late Work at the Kitchen Table: Phyllis Webb's *Water and Light*', *West Coast Line*, 6 (Winter 1991–92), pp. 108–109.
9. Webb has stressed the importance of being true in her art to 'how I really speak, how my feelings come out on the page', *Talking*, p. 47.
10. The Shah abdicated in 1979. John F. Hulcoop, 'Phyllis Webb (1927–)', in *Canadian Writers and Their Works*, eds. Robert Lecker, Jack David,

Ellen Quigley, vol. 7 (Toronto: ECW Press, 1990), p. 297.

11. See Phyllis Webb, 'Message Machine', in *Language in her Eye: Views on Writing and Gender by Canadian Women Writing in English*, eds., Libby Scheier, Sarah Sheard, Eleanor Wachtel (Toronto: Coach House Press, 1990), p. 293; and 'Polishing up the View', in *Talking, op. cit.*, p. 47.

12. Dorothy Livesay's term for characterising the Canadian long poem which, unlike the American pattern, is 'based on topical data but held together by descriptive, lyrical, and didactic elements'. See Dorothy Livesay, 'The Documentary Poem: A Canadian Genre', in *Contexts of Canadian Criticism*, ed., Eli Mandel (Chicago: University of Chicago Press, 1971), pp. 267–281.

13. Aijaz Ahmad, see footnote 4 above.

14. See A.L. Basham, *The Wonder that was India* (London, Sidgwick & Jackson, 1988), pp. 305, 308.

15. John Thompson, *Stilt Jack* (Toronto: Anansi Press, 1978). Thompson was clearly more excited by the form of the ghazal, 'the poem of contrasts, dreams, astonishing leaps', than by its traditional contents, 'full of conventions, required images, and predetermined postures'. See 'Ghazals', in *Stilt Jack*, p. 5.

16. Leila Sujir, 'Addressing a Presence: An Interview with Phyllis Webb, *Prairie Fire* 9.1 (Spring 1988), p. 35. 'I haven't written a word for over a year and a half – not a word of anything, except notes . . . And I am not pushing it. I am quite content to wait and see because I feel that when psychically I am prepared and strong enough to move into poetry, which for me is a very encompassing thing, then it happens.'

17. See also 'Muttering and casting about each morning / for the secret heart of a poem.' *Water and Light*, p. 14.

18. A reworking of Gerard Manley Hopkins's 'Because the Holy Ghost over the bent / World broods with warm breast and with ah! bright wings' ('God's Grandeur')?

19. Daphne Marlatt, 'Difference (em)bracing', in Shirley Chew and Anna Rutherford, eds., *Unbecoming Daughters of the Empire* (Aarhus: Dangaroo Press, 1993), p. 182.

20. The general agreement is that the Book of Daniel was produced in the reign of Antiochus Epiphanes (second century B.C.E.) amid his persecution of the Jews, and the account of the legendary figure living through the days of the last Babylonian kings into the reigns of the Persian kings, 600 to about 520 B.C.E., was intended to console and exhort the faithful. I have found the following works particularly useful: Robert Alter and Frank Kermode, eds., *The Literary Guide to the Bible* (London: Collins, 1987); John J. Collins, *Daniel with an Introduction to Apocalyptic Literature* (Michigan: Eerdmans Publishing Co., 1984).

21. Frank Kermode, *The Genesis of Secrecy: On the Interpretation of Narrative* (Cambridge, Massachusetts: Harvard University Press, 1979), p. x.

22. See, for example, E.L. Doctorow, *The Book of Daniel* (1971) and Timothy Findley, *Famous Last Words* (1981), two of Webb's inter-texts.

23. I have found particularly useful on the subject, Alan Sinfield, *Dramatic Monologue*, Critical Idiom series (London: Methuen, 1977).

24. The phrase is from Stephen Scobie, 'Signature as Documentary', *Signature Event Cantext* (Edmonton: Ne West Press, 1989), p. 132. In his incisive analysis of this section of Webb's work, he argues for the aptness of the 'doubling gesture' to the documentary poem with its 'doubling of fact and imagination, of persona and poet, of history and writing', p. 128.

25. I am grateful to Alistair Stead for discussing the last line of this ghazad with me and for the reference to Donne.

26. In interviews and her essays, as well as her poetry, Webb has drawn attention to the pervasive violence of our time, utopian visions betrayed, the loss of creativity. See, for example, the Foreword and poems in *Wilson's Bowl* (Toronto: Coach House Press, 1980).

27. See Ahmad, *op. cit.*, pp. 66–71.

11

Bodily Functions in Cartesian Space: Working on Women's Writing

Lynette Hunter

Since the late 1970s there has been an undercurrent rumbling about theory and language-focused writing, and the high profile that this writing appears to maintain in Canadian literary culture. To an outsider listening casually to conversation in a variety of literary sites in Canada from writers' workshops to libraries to academic institutions, this rumbling has centred on the erstwhile Canada Council grants system and particularly on the makeup of its juries. Another crude analysis will throw forward the unusually close connections between academics, small publishing houses and language-focused writers. This essay will not attempt any detailed historical analysis of this background, but the frequency of related comments indicates the problems of socio-cultural reception encountered by such poetics in Canada. What I am particularly keen to study here is the way that women's 'language-poetry' in Canada has been traversed by the politics of Freudian/Lacanian language theory and its associations with recent French philosophy. I am not concerned with commenting on the poetic texts themselves, but on the philosophical and cultural filter they acquire in critical and academic responses. The discussion attempted here assumes that philosophical thinking is always a political act, with a greater or lesser social effect.

An Analysis

The debate between language-focused writers and generically accessible writers involves the public perception of a number of issues on both sides. J. Marchessault in 'Is the Dead Author a Woman?' suggests that the two are oppositional.[1] She notes that 'the critique of realism that evolved out of psychoanalytic feminism in the mid-1970s was an essential step in confronting the oppressiveness of prevailing forms of narration and representation . . . Our thinking continues to be informed by the rigid opposition of realism and modernism, of truth and its negative' (p. 87). Yet an analysis of these, indicating quite similar constraints on each, could proceed in the following way:

a) Public perception of philosophy
b) Public reception of language-focused writing

OR

ai) Philosophy *as* philosophy: logic-chopping, male discourse
aii) Philosophy as Freud/Lacan: focus on language

bi) Language-writing as difficult
bii) Language-writing as male discourse

BUT

ai) Philosophy/theory needs to be seen as a site for work on articulation, therefore a moral site bound to daily living
aii) Freud/Lacan is part of Cartesian space, and relegates the woman to the silent or sacrificial. There is a need to work through Cartesian space to the other side, and find other images: not for the sake of new metaphor/metonymy but for the sake of moral action/stance

AND

bi) Language-writing is not difficult in itself, but in its shift of naturalised common grounds. All writing does this, and language-writing needs to be seen as a site for work on articulation, a moral site
bii) Language-writing's alliance with male discourse ties it to Cartesian space and collusion in women's oppression. There is a need to take on the authority of the voice in order to have effect, and to work through it to other sites: not for the sake of authority but for the sake of women's oppression.

AT THE SAME TIME there is a problem with

c) Public perception of women's discourse
d) Public reception of culturally-foregrounded 'genre'-writing

OR

ci) Women's discourse as private, intimate, with no valid broad common ground
cii) Women's discourse as 'genre'-writing and/or personal autobiography

di) Genre-writing as easy
dii) Genre-writing as culturally safe discourse

BUT

ci) Women's discourse needs to be seen as non-institutional social action: a site for the extension of political rhetoric parallel to the nation state
cii) Autobiography (intimate) and Genre-writing (grand cultural gesture) are accessible and open to complicity. Accessibility and popular culture are places where we could find a place to value women's daily lives. We need to do this not only to be oppositional nor to replace the institutional with a new framework, but also for the sake of defining another discourse field where other things can be said

AND

di) Genre-writing and autobiography are seen as easy because they are accessible. All ideology is accessible; work with these writings needs to be seen as a site for dealing with the sophistication of institutional discourse
dii) Genre-writing/autobiography because they are dealing with institutional discourse are collusive in women's oppression. They need to be taken on despite their collusion partly because of their wide audience and learning potential: not because they are populist but for the sake of articulating a world in which women work, so that it can be spoken, critiqued, changed

Both language-focused writing and autobiography/genre writing are weakened by their potential complicity in the institutional. Both are strengthened by their commitment to the community of women from which they draw their alternative discourses. Here I want to focus on some of the problems deriving from both the public perception of philosophy and the public reception of language-focused writing. The institution of which I am part and of which some of my audience will be part, has been deeply infused by the attitude to philosophy often used to anchor language-writing and particular to the post-Cartesian theory of Freud/Lacan. Much of the authoritative language/vocabulary used by institutional commentators on feminism is still part of this psychoanalytic discourse field. I want to examine the grounds, work through them, and discuss some of their implications as they emerge in feminist discourse in Canada surrounding language-focused writing.

An Opening

The curious compound, 'language-focused' writing, usually refers to writing that radically disrupts the current conventions of verbal linguistic graphic expression. In Anglo-American criticism, commentaries on it have leaked into the gaps left by the narrative impetus of much structuralist and post-structuralist theory dominating literary and cultural analysis since the 1950s. Yet a number of Canadian writers and critics have been particularly responsive to the need for some kind of discussion and critique; for example, the Toronto Research Group papers in *Open Letter*, issues 1973 to 1978 inclusive, are substantial contributions to the discussion.[2] More generally, the philosophical field of literary and linguistic theory has come to be seen not as engaging with the devices of 'language-focused' writing, since both have the common concern of working on historically appropriate articulations, but as language-focused writing. Criticisms of the poetry use the theory as ammunition, and *vice versa*. As a result, despite contributions such as those from the TRG, there is little assessment or critique of either except to dismiss their political effectiveness. Any one theory, from for example Derrida, Lacan or Cixous, is taken variously as (a) prescriptive and speaking in jargon, (b) processual and trying to avoid meaning, or (c) temporarily interruptive and chimerical.[3]

During the 1980s elements of this debate transferred into the commentary of women writers, particularly acutely in Canada where for a variety of reasons a number of women writers have chosen to develop their craft in this way. Erin Mouré has spoken about the suppression she experienced when writing 'anecdotal/conversational poems without reversal (which is to say, without the language confronting itself and its assumptions in the poem)'.[4] Several accounts are brought together in Smaro Kamboureli's 'Theory: Beauty or Beast? Resistance to Theory in the feminine',[5] counterpointed in the same year by Libby Scheier, Sarah Sheard and Eleanor Wachtel's *Language in her Eye: Writing and Gender*.[6] None of this story is straightforward. Part of it is related to a separation between generically specific (and therefore easily publishable/consumable) and generically non-specific (and therefore 'difficult' to read) writings. Generically non-specific writing works largely within techniques and strategies that the society takes as 'naturalised'; its actions are capable of inverting, displacing, changing, the cultural commonplaces of language or linguistic object in ways that call for radical response because they unsettle tacit agreements about communication that are frequently taken as self-evident or axiomatic. For some women writers this generically non-specific writing promises a useful ground for speaking of different lives. Gail Scott for example speaks of the need to write against the 'reader's line of least resistance'.[7] Smaro Kamboureli calls contradiction in language a political act.[8] But allied to this promise is the difficulty of getting the writing published.

Part of the story becomes tied to an anglophone Canadian perception of Quebecoise language-writing, which appears to get published and win respect.[9] The early Tessera editorial collective is at least partly attempting to duplicate not only similar concerns with poetics, but also the publishing platforms their Quebecoise sisters set up during the 1970s in for example *La Nouvelle Barre du Jour*. In the view of anglophone writers Quebec has an intellectual community without the academic institutions which dominate English-Canadian intellectual products and which are predominantly male.[10] For anglophone women therefore, there is by example a promise of an alternative community for the poetics of difference.

The story is complicated by the increasing numbers of women who entered Canadian academic institutions in the 1980s, many of whom appreciate and indeed practise generically non-specific language-writing. These women, and the few who preceded them such as Shirley Neuman, Barbara Godard, Lorraine Weir, Sherrill Grace and Linda Hutcheon, see the success of the tactics of their male colleagues and work on the authorisation of this poetics through criticism. More helpfully, they work on teaching strategies of reading that enable readers to take the chance of commitment to a text, to find ways of reading appropriate to these ways of writing. Now the story is further complicated by a broader movement in Western feminism in which the univocal presence of the articulate, largely white, middle-class women of the 1960s to 1970s makes way for/is shattered by newly articulating voices from different races, classes and genders. This shift, which has been well-documented, often places the 'authorisations' of women's language-writing in a discredited field of masculine poetics, whereas some of those authorisations may also be read precisely as attempts to save women's language-writing from accusations of racism, exclusion and class blindness.

As with any attempt at an alternative movement there are necessary engagements with the dominant modes of power, and neither the anglophone women writers until recently, nor their authorising critics, have addressed that complicity directly, or have attempted to assess how the writing is positioned in the social. The antagonism they set off is understandable.[11]

What is interesting to note is that the impetus from Quebecoise writers occurred at a time in the late 1970s when French feminist theory was becoming available in English translation.[12] This language-focused theory, implicitly and explicitly offering a Lacanian analytic, was profoundly influential on the development of Western feminist discourse especially that focused on writing. However, Quebecoise writers such as Nicole Brossard had already worked through this analytic to a critical and more materialist basis by the early 1980s.[13] Brossard's work was available in translation from 1975,[14] but it is unclear how widely read and critiqued her work and later work by Cixous and Irigaray[15] also critical of Lacanian theory, was until the end of the 1980s. As a result the authority of a Lacanian analytic far outstayed its helpful stage and added to the negative reception of women's language-writing. The conflation of women's language-writing with Lacanian analytics has brought immense criticism from socially based women's studies theory and has led to unnecessarily prolonged divisions.

Many of the negative accounts from Canada condense into an argument that a set of women writers, including Daphne Marlatt, Gail Scott, Lola Lemire Tostevin, Betsy Warland, Kamboureli herself, are too language-centred, too theoretical. What seems to be signified is that this writing is prescriptive, particularly about the need for women to find a different language for expression, and that this writing is difficult to read. Specifically translated, the objections are *first* with the writing's often overt connection with Lacanian feminism and *second* that it is part of an experimental graphical poetics related to concrete/breath poetry that is merely relativist and with no social relevance: either it is process only, with no immediacy, or it is unnecessary, because language is neutral so there is no need for 'feminine' writing. The underlying argument is, *first*, that if these women are the avowedly feminist writers they say they are, then their theoretical jargon/complexity and their linguistic obscurity/difficulty put them so far away from the usual concerns of women as to make them useless.[16] And *second*, that the theoretical concerns of graphic linguistic experiment are part of a masculine tradition and the engagement of these writers with these concerns compromises their work and places them in collusion with women's oppression.

In effect we can take pieces out of the poetry by writers such as Marlatt, Scott, Tostevin, Warland and Kamboureli, and indicate the apparent separation of the words from the concerns of most women in Canada – or elsewhere. And of course it is just because of the decontextualising that the pieces appear to be neutral. For example, there is, from Lemire Tostevin's *Gyno Text*,[17]

mute
skeleton
moves
to
muscle
string
pulled
taut
from
A
to
Zone

or, from Warland's *Proper Deafinitions*,[18]

induction

showing 'our sexts'

women's texts subtext
between
                  the
                          line
context pretext *text*:
'in the original language, as opposed to a translation
or rendering'

                                        pre-text
mother tongue:
'a language from which other languages originate'.

But there is not a single writer here who does not engage in a narrative that can provide a location for the neutrality of out-of-context settings. This writing also tells stories, not merely as a strategic sop to narrative expectation but as a necessary link to practical issues.

In this, the pieces are supposedly unlike comparable writing by male writers, such as Steve McCaffrey or Christopher Dewdney, although this apparent masculine neutrality has increasingly been questioned and challenged, by McCaffrey and Dewdney included, in the pages of *Boundary, Open Letter* and *LANGUAGE*, and in a number of recent

articles and books.[19] Betsy Warland explicitly comments that the mo-
tives moving language-poetry by women are different to those for men.
While for women it is a matter of survival, for men it is often a game
lacking any root analysis of patriarchy. She lists the adjectives 'aggres-
sive', 'cynical', 'witty', 'enervated': which are the melancholy points to
which the gamesmanship of postmodernism rolls. But for Warland this
is not an essentialist split where women go looking for a biologically
feminine sentence, but where we all look for the disallowed language
appropriate to our needs, our 'dialect'.[20] For example, there was/is bp
Nichol as a male writer with an ability to critique gently, to 'circumvent
the despair of the dominator's role' and to 'delight in the daily world
as a coinhabitant' (p. 292). All that Warland says generally about male
writers is repeated by others about women language-poets. And her
conclusions on Nichol can aptly guide the reader to commentary on
herself.

There are problems here raised both by the notion of 'poetics' and
of 'theory': I will begin with those clustered around poetics, and follow them into theory. If we take a step back from the debate, it is
possible to observe an on-going anxiety about any poetics in the post-
Renaissance Western world. A problem with a new and challenging
poetics is the need for mediation into that poetics: first time readers
of Dryden or T. S. Eliot typically have similar problems. Poetics have
always separated, untied, dislocated the *loci communes*, the topics of
society, that keep that society bound together. The activity of poetics
described here is specifically relevant for Western European and hemi-
sphere societies and their affiliates, that have depended upon a classical
education in rhetoric which provides the methodology for all social
agreement from consensus to totalitarianism. Learned in a historical
context poetics works alongside rhetoric to open up the verbal media.
Both writer/rhetor and audience need to be able to assess relevance,
and for today, need particularly to address graphic poetics as they have
developed since the Renaissance within a very small class-dominated
context of power, education and publishing: what is called 'literature'.
In that context we need to ask: What is the relevance of a writer's craft
developed within a state nationalism structured by the closed systems
of club culture? What is the relevance of a reader's craft developed
for an ability to recuperate by appropriation? How do the writer and
reader bring a reflexive application of their skills and craft to a historical context so that they may enable critique? It is not the poetics
that are a problem, for no device or structure is inherently enabling or
disabling, but in the way that poetics crosses the border into rhetoric.

What complicates the issue for Canadian women writers of
language-focused work is partly a social context in which the audience is increasingly varied in terms of culture, education and political

expectation; and partly the stand these writers make regarding theory *and* the specific theoretical ground which they claim. Association with theory and philosophy should never disable poetics, for all are concerned with articulating the immediately pressing needs of life; but the association can jar badly where the philosophy is one that can be elaborated without attention to the contingencies of daily experience. That's the problem with the public perception of current theory.

More serious a consideration is that the theoretical ground that is understood from much of this language-centred writing, as *A Mazing Space* repeatedly points out, is the Freudian-Lacanian psychoanalytic discourse that has infused Western feminist discussions about language. While it seems quite clear that the writing deals with women's oppression on the grounds of the world it inhabits, and that this discourse has been one of the most enabling, albeit authoritative, devices for articulating that oppression, the discourse also sets up conceptual barriers. Those who speak it have large authority because they speak the language of men and men listen to them, doors open to publication, distribution and dissemination, but at what cost? Being imprinted, impressed, put to bed and made public. Those who speak the discourse appear to be an anathema to the feminism of community activism, social policy and women's studies. The 'academic' or intellectual woman writer working in this discourse acquires a public persona that separates her radically from other communities of women.[21] It is not a rhetoric that encourages commitment from the reader, indeed it leads either to alienation or to a sense of collusion.

Cartesian Space: Fantasy, commodity/fetish and reciprocity

To look at the kind of crossings between poetics and rhetoric that have been imagined in recent theory, I wish first to put forward a classical text, the *Phaedrus*, that offers metaphors for working on this problem. It is a text where Plato is concerned not with a 'true' but with the social, the body action of the 'good'. *Phaedrus* explicitly addresses the relationship between social conventions for communication in both oral and written media, and the need to negotiate these in response to immediate needs, by way of a metaphor of 'love'. To keep it brief, the text looks at love gained for money: i.e. acquisitive; love exchanged for the pleasure of regarding oneself: i.e. for power; and love which works by allowing oneself to be changed: i.e. by receiving the gift of the other, this third being the ground for a proper interaction between poetic and rhetoric.[22] This metaphorical triptic insistently throbs through Western philosophy from Plato to Derrida. What is interesting here is what happens to it in Cartesian space – or to be more exact, in post-Cartesian space.

Cartesian dualism, conventionally read, splits the brain/body from the mind. Descartes proposes this as one way of explaining the limitations of language in its attempt to re-present the phenomenological actuality of the world. While Descartes recognises this as unstable, the suggestion gains actual currency via for example Port-Royal logicians, and even the Royal Society.[23] The possibility of progress toward a stable representation of referential actuality, phenomena, occurs concurrent with and no doubt as part of the political necessity for the emerging nation states of Europe to present a coherent argumentative ethos to each other. It has withstood the tensions of the rational via Kant's relational twist to ideological representations, which (simply) throws into relief the elements of structure that need to be readjusted to keep the status quo static. The Cartesian split becomes an appropriate common ground, self-evident fact, and generates two interlinked spin-offs about the body and about language that in contemporary cultural theory are both linked to desire.

First, the body: of the many developments from the mind-body split, the most urgent for women has been its use in sexual and gender oppression. Currently laid out in Freudian-Lacanian theory,[24] the split allows for the suggestion that if you have a different body you must have a different mind – but technically this is illogical, for if there is a *split* there may be no connection between the two: just one of the enabling contradictions of this theory that Freud emphasised increasingly in his later writings. Lacan describes the system of stable representation of the state ethos as the symbolic: made by men for men because they control economic and governing power; they hold political office; they operate within and strengthen the ideological stability necessary to the nation state. Because women are somatically/physiologically different, they cannot conceptualise in the same way and cannot fully enter the symbolic.

But also, Freud and Lacan work in Cartesian space because they need the split to cope with their fear. This fear is hydra-headed, but the one analogical example I shall pursue in the next section is the fear of inadequate language. To cope with fear the concept of a split self, found in abundant psychological metaphors throughout the nineteenth century is formalised/scientised: the self is accompanied by the 'other' in different ways that generate the classic psychoanalytical terms of narcissism, neurosis and psychosis, and that indicate desire at work. The underwriting of stable ideology via an elaboration of the Cartesian split into the imaginary (body) and the symbolic (mind), tautologically sets the ground out to enable a justification of the self as a split subject. The search for any completion of the self becomes, by definition, a denial of the subject, a fantasy, something that drives desire. But fantasy doesn't search for the complete, it invents strategies to suppress awareness or knowledge of the other: sometimes with the intention of realising the other most acutely at the moment of suppression (the fantastic), yet most frequently leading to a dominating process that seeks to create ignorance/to repress – a repression which lies at the root of narcissism,[25] and at the centre of the fetish.[26]

This reworking of Cartesian dualism does interesting things to the Phaedrean triptic. From money/power/change:gift as metaphors for verbal communication describing different ways of interaction and engagement with the social, money is eliminated (cancelled by the professional exchange of psychoanalysis) and the remainder is inverted. The interaction of poetics and rhetoric in the metaphor of love as change:gift is found only in the semiotic, the imaginary, the chora; while the exchange of love for a version of oneself that describes the narcissistic and dominating gesture, provides the necessary stability for the representation of ideology and becomes the central metaphor for the symbolic. The reversal allowed Lacan to gender the account of ideology via power: to provide a vocabulary for talking about the subordination and oppression of women; and to imply that there is a place pre-power, pre-symbolic.

Unfortunately, what Descartes remembered as unstable, and what Freud described as repression, Lacanianism sets into the possible as the ideal strategy for the power abuses of Western state nationalism: doublethink: you accept that there is an 'other' and simultaneously repress it; you remember to forget the other. The psychoanalytic stance foregrounds ideological power as the determining characteristic for both gender and language, and then analyses how we ignore it. This dis-membering forgetfulness has emerged in the multinational state as ethnocentricity and can be read as a backlash, similar to the backlash against feminism in the 1980s, against the moral intensity of theorists/philosophers such as Derrida and Brossard who use the Phaedrean triptic in its fulness, as well as a backlash against the overwhelming needs of the disempowered 'other' as presented to the empowered by their own media/communications technology.

The shift of the Phaedrean tryptic to a hierarchical duality of an initial change:gift, and then more important, exchange/power, also has implications for the social understanding of poetics. Freudian/Lacanian theory is built on post-Cartesian thinkers and their conceptualisations of the self, and it achieves a flexible and popular discourse for these ideas. Just so, the implications of the theory for nationalism lie in the discourse field that opens up to the concepts already articulated in another domain; and the implications of the theory for poetics are most evident in the sophisticating of a vocabulary for contemporary practices. The dominating metaphor for poetics becomes individual sacrifice within and to a system of power,[27] that elaborates on the essential activity of fantasy, the role of commodification within fantasy, and the difficulties of reciprocal exchange that make the fetish both banal and constructive:[28] all of which is predicated on the concept of the inadequacy of language.

Now, language: if Descartes dreamed of a language that could fully represent phenomena, he knew the limitations of language as a condition. But those working in Cartesian space took the dream as a possibility. This possibility held within it a multitude of utopias, including the hope that the new political systems of increasing state government could create a large and cohesive commonwealth to replace the feudal: no small dream. However, while the poets always knew differently, the politicians, scientists, philosophers, theologians (who had always had this tendency to forget) began, at least on the printed pages we still keep, to forget that representation is *necessarily* limited, and to think of the limitation as a problematic inadequacy. What Freud made accessible to everyone was a vocabulary for discussing this idea that representation is inadequate.

If Cartesian space splits the body from the mind, thought becomes articulable and separate from the body. Further, the mind cannot deal with the possibility of inarticulated knowledge. The history of psychology since the seventeenth century is an attempt to deal with the detritus flung from this severance which makes the inarticulated/able (i.e. not systematic/ideological) 'mad', located in the body, deranged. Just as there are tensions in Freud's simultaneous and contradictory linkage and separation of the body/mind, so there are tensions in his contradictory separation and hope for linkage between the articulated and the inarticulable. At the centre of Freud's definition of psychosis, neurosis and narcissism, is the 'other' as inarticulable. The 'other' becomes allied with the inarticulable body, hence what *is* articulated is never complete, never adequate to reality because it doesn't deal with all phenomena. To articulate, to *think*, in Cartesian space is to enter a system of representation increasingly dominated by the need for stable representations of ideology. The more pervasive this ideological discourse becomes, the more stable the representation, the more inadequate the inarticulable. This is the strategy that invents desire.

When Lacan extends this inadequacy into the split between the imaginary and the symbolic, the symbolic, like the mind, becomes what is articulated, what can be said; and the imaginary becomes the 'body', what cannot be articulated and is pre-symbolic. This is a necessary move if he is to make a case for the split subject and the structure of fantasy, and to prove his point he introduces the different bodies of women, using them with a casual curiosity. When you enter language you lose 'phenomenological plenitude'. This loss divides the self, leaving a desire for wholeness. The subject is always made up of the symbolic (necessarily masculine and phallic) and this inarticulable 'other', which is constantly desired via Lacan's notion of reciprocity. 'Reciprocity' has been developed in terms of fantasy and resistance to commodification, of considerable interest to women given that because women can't fully enter the symbolic they are 'other', and because they are 'other' they can't enter the symbolic.[29] The movement between desire and knowledge as a movement between inarticulated and articulated, is one that depends on a notion of linguistic adequacy underpinned by a profoundly post-Renaissance Christian ideology. A desirable object becomes known by being commodified, fully represented. The pleasure of such commodifying practice reinforces the sense that people live in an ordered, rational world of stable representation. Desire becomes something that leads to the satisfaction of repeating that order (repetition compulsion); or, it may lead to the terror felt at the edge of chaos (death), coincident with bliss or jouissance. Bliss is felt to be closer to the real because it's as if we make order out of chaos, risk ourselves in a metaphorical sacrifice. This also accords with a post-Renaissance concept of 'beauty'.

But in effect it is impossible to distinguish between the two because you can never know whether 'risk' and 'chaos' is simply the result of not understanding the systematic order all around you. The one is fully-fledged narcissism, suppressing the absent term and projecting completions/commodities such as God or woman from the phallic symbolic: the economy of the same. The other is a fetishisation of desire that locates the 'other', displaces into commodity rather than completes the subject: an economy of displacement, the failure of which makes necessary sacrifices. Both operate within the structure of fantasy and assume an inadequacy of language. The problem for women is that in either economy they are not only a central metaphor for desire, power and commodity, but also they are inarticulable and therefore unable to articulate.

The reciprocity that fantasy enables can devolve, as just drawn, into commodity or banal fetish, but some readings offer reciprocity as a version of dialectical reasoning, constant exchange between self and other, so that identity is internally alienated, the subject is never complete. In this version, women cannot be offered linguistic adequacy but neither are they commodified by others. The 'other' here is rooted in the body and the inarticulable, but can be written into the symbolic as the mystical, the religious. Of course in one sense this is Lacan (and others) simply re-discovering through poetics the limited rather than inadequate work of language, in a political world which has denied the instability of representation; but in another, it is a dangerous sidelining into experience marginal to ideological stability. In the face of theories that deal otherwise with the fear of chaos via concepts of total system (Althusser) and total inadequacy of representation (Baudrillard), Lacan has tried hard to deal with the sense of individual response, yet like them is still caught in the ambergris of Cartesian space.

Contacting Reality in Cartesian Space: Inadequacies and Practices

BUT, there are different approaches to the limitations of language made possible by reading Freud in alternative ways. To return to Descartes: by remembering the instability of language, part of the common ground for Descartes' thinking is that 'thought' is a way of working toward articulating the not-yet-articulated. Like 'theory' which in many contemporary discourses tends to get separated from practice but which is in effect the same thing, his 'thought' is trying for appropriate representations of practice: but why? Articulating practice is understood variously as a way of contacting 'reality' and as a way of making individual practice social.[30] Freud described the inarticulable as the repressed, focusing on two different kinds of repression: into the unconscious (not possible to articulate) and the subconscious (possible to articulate). The 'unconscious' becomes a concept responding to the sense of a systematic stable ideology inaugurated by nation state governments that emerge in post-Renaissance Europe. It is a way of providing an origin or raison d'être for the 'private', and links the private with the body, particularly the body we cannot articulate.

If the unconscious is understood as a constructed political response to authoritarian politics, then there is a clear transition into a wide variety of social repressions under state governments which institutionalise community functions. If the state is authoritarian but also powerful and systematic, then the disempowered are not just partially repressed but completely repressed, eradicated from participation. The terms become unconscious vs. system; private vs. state; isolated individual vs. nation. But what this also does, apart from providing a political rather than a biological reason for the unconscious, is ally the impossibility of articulation with disempowerment.

The alliance has a curious effect on people who are in effect empowered and should thereby be able to articulate because the system works for them. They hold the position they are in because a state system defines them as powerful in a particular way, so if people are empowered then their inability to articulate must be a result of the system. This seems to make sense because the system is presented as a symbolic mode of representation that is taken as necessarily (and hopelessly) inadequate. It is only those who are disempowered who understand that (in)articulation is work. The unconscious as the split self, is the response of the powerful/empowered to their own sense of the hopeless inadequacy of the public representation of the symbolic to their individual and 'private' lives. And it is those who have been *relatively* empowered who have used the 'unconscious' as an analytical tool for articulating systems of authoritative power: for example, Franz Fanon on the colonial subject or Juliet Mitchell (among others)[31] on the repressed woman.

It is vitally important that authoritative systems of power are analysed critically from within their own terms. They cannot 'hear' anything else because it is repressed, absent, dis-membered by forgetfulness. But those relatively empowered speakers are in a highly ambivalent position, dependent on the degree of their disempowered status. Within this powerful system of discourse, in order to talk about the disempowered, they have to talk about the unconscious, but in talking about the unconscious they accept the framework of authoritative state vs. private that creates disempowerment. If their aim is to interpellate a disempowered subject into the representative system (already taken to be inadequate) this is valuable because then that subject can be 'heard', but simultaneously that subject is dismissable as inadequate. This inadequacy only diminishes as the representation moves closer to the sufficiently adequate and the subject is systematised.

In the eyes and ears and mouths of the powerful, the disempowered are dismembered, part of the unconscious, the body, the private. Like the unconscious/body/private, they are part of the 'natural', the 'intuitive', the 'primitive', the 'not-civilised', the not-articulated. For example, until recently the metaphors for women make no separation between gender and sexuality because the body defines their position outside the symbolic. Just so, the body defines the position of visibly 'different' people outside the system. This is one reason why class analysis was effective for so long: it was difficult to locate the 'poor' outside the system on body terms, so it was done in terms of the 'private' – although the spurious connecting of a working class with sexual 'perversion' or the cultural battle over fashion are indications of the way the media are used to transfer 'poor' into bodily 'difference'.

The relegation to the unconscious by state ideology, of women and other physically 'different' groups of people had been so effective a political strategy for stable representation that Freud's popularisation of an emerging vocabulary for discussing this repression was of course profoundly unsettling. By definition the unconscious should have remained inarticulable. With psychological and psychoanalytic methodology, a discourse was formed both to enable people to talk about the language as inadequate and why representations are to be distrusted, and even ignored as in the forgetfulness of ethnocentricity;

and to encourage people to attempt articulations of the 'different', often using the body as the site for alternative articulations as in feminism's 'writing the body': re-membering and dismembering the individual in Cartesian space. But this version of language underwrites the sacrificial metaphor for poetics. Women, and others, can begin to talk and insert themselves into the dominant, but only at the cost of severance and mutilation. *The symbolic is powerful because it is defined by conditions of inadequacy materially realised by 'others': women are by definition inadequate.*

This is where it gets really difficult: this version of 'writing the body', re-membering the individual, within a system based on notions of linguistic inadequacy is always going to run close to accepting the concept of the unconscious as biological and hence of a private, owned and commodifiable, sexuality and writing. Brossard speaks of writing as different from text, and 'thought of as a machine capable of helping us resolve problems of sense, puts us in a position where we think we are able to produce truth, that is, reality',[32] or that is, adequate representation. The urgency of Cixous' early writing, which reclaimed the body from metaphors in the symbolic system, is carried out by repetition – repetition that can never be exact and is therefore potentially various, yet repetition always under hideous constraints demanding that poetics becomes a heroic attempt at individual adequacy, challenging the *a priori* inadequacy of anything without ideology. Or Kristeva's linguistic terror/ism. The violence of this enforced opposition describes precisely the system's brutality to all who are different, here women. At the same time it participates in the sacrificial metaphor, the writer undergoing mutilation and severance on behalf of a community.

Put in this abstract and rather dry manner, the sacrificial metaphor appears obvious in its futility. Yet it is not surprising that women writers exposed to a pervasive philosophical discourse field that defines poetics in this way should try to write back through it, as I am doing here, to other philosophical authorities in a search for another metaphor. For example, there is Daphne Marlatt's writing in *Musing with the Mothertongue*, through etymology and myth to the Kristevan chora. Or there is Erin Mouré's stab at Aristotle by way of a peculiarly Canadian emphasis that has been provided via the large number of writers who came into contact with the work of George Whalley: i.e. Plato's Aristotle. Brossard speaks of this in *Picture theory*[33] saying,

> No matter which cities, books repeat us, take the form of our emotions. The necessity for certain positions prior to feminist thought. Yes this body takes up a strategic stand in the streets of the Polis of men, yes, this body dis/places the horizon of thought, if it wants, this body is generic. (p. 143)

Generic bodies, articulatable bodies, have to work through the sites of philosophical discourse to understand both how they come to be articulated and whether they can be articulated differently.

The see-saw between system and individual, authority and arbitrary, determined and relativist, nation state ideology and subject, this see-saw is predicated on a notion that there is an externally ordered world: a system. It is predicated on the concept that language should be able to represent that order. However, neither the order nor the representation is ever complete; and yet because it is 'supposed' to be, the incompletion is taken as an inadequacy, a failure, something to drive desire. In turn, individual people are reduced to subjects forever under a naturalised power-relation. Because many Western societies accept a version of this implicitly in their structures of state government, it becomes an immediate reality that has to be dealt with on its own terms. And there are many writers in relatively empowered academic and intellectual communities who attempt to do so. But it can also be addressed, as Brossard addresses the writing of Stein and Wittgenstein, working with the flexibility of a language never intended to be adequate. And it can be addressed on the other terms of 'writing the body' suggested by the political gesture of the unconscious: of making practice social.

Making Practice Social

To 'Write the body' by writing from the practices of life, must partly be in response to institutional systems, yet it is also to do with many areas of non-institutional daily life. I would like to argue that there are many sites where language is not considered a problem of inadequate representation with its penumbra of failure, power, desire and commodification. Rather there are places where we negotiate communications, work with other people to arrive at immediately appropriate uses; places where in effect we sometimes resent the sacrifice-at-a-distance made 'for' us by someone who has the apparent luxury of being *able* to choose to become 'other'. If representation is taken as necessarily limited rather than inadequate, all order is necessarily socially questionable and negotiable.[34] There is no mysteriously (or mystically) externally-ordered world. There is no need for the terror of chaos, and when things get commodified we know about it. Unarticulated knowledge can here be seen to resist commodification to the extent that it cannot be systematised. But the attempt at an articulation of it is helpful: we value the articulated particularly at the moment of its articulation because we know the context and the activity of discussion that made it possible. It becomes part of the way we assess common ground, take decisions and act.[35]

Poetics in Western thought has always been a place to work on articulations that are difficult to make. It has provided a location for focusing on cultural tensions or knots and unpicking them, unravelling the weave of social texts and retexturing, hammering out appropriate words, shifting the common grounds. Prior to the Renaissance other pressures bear upon the direction of poetics, but increasingly since the seventeenth century, poetics has become contextualised within the pervasiveness of state ideology necessary to nation state ethos, and the context has shifted the emphasis to the heroic and sacrificial poet also coincident with Christian humanism, that reinforces the primacy of power over change: gift interaction. Recent Western writers have turned to craft and skilled practice, or the labour of care, in order to find articulations to value daily work without the success/failure criteria of symbolic power.[36] *Phaedrus* offers medicine, gardening, writing as textuality, as examples of the practices, the labour needed to maintain love as change:gift.

What emerges is a metaphor of labour, connotative of class struggle, physical work, birthing. There can be puritanical associations, but 'labour' here is not put forward as some grim duty; it need not be without a sense of Derridean 'play' but it is insistently communal in a way not easy to recognise in Derrida's own direct rejections of inadequacy in his concepts of fold, erasure, difference, supplementarity, etc. And while labour is work, it is not put forward as a mechanical or technical exercise in strategy, as in recent theories of communicative argumentation, but more as in Wittgenstein's own attack on the poverty of the case/silence duality, with his development of justificatory negotiation rather than judgements.[37] 'Labour' for me is also for the moment more enabling than 'sacrifice', partly because sacrifice is cast as individual while labour is more frequently communal and I'm tired of being alone, and partly because I'm also tired of being a sacrifice and continually returning to heroic self-mutilation in face of the symbolic.

Poetics as Labour

The problem with poetics as labour is that it requires commitment to working on a communal agreement of some kind however context dependent. Poetics asks the writer/audience to deal with the difficulties of articulations that untie cultural knots that bind us in particular ways, and reweave them into appropriate texturings. This is difficult work because it requires time and energy, so we need good reasons before we can commit ourselves to it. This is also vulnerable work because between the untying of the knot and the retying of the strands, our common grounds, which we both stand upon and understand, fall away. We need to trust to mutual support before we can do it. Again,

Brossard describes such an 'assemblage' or *contextus* of women work-ing together at a film festival, 'Invigorated, we are women's creative energy gathered together' (*The Aerial Letter*, p. 129); and later, context as 'inspiration' that 'restores to the community of women their energy. The energy of each captivating woman activates women's energy, and it is from this energy that a collective consciousness of who we are is born' (p. 130).

The commitment to the poetics of labour has to come from the re-sponse of an audience that wants to attempt new common ground – but there are many difficulties surrounding both commitment and support. A common way of proceeding is via a small group thrashing things out and hoping by mediation (in print) that others will recognise the appropriateness, see the light. The structure is avant-garde, and runs uncomfortably close to ethnocentric club culture and to much modern science. Larger audiences/communities are more difficult to form un-less one goes for less difficult shifts in common ground. My argument is not that the more difficult it is: the fewer the number of people who will read the writing, or: the more challenging it is. Rather, the argu-ment is that the more dislocating the writing is to a *particular* common ground, the more or less committed people will be to responding to it, and that this commitment is affected by numerous conditions. For example, since dislocations to culturally foregrounded structures are easier than dislocations to more naturalised structures, generic and narrative grounds in which Western education and mass culture spe-cialises are the most likely to gain a large audience in the short term, but just because they are culturally foregrounded they are more con-strained in the extent of their dislocation. It is more difficult to gain a commitment for a dislocation to a naturalised common ground be-cause they are more difficult to see as grounds, but the effects are far reaching.

Given this, dislocation can be an act of desperation, to loosen up the social and cultural restrictions no matter what: a gamesmanship of which language-poetry has been accused. If language-poetry addresses the frames of language itself – syntax, phonemes, morphemes – it will be more difficult simply because people take these grounds as natural. But it doesn't generate much commitment from the disempowered to say, as Jameson does, that since you can't disorganise the fetish of capitalist society the poet must work in the pre-symbolic of language; or to say as Hartley does, that poetics is meta-symbolic: you can't dis-locate the symbolic system but you can comment upon and critique the structure. Both responses are from a position of relative empower-ment, they both assume Freudian/Lacanian linguistic inadequacy and are rootedly anarchic acts which like all anarchy are contained within the system. Yet dislocation can also be a directed act, positioned toward a particular kind of work, with the problem that the positioning may not be recognised because the grounds are so fundamentally shifted, or possibly that this work may be of a kind people do not want to do on that position – they may not think it important enough or they may find it too frightening even with support.

Commitment will come from the perceived or enacted stance of the poetics, mediated by its cultural and social position (race, gender, ethnicity, sexuality . . .) and medium (magazine, book, newspaper, sheet). Commitment comes not from ethos, which is the relatively stable construction of the writing's voice whether generically specific or non-specific, but stance, which invites into shared work on articulation and appropriate significance. A stress on the labour of poetics as change: gift, presumes that the individual is working with other people, doing work that is acted upon but not contained within state discourse, that power is a contingency. It also presumes that the individual is not alone because this would be an impossibility – there is after all no such thing as a private isolated individual. In effect we work with others all the time on a common ground of power relations which, with support, we are always able to attempt to reground by work on appropriateness for our communities.

Lola Lemire Tostevin opens her introduction to *Redrawing the Lines* . . . [38] by proclaiming variety, stating that the women contributing to this issue 'never violate other women's theories, other women's freedom to express' (p. 5), yet notes that not many women of colour responded to the invitation to contribute. Partly this may be to do with the status of *Open Letter* which is from the world of the relatively empowered, the marginal intellectual. Partly one suspects, in the absence of any information about how writers were invited to contribute, that it has to do with the penumbra of Lemire Tostevin = language-focused writing = white/male elite literary culture. However, among the contributors' accounts of their writing lives there is some awareness of this particularly in the essay by Marchessault, cited in the opening to this discussion.

The accounts of women's writing lives consistently describe the importance of finding a textual community. Several do so through the vocabulary of Freudian/Lacanian psychoanalysis as it is mediated by Cixous, Kristeva, Irigaray and others. Many do so through Brossard's theoretical writings. But all do so through lists of other women writers who form their communities and who are spoken of in terms of gift: change, embrace and love. Joanne Arnott says, 'The poem is the vehicle inside of which she and I meet, embrace, and give each other strength for the journey' (p. 8). Anne Michaels says 'not action instead of words, but rather, action and words, Writing is one kind of giving. To become what you wish to give, quite another' (p. 99). Or there is Nancy

Chater's political self-love which is love within a 'collectivity . . . commitment/responsibility/accountability to a community or larger social context' (p. 32). Perhaps because these accounts are autobiographical they do occasionally construct a curious intersection between genre-writing and language-focused writing, that moves toward the kind of materiality of labour for writer and reader that Brossard and Marlatt work within. This is the kind of stance that engenders commitment. It offers recognisable common grounds and provides a poetics to challenge, unpick and retextualise. In this it is no different from genre-writing texts, Marchessault's 'realism', where working on materiality also goes on.

Coda

Work on materiality and common ground is often unexpected. It is not to do with identity politics, solidarity or authentic voice, but with being part of work with other people on the articulation of aspects of life different to those defined by ideological representation. That difference, and the perception of it, is important to our awareness of the limitations of the ideological. But simply noting difference in say class, gender or race, is to note only the representation of it, not its agency. To understand the agency you need to be part of the communal work. Representations of difference are important but need to be contextualised within their complex relationship with ideology, for ideology is itself the strategy of a stable ruling system of permitted representaions that position the subject.

Psychoanalytic vocabularies offered by Freud and Lacan provided a way of describing and analysing this relationship between the individual and the nation state, and their focus has been on ways that sexuality had been constructed into a statement about the position of the subject within ideology. Writers such as Foucault have of course elaborated on sexuality not as the bodily erotic, but precisely as permissable representations of the body within the state system. Indeed, the erotic is rather a mode of agency: the eroticisation of desire occurs at the moment when the physical body fits the sexual/sexuality; eroticisation can be viewed as a way of bringing the subject into the representations of ideology. Just so, beauty can be the individual eroticising actuality into representations of reality defined by ideology. Power can be constructed similarly as an eroticisation of ruling.

But if the agency of eroticisation brings individuals into representation, it also indicates that there are moments when individuals are not represented within ideology. The moment of instantiation into representation is at the same time the moment of commodification, and ideology simultaneously gives that sense of 'fit' to representation and necessitates the activity that leads to it. You could think of ideology as the source of contemporary Western aesthetics, the bliss/jouissance of instantiation being dependent upon it. The simultaneity of bliss/jouissance with commodification in 'fit' is also the source of the attempts to maintain that moment, to extend recognition of beauty/desire/power beyond the moment of its occurrence, which lead to the frustration of desire and yet also to the satisfactions of pleasure.

The possibility of 'fit' implies both notions of adequacy/adequate representation and of places without 'fit'. Those places without 'fit' may be preliminary unarticulated desires, or they may be quite different to the limited articulations of the ideology-subject axis. Within that axis all need becomes desire, and deprives the individual of further agency, leaving them overdetermined in commodified representations. Yet living together with other people alongside the operations of ruling state systems as one set of events currently defined by the ideology-subject axis, need is not turned into desire but is held in the middle of many contingencies. Here, alongside, agency becomes the inability to turn need into desire.

Many language-focused writers, writing through the vocabularies of Freud and Lacan, write at the centre of the ideology-subject axis, because that vocabulary is located precisely there, between the nation state and the individual. Yet many also write through to the other side of representations, dealing in the middle of the difficulty of articulation with the agency of words that net together a material ground. This work is not representative; hence it can easily also be taken as undemocratic. But if we work with it, rather than merely note or observe its lack of representation, we may find unexpected commonality in the labour.

Notes

1. In *Open Letter*, series 8, 4, Summer 1992.
2. A recent summary is provided by A. Karasick, 'Tract Marks' in *Open Letter*, Series 8, 3, Spring 1992. Karasick tries to makes a case for Marxian connections, but at least in the emphases she chooses I see more in common with American culturalism: i.e. cultural not economic production.
3. For a longer list see B. Godard, *'Canadian? Literary? Theory?'* in *Open Letter*, Series 8, 3, Spring 1992.
4. E. Mouré, 'Poetry, memory and the polis', p. 205.
5. Smaro Kamboureli, 'Theory: Beauty and Beast? Resistance to Theory in the Feminine' in *Open Letter*, 7, 8, Summer 1990.
6. Libby Scheier, Sarah Sheard and Eleanor Wachtel, eds., *Language in her Eye: Writing and Gender*.
7. G. Scott, 'A feminist at the carnival', p. 250.
8. S. Kamboureli, Interview with R. Kroetsch.

9. Despite for example L. Bersianik, 'Aristotle's Lantern' in *A Mazing Space*, eds., Kamboureli and Neuman (1986).
10. The tape of the editorial collective is held in the Special Collections section of the National Library of Canada. A much shortened version containing some of this material is found in the editorial statement made in the first issue of *Tessera*, published as *A Room on One's Own*, 8, 4, Jan. 1984.
11. Although some writers clearly show this response operating and document their answer to it. See Libby Scheier, in 'Chopped Liver', *Language in her Eye*.
12. Especially essays such as Cixous' 'Sorties' and 'The laugh of the Medusa' and Kristeva's 'Woman's Time'.
13. N. Brossard, *These Our Mothers*.
14. Indeed Brossard was invited to tour the UK courtesy of Cedric May of the University of Birmingham while I was working at the University of Liverpool in 1978/79.
15. Such as 'Coming to writing' or *Vivre l'Orange* by Cixous, and *Speculum of the other woman* by Irigaray.
16. This was the argument of Bronwen Wallace as well as Dorothy Livesay.
17. L. Lemire Tostevin, *Gyno Text*.
18. B. Warland, *Proper Deafinitions, Collected Theorograms*.
19. See for example M. Perloff and G. Hartley.
20. B. Warland, 'the breasts refuse: suffixscript' in Scheier *et al*.
21. See D. Marlatt, *Telling It, women and language across cultures*, ed. Telling It collective, p. 12.
22. L. Hunter, *Rhetorical Stance in Modern Literature*, chapter two.
23. As above, chapter three.
24. See the bibliography for much-referred to primary texts, and for widely disseminated secondary commentaries.
25. L. Hunter, *Modern Allegory and Fantasy*.
26. T. Modleski, *Feminism without Women*, p. 162.
27. See M. Whitford, *Luce Irigaray: Philosophy in the Feminine*.
28. T. Modleski, *Feminism without women*, p. 163.
29. Many commentators have discussed this element; Marchessault uses it to focus her argument about the oppositional in 'Is the Dead Author a Woman?', as above.
30. See L. Hunter, 'Artificial Intelligence and Representation: An argument for legitimation' in *Artificial Intelligence and Society*, 1993.
31. See bibliography for several commentators on psychoanalysis and feminism.
32. N. Brossard, 'Intercepting what's real' in *The Aerial letter*.
33. N. Brossard, *Picture Theory*.
34. L. Wittgenstein is particularly helpful on this in *Philosophical Investigations*.
35. A. Tanesini, 'Whose Language?'
36. L. Hunter, 'Artificial Intelligence and Representation: An argument for legitimation' in *Artificial Intelligence and Society*, 1993. See also the work on tacit knowledge by A. Janik and the Swedish Centre for Working Life studies; or the vocabulary of care, in for example, D. Smith, *The*

Everyday World as Problematic: A Feminist Sociology (Milton Keynes: Open University Press, 1987).

37. A. Tanesini, 'Whose Language?'
38. *Open Letter*, series 8, 4, Summer 1992.

List of Contributors

Shirley Chew, Professor of Commonwealth and Post-colonial Literatures, University of Leeds, UK.

Peter Easingwood, Lecturer, University of Dundee, UK.

Coral Ann Howells, Reader in Canadian Literature, University of Reading, UK.

Lynette Hunter, Reader in Rhetoric, University of Leeds, UK.

Jill LeBihan, Lecturer, Sheffield Hallam University, UK.

David Richards, Senior Lecturer, University of Leeds, UK.

Susan Spearey, Lecturer, Brock University, Canada.

Lee Spinks, Lecturer, University of Edinburgh, UK.

Alistair Stead, Senior Lecturer, University of Leeds, UK.

John O. Thompson, Lecturer, Cardiff University of Wales, UK.

Marion Wynne-Davies, Senior Lecturer, University of Dundee, UK.

Select Bibliography

Adam, Ian, and Tiffin, Helen, eds., *Past the Last Post: Theorizing the Post-Colonial and the Postmodern* (London: Harvester Press, 1991).

Ahmad, Aijaz, ed., *Ghazals of Ghalib: Versions from the Urdu* (New York: Columbia University Press, 1971).

Ahmad, Rukhsana, trans. and ed., *We Sinful Women: Contemporary Urdu Feminist Poetry* (London: The Women's Press, 1991).

Alter, Robert and Kermode, Frank, eds., *The Literary Guide to the Bible* (London: Collins, 1987).

Andrews, B., 'Writing Social Work and Political Practice', in LANGUAGE, 2, 9/10, October 1979.

Attridge, Derek, *Peculiar Language: Literature as Difference from the Renaissance to James Joyce* (Ithaca: Cornell University Press, 1988).

Atwood, Margaret, *The Journals of Susanna Moodie* (Ontario: Oxford University Press, 1970).

— *Survival: A Thematic Guide to Canadian Literature* (Toronto: Anansi, 1972).

— *Surfacing* (London: Virago, 1979).

— *Bluebeard's Egg* (Toronto: McClelland and Stewart, 1983).

— *Wilderness Tips* (London: Virago, 1992).

Bakhtin, M., *The Dialogic Imagination*, trans., C. Emerson and M. Holquist (Austin: University of Texas Press, 1981).

Barbour, Douglas, 'Late Work at the Kitchen Table: Phyllis Webb's *Water and Light*', *West Coast Line*, 6 (Winter 1991–92).

Barthes, Rowland, *Writing Degree Zero and Elements of Semiology*, trans., Annette Lavers and Colin Smith (London: Cape, 1984).

— *The Grain of the Voice: Interviews 1962–1980*, trans., Linda Coverdale (New York: Hill and Wang, 1986).

Basham, A. L., *The Wonder that was India* (London: Sidgewick & Jackson, 1988).

Bayard, C., *The New Poetics in Canada and Quebec: from Concretism to Post-modernism* (Toronto: University of Toronto Press, 1989).

Belsey, C. and Moore, J, eds., *The Feminist Reader: Essays in Gender and the Politics of Literary Criticism* (London: Macmillan, 1989).

Berger, John, *The Look of Things* (New York: Viking Press, 1974).

Bhabha, Homi K., 'Interrogating Identity', ICA Documents, 6, 1987.

Binns, Ronald, *Malcolm Lowry*, Contemporary Writers series (London: Methuen, 1984).

Blumberg, M., 'Rereading Gail Scott's Heroine' in *Open Letter*, series 8, 2, Winter 1992.

Bordo, Jonathan, 'Jack Pine – Wilderness Sublime or the Erasure of the Aboriginal Presence from the Landscape' in *Journal of Canadian Studies/Revue d'etudes canadiennes*, 27.4 (1992–93).

Bowker, Gordon, *Pursued By Furies: A Life of Malcolm Lowry* (London: Harper Collins, 1993).

Breit, Harvey, and Lowry, Margaret Bonner, eds., *Selected Letters of Malcolm Lowry* (Harmondsworth: Penguin, 1965).

Brewer, Derek, ed., *Chaucer: The Critical Heritage* (London: Routledge, 1978).

Brossard, Nicole, *Daydream Mechanics*, trans., L. Shouldice (1974; Toronto: Coach House Quebec Translations, 1980).

— *These our mothers*, trans., B. Godard (1977; Toronto: Coach House Quebec Translations, 1983).

— *The Aerial Letter*, trans., M. Wildeman (1985; Toronto: The Women's Press, 1988).

— *French Kiss*, trans., P. Claxton (1986; Toronto: Coach House Quebec Translations).

— *Surfaces of Sense*, trans., F. Strachan (1980; Toronto: Coach House Quebec Translations, 1989).

— *Mauve Desert*, trans., S. de Lotbini re-Harwood (1987; Toronto: Coach House, 1990).

— 'Poetic Politics' in *The Politics of Poetic Form*, ed., Charles Bernstein (New York: Roof Books, 1990).

— *Lovhers*, trans., B. Godard (1980; Montreal: Guernica, 1991).

— *Picture theory*, trans., B. Godard (1982; Montreal: Guernica, 1991).

Capra, Fritjof, *The Tao of Physics* (Berkeley, California: Shambhala, 1975).

Carrithers, Martin, Collins, Steven, and Lukes, Steven, eds., *The Category of the Person* (Cambridge: Cambridge University Press, 1985).

Césaire, Aimé, *Corps perdu/Lost Body*, trans., Smith and Eshleman (New York: G. Braziller, 1986).

Cixous, H. and Clement, C., *The Newly Born Woman*, trans., B. Wing (Manchester: Manchester University Press, 1986).

Cixous, H., *L'Heure de Clarice Lispector Precede de Vivre l'Orange* (Paris: des femmes, 1979).

— 'Coming to writing' and other essays, ed., D. Jenson (Cambridge, Mass: Harvard University Press, 1991).

Collins, John J, *Daniel with an Introduction to Apocalyptic Literature* (Michigan: Eerdmans Publishing Co., 1984).

Culler, Jonathan, ed., *On Puns: The Foundation of Letters* (Oxford: Basil Blackwell, 1988).

Cunningham, Valentine, *In the Reading Gaol: Postmodernity, Texts and History* (Oxford: Basil Blackwell, 1994).

Daniel, Helen, 'Introduction' to Janette Turner Hospital, *Borderline* (London: Virago, 1990).

— 'Janette Turner Hospital', *Contemporary Novelists*, Fifth Edition, ed., Leslie Henderson (Chicago and London: St James's Press, 1991).

De Lauretis, T., *Technologies of Gender* (London: Macmillan, 1987).

di Michele, M., *Luminous Emergencies* (Toronto: McClelland and Stewart, 1990).

Eco, Umberto, *The Role of the Reader: Explorations in the Semiotics of Texts* (Bloomington: Indiana University Press, 1979).
— *Reflections on 'The Name of the Rose'* (London: Secker and Warburg, 1989).
Eliot, George, *Collected Poems*, ed., Lucien Jenkins (London: SKOOB books, 1989).
Fanon, Frantz, *Black Skin, White Masks [Peau Noir, Masques Blancs]*, trans., Charles Lam Markmann (1952; London: Pluto Press, 1986).
Felman, S., ed., *Literature and Psychoanalysis: the Question of Reading: Otherwise (Baltimore: John Hopkins University Press, 1982)*.
— *Jacques Lacan and the Adventure of Insight* (Cambridge, Mass: Harvard University Press, 1987).
Fitzgerald, Judith, ed., *SP/ELLES. Poetry by Canadian Women* (Windsor, Ontario: Black Moss Press, 1986).
Foucault, Michel, *Power/Knowledge: Selected Interviews and Other Writings, 1972–1977*, ed. and trans., Colin Gordon (Brighton: Harvester, 1980).
Freccero, John, Dante: *The Poetics of Conversion*, ed., Rachel Jacoff (Cambridge, Mass: Harvard University Press, 1986).
Freud, S., 'Das Unheimliche' in *The Standard Edition of the complete psychological works of Sigmund Freud, Vol XVII*, trans., J. Strachey (1919; London: Hogarth Press, 1955).
— *Beyond the Pleasure Principle*, trans. J. Strachey (1920; London, 1961).
Gallop, Jane, *Feminism and Psychoanalysis: The Daughter's Seduction*, (London: Macmillan, 1982).
Godard, Barbara, 'Canadian? Literary? Theory?' *Open Letter*, series 8, 3, 1992.
— 'Ex-centriques, Eccentric, Avant-Garde', *Room of One's Own*, 8, 4 (1984).
Goldie, Terry, *Fear and Temptation: The Image of the Indigene in Canadian, Australian and New Zealand Literature* (Montreal: McGill-Queen's, 1989).
Greene, G. and Kahn, C., eds., *Making a Difference: Feminist Literary Criticism* (London: Methuen, 1985).
Greenstein, Michael, 'Ondaatje's Metamorphoses: "In the Skin of a Lion"', *Canadian Literature*, 126 (Autumn 1990).
Grosz, E., *Jacques Lacan: A Feminist Introduction* (London: Routledge, 1990).
Hall, Chris, '"Behind the Hieroglyphic Streets": Pynchon's Oedipa Maas and the Dialect of Reading', *Critique*, 33, 1 (Fall 1991).
Haraway, Donna, *Primate Visions* (London: Routledge, 1989).
Harpham, Geoffrey Galt, *The Ascetic Imperative in Culture and Criticism* (Chicago: University of Chicago Press, 1987).
Hartley, G., *Textual Politics and the Language Poets* (Bloomington: Indiana University Press, 1989).
Hayman, David, *Reforming the Narrative* (Ithaca: Cornell University Press, 1987).
Heller, Thomas C. and others, eds., *Reconstructing Individualism* (Stanford: Stanford University Press, 1986).
Hospital, Janette Turner, *The Ivory Swing* (Toronto: McClelland and Stewart, 1982).
— *The Tiger in the Tiger Pit* (Toronto: McClelland and Stewart, 1983).

— *Borderline* (Toronto: McClelland and Stewart, 1985).
— *Dislocations* (Toronto: McClelland and Stewart, 1986).
— 'Letter to a New York Agent', *Meanjin Quarterly*, 47 (1988).
— *Charades* (Toronto: McClelland and Stewart, 1989).
—*A Very Proper death* [as Alex Juniper] (Ringwood, Victoria: Penguin, 1990).
'Janette Turner Hospital', *Writers in Action: The Writer's Choice Evenings*, ed., George Turcotte (Sydney: Currency Press, 1990).
— *Isobars* (St Lucia: University of Queensland Press, 1990).
— *The Last Magician* (London: Virago, 1992)
Hulcoop, John, 'Webb's "Water and Light"', *Canadian Literature*, 109 (Summer 1986).
— 'Phyllis Webb (1927 -)' in *Canadian Writers and their Works*, 7, eds., Robert Lecker, Jack David, Ellen Quigley (Toronto: EWC Press, 1990).
Hurley, Michael, *The Borders of Nightmare: The Fiction of John Richardson* (Toronto: University of Toronto Press, 1992).
Hutcheon, Linda, *A Poetics of Postmodernism: History, Theory, Fiction* (London: Routledge, 1988).
— *The Canadian Postmodern: A Study of Contemporary English-Canadian Fiction* (Toronto: Oxford University Press, 1988).
In the feminine ed. coll., *In the Feminine: Women and Word/les femmes et les mots* (Edmonton: Longspoon Press, 1983).
Irigaray, L., *Speculum of the Other Woman*, trans., G. Gill (Ithaca: Cornell University Press, 1985).
Jolly, R., 'Transformations of Caliban and Ariel: Imagination and Language in David Malouf, Margaret Atwood and Seamus Heaney', *World Literature Written in English*, 26, 2 (1986).
Kamboureli, Smaro, 'Interview with R. Kroetsch', Open Letter, series 5, 8–9, 1981.
—'Theory: Beauty or Beast? Resistance to theory in the feminine', *Open Letter*, series 7, 8, Summer 1990.
Kermode, Frank, *The Genesis of Secrecy: On the Interpretation of Narrative* (Cambridge, Mass: Harvard University Press, 1979).
Kroetsch, Robert, *The Lovely Treachery of Words* (Toronto: Oxford University Press, 1989).
Lacan, Jacques, *Ecrits: A Selection* (1966), trans., A. Sheridan (London: Routledge, 1977).
LaCapra, Dominick, *History and Criticism* (Ithaca: Cornell University Press, 1985).
Lodge, David, *The Modes of Modern Writing* (London: Routledge, 1977).
Lonoff, Sue, *Wilkie Collins and his Victorian Readers* (New York: AMS, 1982).
Lowry, Malcolm, *Under the Volcano* (London: Cape, 1947).
—*Hear Us O Lord From Heaven Thy Dwelling Place* (Harmondsworth: Penguin, 1979).
Lyotard, Jean-Francois, *The Inhuman*, trans., Geoffrey Bennington and Rachel Bowlby (1988; Cambridge: Polity Press, 1991).
MacCannell, J. Flower, *Figuring Lacan: Criticism and the Cultural Unconscious* (London: Croom Helm, 1986).

Mandel Eli, ed., *Contexts of Canadian Criticism* (Chicago: University of Chicago Press, 1971)

Marlatt, Daphne, *Steveston* (Edmonton: Longspoon Press, 1984).

— *Touch to my tongue, and Musing with mothertongue, with Memory Room,* photographs by *Cheryl Sourkes* (Edmonton: Longspoon Press, 1984).

— *Ana historic* (Toronto: Coach House Press, 1988).

— *Salvage* (Red Deer: Red Deer College Press, 1991).

— 'Difference (em)bracing' in *Unbecoming Daughters of the Empire, eds., Shirley Chew and Anna Rutherford* (Aarhus: Dangaroo Press, 1993).

Matthews, D. J., Shackle, C., Husain, Shahrukh, *Urdu Literature (London: Third World Foundation, 1985).*

McDougall, R., '"A Portable Kit of Images"': Photography in Australian and Canadian Literature in English', *Kunapipi*, IX, 1 (1987).

McGregor, G., *The Wacoust Syndrome: Explorations in the Canadian Langscape* (Toronto: University of Toronto Press, 1985).

McHale, Brian, *Postmodernist Fiction* (London: Methuen, 1987).

Moi, Toril, ed., *The Kristeva Reader (Oxford: Basil Blackwell, 1986).*

— *Sexual/Textual Politics: Feminist Literary Theory (London: Methuen, 1985).*

Morrissey, K., *Batoche* (Saskatchewan: Coteau Books, 1989).

Mour ,E., *Wanted Alive* (Toronto: House of Anansi, 1983).

— *Domestic Fuel* (Toronto: House of Anansi, 1985).

— *Furious* (Toronto: House of Anansi, 1988).

— *WSW* (West South West) (Montreal: V hicule,1989).

— 'Poetry, memory and polis' in Libby Scheier, Sarah Sheard, Eleanor Wachtel, eds., *Language in her Eye: Views on Writing and Gender by Canadian Women Writing in English* (Toronto: Coach House Press, 1990).

— *Sheepish Beauty, Civilian Love* (Montreal: Vehicule Press, 1992).

Munro, Alice, *The Progress of Love* (London: Fontana, 1988).

Neumann, S. and Kamboureli, S., eds., *A Mazing Space: Writing Canadian Women Writing* (Edmonton: Longspoon/NeWest Press, 1986).

Neumann, Shirley and Wilson, Robert, eds., *Labyrinths of Voice: Conversations with Robert Kroetsch (Edmonton: NeWest Press, 1982).*

Nicolaisen, W. F. H., 'Ordering the Chaos: Name Strategies in Robert Kroetsch's Novels', *Essays on Canadian Writing*, 11 (Summer 1978).

Noble, Charles, *Let's Hear It For Them* (Saskatoon: Thistledown Press, 1990).

Ondaatje, Michael, *Coming Through Slaughter* (London: Marion Boyars, 1979).

— *The Collected Works of Billy The Kid* (London: Marion Boyars, 1981).

— *Running in the Family* (London: Picador, 1984).

— *In The Skin of a Lion* (London: Picador, 1988).

Open Letter, *Open Letter*, series 6, 9, Fall 1987.

— ed., bp Nichol, *Victor Coleman: a selection of art writing and literary commentary 1966–83*, series 7, 4, (Winter 1988).

— ed., S. Dorscht and E. Savoy, *Particular arguments: a special issue on Bronwen Wallace*, 1991.

— ed., L. Tostevin, *Redrawing the lines: the next generation*, series 8, 4 (Summer 1992).

Parker, Patricia, *Inescapable Romance: Studies in the Poetics of a Mode* (Princeton, NJ: Princeton University Press, 1979).

Paulhan, Jean, *la preuve par l'etymologie* (Cognac: Le temps qu'il fait, 1988).

Perloff, M., *Poetic License: Essays on Modernist and Postmodernist Lyric* (Evanston: Northwestern University Press, 1990).

Philip, Marlene Nourbese, 'Making the House our Own: Colonized Language and the Civil War of Words', *Fuse*, 8, 6 (Spring 1985).

— *She Tries Her Tongue; Her Silence Softly Breaks* (Charlottetown: Ragweed Press, 1989).

— *Looking for Livingstone, An Odyssey of Silence* (Stratford, Ontario: Mercury Press, 1991).

Quilligan, Maureen, *The Language of Allegory: Defining the Genre* (Ithaca: Cornell University Press, 1979).

Raban, Jonathan, *Soft City* (London: Hamish Hamilton, 1974).

Redfern, Walter, *Puns* (Oxford: Basil Blackwell, 1984).

Ricoeur, Paul, *Time and Narrative* (3 vols.), trans., Kathleen McLaughlin and David Pellauer (Chicago: University of Chicago Press, 1984–88).

Robinson, F. N., ed., *The Works of Geoffrey Chaucer* (London: Oxford University Press, 1957).

Rooke, Connie, 'Getting into Heaven', *Malahat Review*, 85 (Summer 1988).

Rose, Jacqueline, *Sexuality in the Field of Vision* (London: 1986).

Rossetti, Christina, *Time Flies: A Reading Diary* (London S.P.C.K., 1885).

Russell, Ralph, trans. and ed., *Hidden in the Lute: an Anthology of Two Centuries of Urdu Literature* (Manchester: Carcanet Press, 1995).

Scheier, Libby, Sheard, Sarah, Wachtel, Eleanor, eds., *Language in her Eye: Views on Writing and Gender by Canadian Women Writing in English* (Toronto: Coach House Press, 1990).

Scobie, Stephen, *Signature Event Cantext* (Edmonton: NeWest Press, 1989).

Scott, Gail, *Heroine* (Toronto: Coach House Press, 1987).

— *Main brides, against ochre pediment and aztec sky* (Toronto: Coach House Press, 1993).

Seed, David, 'Naming and Identity in Modern American Fiction', *Dutch Quarterly Review of Anglo-American Letters*, 20 (1990–92).

Sellers, S., ed., *Writing differences: Readings from the Seminar of Helene Cixous* (Milton Keynes: Open University Press, 1988).

Shiach, M., *Helene Cixous: A Politics of Writing* (London: Routledge, 1991).

Showalter, Elaine, ed., *The New Feminist Criticism* (London: Virago, 1986).

Sinfield, Alan, *Dramatic Monologue*, Critical Idiom series (London: Methuen, 1977).

Soja, E., *Postmodern Geographies: The Reassertion of Space in Critical Social Theory* (London: Verso, 1989).

Solecki, Sam, ed., *Spider Blues* (Montreal: Vehicule Press, 1985).

Sontag, S., *On Photography* (Harmondsworth: Penguin, 1979).

Sparrow, F., '"This place is some kind of a garden": Clearings in the bush in the works of Susanna Moodie, Catharine Parr Traill, Margaret Atwood and Margaret Laurence', *The Journal of Commonwealth Literature*, XXV, 1 (1990).

Staines, David, ed., *The Canadian Imagination: Dimensions of a Literary Culture* (Cambridge, Mass.: Harvard University Press, 1977).

von Strasburg, Gottfied, *Tristan*, trans., A.T. Hatto (Harmondsworth: Penguin 1960).

Sujir, Leila, 'Addressing a Presence: An Interview with Phyllis Webb', *Prairie Fire*, 9.1 (Spring 1988).

Tanesini, A., 'Whose Language?', unpublished ms, 1993.

Telling It ed. coll., *Telling it: Women and language across cultures* (Vancouver: Press Gang, 1990).

Tessera ed. coll., Cassette tape of editorial meeting, held in the archives of the National Library of Canada, 1982?

Tessera ed. coll., Vol 1 in *A Room of one's Own*, 8, 4 (January 1984).

Thompson, John, *Stilt Jack* (Toronto: Anansi Press, 1978).

Tostevin, L. Lemire, *The Color of Her Speech* (Toronto: Coach House Press, 1982).

— *Gyno text* (Toronto: Underwhich, 1983).

— *Sophie* (Toronto: Coach House Press, 1988).

— 'Interview with C. Dewdney', *Open Letter*, series 7, 7, 1990.

Tyler, S. A., 'The Poetic Turn in Postmodern Anthropology: The Poetry of Paul Friedrich', *American Anthropologist*, 86:2 (1984)

Vice, Sue, ed., *Malcolm Lowry Eighty Years On* (London: Macmillan, 1989).

Vogel, Susan and Ebong, Ima, eds., *Africa Explores: Twentieth Century African Art* (New York: Centre for African Arts, 1991)

Wachtel, E., 'Putting up fences in the garden', *Tessera*, 5 (September 1988).

Wallace, Bronwen, *The Stubborn Particulars of Grace* (Toronto: McClelland and Stewart, 1987).

Warland, B., *Proper Deafinitions, Collected Theorograms*, (Vancouver: Press Gang Publishers, 1990).

Wayne, Valerie, ed., *The Matter of Difference* (Hemel Hempstead: Harvester Wheatsheaf, 1991).

Webb, Phyllis, *Talking* (Quebec: Quadrant Editions, 1982).

— *Water and Light: Ghazals and Anti Ghazals* (Toronto: Coach House Press, 1984).

Wells, S., and Taylor, G., *William Shakespeare. The Complete Works* (Oxford: Clarendon Press, 1986).

Whitford, M., *Luce Irigaray: Philosophy in the Feminine* (London: Routledge, 1991).

Wittgenstein, L., *Philosophical Investigations*, trans., G. Anscombe (1953; Oxford: Basil Blackwell, 1967).

Yale French Studies, *French Freud: Structural Studies in Psychoanalysis*, 48 (1972).

Index